# Myth and Philosophy in Platonic Dialogues

Omid Tofighian

# Myth and Philosophy in Platonic Dialogues

Omid Tofighian
Lecturer in Rhetoric and Composition in the School of Literature, Art, and Media, and Honorary Research Associate in the School of Philosophical and Historical Inquiry.
Both in Faculty of Arts and Social Sciences at University of Sydney
Sydney, Australia

ISBN 978-1-137-58043-6     ISBN 978-1-137-58044-3  (eBook)
DOI 10.1057/978-1-137-58044-3

Library of Congress Control Number: 2016953618

© The Editor(s) (if applicable) and The Author(s) 2016
The author(s) has/have asserted their right(s) to be identified as the author(s) of this work in accordance with the Copyright, Designs and Patents Act 1988.
This work is subject to copyright. All rights are solely and exclusively licensed by the Publisher, whether the whole or part of the material is concerned, specifically the rights of translation, reprinting, reuse of illustrations, recitation, broadcasting, reproduction on microfilms or in any other physical way, and transmission or information storage and retrieval, electronic adaptation, computer software, or by similar or dissimilar methodology now known or hereafter developed.
The use of general descriptive names, registered names, trademarks, service marks, etc. in this publication does not imply, even in the absence of a specific statement, that such names are exempt from the relevant protective laws and regulations and therefore free for general use.
The publisher, the authors and the editors are safe to assume that the advice and information in this book are believed to be true and accurate at the date of publication. Neither the publisher nor the authors or the editors give a warranty, express or implied, with respect to the material contained herein or for any errors or omissions that may have been made.

Cover image © Jozef Klopacka / Alamy Stock Photo

Printed on acid-free paper

This Palgrave Macmillan imprint is published by Springer Nature
The registered company is Macmillan Publishers Ltd.
The registered company address is: The Campus, 4 Crinan Street, London, N1 9XW, United Kingdom

*For Manoutchehr and Iradj*

# Acknowledgments

The ideas and research for this book benefited greatly from nearly three years of work on the Australian Research Council (ARC) research project at the University of Sydney, 'Plato's Myth Voice: The Identification and Interpretation of Inspired Speech in Plato', headed by Rick Benitez. I am grateful to Rick for including me in this project, giving me the liberty to explore various directions, and involving me in the planning, direction and outcome of the project. Rick has been a mentor and friend since my undergraduate years supporting my academic, cultural, and community work.

I also extend a special thank you to Lily Zubaidah Rahim for many years of support and guidance. I am grateful to Lily for involving me in the Religion, State & Society Research Network at the University of Sydney and giving me opportunities to conduct special research, combine my diverse academic, cultural, and community activities, and gain insight and experience into the way projects are developed and carried through.

The earlier years of this project benefited from working with Frans de Haas. I am grateful to Frans for advising me on ways to integrate various scholarly interests. I also extend thanks to Asghar Seyed-Gohrab, who has been instrumental in helping me pursue transnational academic and cultural projects.

I acknowledge and thank Martine Antle for her encouragement and mentoring. Her support and advice have played a significant role in my academic work and career development. I am grateful to Sahar Amer for contributing to my work in important ways by providing me with encouragement, support, and valuable opportunities.

I appreciate the help of Sebastiana Nervegna, who read my manuscript and made important corrections and suggestions. Her extremely valuable contribution improved my work immensely, instilled confidence in me, and gave me perspective on key themes and topics.

I thank Moira Gatens for years of mentoring and assistance. I am grateful to Susan Thomas for her support and advice over the last few years. And I thank Vanessa Smith for her interest in my research and community advocacy.

I am also grateful for the support I received during different periods of my research from Harrold Tarrant, Pauline Kleingeld, Carlos Steele, Gerd Van Riel, and Luc Brisson. And I thank Merran Laver for editing the bibliography. I originally acquired the book contract with Palgrave Macmillan through Esme Chapman and carried the project through to completion with Grace Jackson. I am grateful to both assistant editors for their work. I also acknowledge the work of Swamikannu Sowmiya, Raghupathy Kalynaraman, and Sarah Blake throughout the production process.

I am grateful to the following people for collaborating with me on initiatives aimed at promoting cross-cultural understanding, and challenging and transforming the curriculum in higher education: Juanita Sherwood, Melinda Lewis, Arlene Harvey, Amani Bell, Gabrielle Russell-Mundine, National Centre for Cultural Competence (University of Sydney), Behrouz Boochani, Hani Abdile, Mahmoud Salameh, Zahra Al-Mudhafar, Sana Al-Ahmar, Hussein Nabeel, Alwy Fadhel, Kween G Kibone, Candy Royalle, Mark Munk Ross, Renee Williamson, Frank Trotman-Golden, Sharon F. Gooding, Frederick Gooding Jr, Rebecca Sheehan, Kaiya Aboagye, Jonathon Potskin, Jakelin Troy, Preston Peachy, Rhyan Clapham, Delise Kerehona, Matthew Peet, Jacob Ballard, Omar Offendum, Zainab Kadhim, Mohammad Al Mayahi, Ian Escandor, Spice Bezzina, Thomas Rock Dent, Silas (Mohammad Gholami), Ali Razivand, Vyvienne Abla, Kazi A Mamun, Luka Haralampou, Helen Ngo,

Sherene Idriss, Rayila Maimaiti, Evelyn Araluen Corr, Ailin Naderbegi, Mythily Meher, Antoinette Abboud, Andrew Viller, the Free University of Western Sydney project, Nathaniel Adam Tobias ~~Coleman~~, Pedro Tabensky, Adam Elliott-Cooper, the Why Is My Curriculum White? initiative (UK), the Why Is My Curriculum White? – Australasia initiative, Liz Thompson, xborder (Crossborder Operational Matters), Raha Faridi, Meysam Sefidkhosh, Mehrdad Oskouei, Vedad Famourzadeh, Omid Shayan, Gizella Varga Sinai, Farah Ossouli, Khosrow Sinai, Ranaa Farnoud, Mitra Kavian, Arya Shokouhi Eghbal, Shahrzad Ossouli, Masoumeh Mozafari, Naghmeh Ghasemlou, Mohammad Hamzeh, Éric Rolland Bellagamba, Elham Etemadi, Omid Azadibougar, Armin Miladi, Iranian Film Festival Australia, Tilman Andreas Grünewald, Autonomous Collective Against Racism (ACAR) – University of Sydney, Stephanie Barahona, David Bovey Wang, Samuel Kaldas, Eve Mayes, Jyhene Kebsi, Shima Shahbazi, Arezoo Farazandeh, Sajad Kabgani, Linda Briskman, Umut Azak, Emrah Gürsel, Derya Acuner, the Karakutu project, the Iran Academia project, Michael A. Peters, and Tina Besley.

My family has been a great source of hope and inspiration throughout my life and especially during the process of writing this book. I express my deepest gratitude to my mother Akhtar, my brothers Navid and Naysan, my father Manoutchehr, and my uncle Iradj. I also wish to acknowledge my god-daughters Talisah Jordan Caruana and Brionny Mia Watson, and godsons Zachary Jhi Caruana and Terrell David Watson.

# Introduction

Mythology, myth studies and comparative mythology, like religious studies or comparative religion, are part of a specific area of study, consist of specialized research, emerged relatively recently, and correspond with the contemporary history of scholarship on Plato's myths. Scholars theorizing and analyzing myth have been operating in certain traditions and imported and acknowledged views and methods from philosophy, theology, classics, and the social sciences.[1] And scholars working on ancient philosophy develop their own analytic methods and philosophical perspectives which they implement and express in studies of Plato. However, when addressing the topic of Plato's myths, one notices how in most cases the analyst has visited an 'intellectual storehouse' to assist his or her critical evaluation and description of myth—an understudied issue in contemporary philosophy. After over a century of specialized work on the mythical aspects of Plato's dialogues, it is critical that research continue identifying and defining this ambiguous intellectual storehouse drawn upon by Plato scholars.

---

[1] For general schools of thought and originators/leading practitioners, themes, movements, developments, and influential figures in myth studies, see Doty (1986); Feldman and Richardson (1972); Lincoln (1999); Segal (1999, 2004); Csapo (2005); and Dundes (1984) and, in relation to the study of Greek mythology, see Bremmer (2011). An important study addressing research and perspectives from different disciplines and examining non-European cultures is Kirk (1970). And for Eastern influences on Greek myth and culture, see Burkert (2007).

I investigate different connections between Plato studies and myth studies, taking into account certain intellectual developments that have been marginalized or ignored. I also suggest possible multidisciplinary approaches for understanding Plato's myths; I introduce methods that engage with particular features of the dialogues largely neglected or taken as peripheral. Chapter 2 outlines a technique I term 'mutual scaffolding' used to examine Plato's philosophical project in a way that resists restricting the role of myth to a single definition or explanation and categorizing it in contradistinction to argument. I also avoid reducing myth to one or a limited number of functions and interpret selected myths in their own philosophical, literary, and thematic contexts. My methodology is based on the notion that in specific cases myth cooperates with philosophy within an interdependent unity rather than as two separate genres with their own meanings, aims, and agendas.

Myth studies, also referred to as mythography, is an interdisciplinary subject that has advanced and diversified over the past half century. I consider some of the most progressive and sophisticated ideas and theories introduced and applied by myth scholars, including philosophical studies of myth, and incorporate them into my approach to test the extent to which they advance Plato scholarship. My study of Plato's myths involves an analysis of six dialogues and rests heavily on the identification and recognition of the integral and complex role of narrative plot. I analyze plot structure and how it accommodates the dynamic links between the literary and philosophical features represented in key sections. I also give special consideration to seemingly minor symbolic and thematic elements and examine how they inform the authority of the plot. Each dialogue presents myth and philosophy as interdependent parts of an orchestrated totality; *mythos* and *logos* interact differently depending on the topic and goal of the text but are put on stage in Plato to work in unison. My choice of dialogues is influenced by topic, aim, and style. My selections stand as strong illustrations of powerful mythic themes, ideas, and corresponding arguments; they contain vivid, elaborate, and influential myths and provide accessible examples for the application of my mutual scaffolding technique.

My case studies include the following:

1. *Meno* (Chapter 3): I examine how references to myth function to characterize the text as an instruction manual that guides readers in how to do one form of philosophy correctly. I integrate research of the mythical trickster character to reveal plot structure and related themes pertaining to liminality, transformation, and renewal.
2. *Protagoras* (Chapter 4): Plato provides an advanced dual between a sophist who presents a myth and alternative lines of argument submitted by Socrates. A philosophical exploration of partnership in intellectual inquiry is central. I consider Laurence Coupe's radical typology approach and explore appropriations of myth for creating conditions that illuminate philosophical debate.
3. *Phaedo* (Chapter 5): Myth acts as a regulating code that maps arguments, opposing arguments, and connections between arguments in the text. Drawing on Lévi-Strauss's theory of binary systems in myth, I examine the tale of the soul's journey in the *Phaedo* and decipher how binary oppositions are imposed on various dramatic sequences and the levels of philosophical discussion, producing literary rhythm and theoretical cohesion.
4. *Phaedrus* (Chapter 6): Plato introduces myth as a device facilitating transition between phases of philosophical theory and vision. With reference to William Doty's advanced reading of myth in *Mythography* (1986), I employ an expanded and inclusive working definition of myth. My analysis elucidates a number of key epistemological and metaphysical shifts and developments pertaining to Plato's view of love and the body.
5. The Atlantis myth in both the *Timaeus* and *Critias* (Chapter 7): The myth described in the two texts operates as a tool for Plato's self-reflection and criticism. I develop Bruce Lincoln's critique of the relationship between myth studies and nationalism from *Theorizing Myth* (1999) to disclose the Atlantis myth's strong themes of patriotism, Athenian pride, and exaggerated promotion of an exclusive form of cultural identity.

I structure the interpretation of each case study consistently and order my analysis by focusing on a series of features sensitive to literary, philosophical, and culture elements. I pay special attention to particular details constituting the opening scenes of the dialogues and the status of narrators (theme introduction, setting, and narrative mode). I conduct a theme-based analysis of the myth itself (myth analysis) and the arguments (the philosophical arguments). Next, I apply mutual scaffolding in order to illustrate the interdependent relationship between both discourses and the harmony between this unity and other aspects of the dialogue (mutual scaffolding). And I disclose the complexities of the plot (plot structure) and Plato's strategic choice of personalities (character selection).[2] As both myth-maker and philosopher, Plato includes selected mythic elements and ideas and chooses to exclude others. My study of different dialogues elucidates how selection is determined in each case by an intention to construct nuanced narrative situations that inform and communicate complex philosophical paradigms and messages. Myth is strongly associated with Plato's philosophical thinking and can be analyzed as being interdependent with it.[3]

---

[2] The nature of this study resembles a number of significant structural features found in *Funf platonische Mythen im Verhaltnis zu ihrem Textumfeldern* by Colloud-Streit (2005). Also, consider Blondell (2002) for insights into the dramatic elements of the dialogues with a focus on Plato's characters.

[3] My methodology is applicable to other important myths from Plato's corpus; the interdependence between myth and argument reflects Plato's overall philosophical vision and approach, and many modern theories of myth are suited to illuminating the unity. However, I decided against addressing the myth of Er or the allegory of the cave because of the scale of such an analysis. Applying my method to the *Republic* and interpreting the myth/philosophy relationship with the rigor it deserves would require much more than one chapter in this book. Also, the myths, literary themes, and philosophical issues from dialogues such as the *Gorgias*, *Symposium*, *Statesman*, and *Laws* could have presented compelling and revealing case studies; the dialogues are also important examples that invite numerous theories of myth. However, I have selected dialogues for the present study on the basis of the clarity with which they demonstrate the relevance and importance of my approach and the lucidity characterising their match with particular theories. The five chapters examined here are exemplary in that they introduce the broad range of ways that Plato orchestrates the myth/philosophy interrelation in order to stimulate interest in a topic, achieve his aim, and represent intellectual style.

# Bibliography

Blondell, R. (2002). *The Play of Characters in Plato's Dialogues*. Cambridge: Cambridge University Press.
Bremmer, J.N. (2011). 'A Brief History of the Study of Greek Mythology', in *A Companion to Greek Mythology*. K. Dowden and N. Livingstone (eds.) Oxford: Wiley-Blackwell, 527–547.
Burkert, W. (2007). *Babylon, Memphis, Persepolis: Eastern Contexts of Greek Culture*. Massachusetts: Harvard University Press.
Colloud-Streit, M. (2005). *Funf platonische Mythen im Verhaltnis zu ihrem Textumfeldern*. Fribourg: Academic Press.
Csapo, E. (2005). *Theories of Mythology*. Oxford: Wiley-Blackwell.
Doty, W. (1986). *Mythography*. Alabama: University Alabama Press.
Dundes. A. (ed.). (1984). *Sacred Narrative. Readings in the Theory of Myth*. Berkeley: University of California Press.
Feldman, B. and Richardson, R.D. (1972). *The Rise of Modern Mythology: 1680–1860*. Bloomington: Indiana University Press.
Kirk, G.S. (1970). *Myth: Its Meaning and Functions in Ancient and Other Cultures*. Cambridge: Cambridge University Press.
Lincoln, B. (1999). *Theorizing Myth: Narrative, Ideology, and Scholarship*. Chicago: University of Chicago Press.
Segal, R.A. (1999). *Theorizing About Myth*. Amherst: University of Massachusetts Press.
Segal, R.A. (2004). *Myth: A Very Short Introduction*. Oxford: Oxford University Press.

# Contents

| | | |
|---|---|---|
| **1** | **Myth and Philosophy on Stage: Connections, Divisions, and Interdependence** | 1 |
| | 1.1 What Do We Mean by Myth? The Study of Myth in General | 1 |
| | 1.2 The Study of Myth in Philosophy | 13 |
| | 1.3 The Study of Myth in Plato | 18 |
| | 1.4 Methodology and Genre | 27 |
| **2** | **Mutual Scaffolding: Unifying Myth and Philosophy** | 33 |
| | 2.1 Mutual Scaffolding (A Dialectical Unity) | 35 |
| | **Dialogue Analysis** | 53 |
| **3** | **Myth and Instruction: *Meno*** | 55 |
| | 3.1 Introducing the Trickster | 55 |
| | 3.2 Theme Introduction, Setting, and Narrative Mode | 60 |
| | 3.3 Myth Analysis | 63 |
| | 3.4 The Philosophical Arguments | 68 |
| | 3.5 Mutual Scaffolding | 70 |
| | 3.6 Plot Structure | 73 |

|     |       |                                                  |     |
| --- | ----- | ------------------------------------------------ | --- |
|     | 3.7   | Character Selection                              | 75  |
|     | 3.7.1 | Meno                                             | 75  |
|     | 3.7.2 | Socrates                                         | 76  |
|     | 3.7.3 | The Slave                                        | 78  |
|     | 3.8   | Conclusion                                       | 79  |
| **4** | **Myth and Partnership: *Protagoras***         |                                                | 83  |
|     | 4.1   | Radical Typology                                 | 83  |
|     | 4.2   | Theme Introduction, Setting, and Narrative Mode  | 87  |
|     | 4.3   | Myth Analysis                                    | 90  |
|     | 4.4   | The Philosophical Arguments                      | 94  |
|     | 4.5   | Mutual Scaffolding                               | 96  |
|     | 4.6   | Plot Structure                                   | 101 |
|     | 4.7   | Character Selection                              | 105 |
|     | 4.7.1 | Socrates                                         | 105 |
|     | 4.7.2 | Protagoras                                       | 106 |
|     | 4.7.3 | The Attendees                                    | 107 |
|     | 4.8   | Conclusion                                       | 107 |
| **5** | **Myth and Regulation: *Phaedo***              |                                                | 111 |
|     | 5.1   | Binary Systems and Myth                          | 111 |
|     | 5.2   | Theme Introduction, Setting, and Narrative Mode  | 115 |
|     | 5.3   | Myth Analysis                                    | 120 |
|     | 5.4   | The Philosophical Arguments                      | 123 |
|     | 5.5   | Mutual Scaffolding                               | 130 |
|     | 5.6   | Plot Structure                                   | 135 |
|     | 5.7   | Character Selection                              | 137 |
|     | 5.7.1 | Phaedo                                           | 137 |
|     | 5.7.2 | Echecrates                                       | 138 |
|     | 5.7.3 | Socrates                                         | 138 |
|     | 5.7.4 | Simmias and Cebes                                | 139 |
|     | 5.8   | Conclusion                                       | 140 |
| **6** | **Myth and Transition: *Phaedrus***            |                                                | 143 |
|     | 6.1   | Cultural Standpoint and Myth                     | 143 |
|     | 6.2   | Theme Introduction, Setting, and Narrative Mode  | 149 |

|     |       |                                          |     |
| --- | ----- | ---------------------------------------- | --- |
|     | 6.3   | Myth Analysis                            | 153 |
|     | 6.4   | The Philosophical Arguments              | 158 |
|     | 6.5   | Mutual Scaffolding                       | 159 |
|     | 6.6   | Plot Structure                           | 167 |
|     | 6.7   | Character Selection                      | 169 |
|     |       | 6.7.1 Master                             | 169 |
|     |       | 6.7.2 Student                            | 169 |
|     | 6.8   | Conclusion                               | 170 |

7 **The Atlantis Myth and Cultural Identity: *Timaeus* and *Critias*** — 173
    7.1 Nationalism and Myth — 173
    7.2 Theme Introduction, Setting, and Narrative Mode — 179
    7.3 Myth Aanalysis — 184
    7.4 The Philosophical Arguments — 187
    7.5 Mutual Scaffolding — 188
        7.5.1 Rethinking Recollection — 190
        7.5.2 Revisiting the Ideal State — 192
        7.5.3 Metaphysics — 194
    7.6 Plot Structure — 195
    7.7 Character Selection — 198
        7.7.1 Socrates — 198
        7.7.2 Critias — 198
        7.7.3 Timaeus — 199
        7.7.4 Hermocrates — 199
        7.7.5 Egypt and the Egyptian Priest — 200
        7.7.6 Solon — 201
        7.7.7 Atlantis — 201
    7.8 Conclusion — 202

8 **Where Does Myth Belong?** — 205

**Bibliography** — 219

**Index** — 239

# 1

# Myth and Philosophy on Stage: Connections, Divisions, and Interdependence

## 1.1 What Do We Mean by Myth? The Study of Myth in General

Contemporary scholarly approaches to myth must critically engage some of the most salient twists, turns, developments, and obstacles facing myth studies since becoming a recognized academic area of study. This section identifies a tradition in order to systematically connect debates, ideas, methods, movements, and positions. To assess the historicity of certain approaches and claims regarding Plato's myths, one must associate them with a modern history of knowledge production related to mythology. These connections help clarify the status of particular perspectives and aid in critically evaluating interpretations of myth in Plato scholarship. Contextualizing approaches to myth in social, cultural, and intellectual history enables one to draw distinctions between methods, concepts, and techniques from various disciplines, identify

An earlier and shorter version of this chapter is published in Tofighian (2010).

© The Editor(s) (if applicable) and The Author(s) 2016
O. Tofighian, *Myth and Philosophy in Platonic Dialogues*,
DOI 10.1057/978-1-137-58044-3_1

lineage, recognize far-reaching historical impact, and identify contemporary scholarly influence.

In the modern era, the word 'myth' has become a general term referring to revelation, folktales, sacred scripture, fairy tales, legend, epic, and even community hearsay.[1] Myth is understood to narrate the exploits of humans (from ancestors until the present) and gods and a host of other supernatural beings.[2] Some myths depict the history of a family or dynasty; the glory or demise of a city or civilization; the adventures or fate of different kinds of souls; the origins of the universe, the structure of the universe and the coming end of the universe. These plots, themes or motifs (the tropes differ in their roles based on their incorporation and application), in addition to a vast range of other recurring topics, often feature with story lines familiar to us such as 'the death and resurrection of a god or hero',[3] 'deliverance',[4] 'recurrence',[5] 'cyclical time', 'linear time', 'progress',[6] 'regress', reciprocity', 'alchemical transformation', 'salvation', 'damnation' and, more generally, tragedy, comedy, romance,

---

[1] In the introduction to the second edition of Vladimir Propp's *Morphology of the Folktale*, Alan Dundes explains that the affinities between these different forms of narrative have been based primarily on content rather than structure. He indicates that one of the virtues of Propp's study is that it illustrates how important cultural patterns are manifested in cultural production, including novels, plays, comic strips, and motion picture and television plots (Propp [1968] pp. xiv–xv). Appreciation of similar factors can be traced back to Fontenelle's ground-breaking essay 'On the Origin of Fables' (1724); see Feldman and Richardson (1972) pp. 7–18. For an explanation of Heyne's (1729–1812) contribution to the emergence of modern myth studies and the modern use of the term myth, see Bremmer (2011) pp. 532–533; Feldman and Richardson (1972) pp. 215–223.

[2] Doty collected fifty individual definitions of myth. He groups them into eight types: myth as aesthetic device, narrative, or literary form; subject matter pertaining to gods or a realm beyond ours; etiology; early, weak, or inaccurate science; myth as the literal or verbal concomitant to ritual; an accessible account of universals; explicating beliefs, collective experiences, or values; and the expression of 'spiritual' or 'psychic' states (Doty [1986] p. 9).

[3] For examples of themes, motifs, and plots of this nature, see Compton (2006); Campbell (1949); Coupe (2006) pp. 63–65; and Segal (1990).

[4] Consider Coupe's various references to the theme of deliverance in his book *Myth* (2006).

[5] For an example of the significance of recurrence in myth, see Hatab (2005).

[6] For a study of the notion of progress, see Mehta (1985) pp. 69–82.

and satire.[7] In some myths, these topics are exclusive, and in others they are combined.[8]

In his monumental study of myths and rituals, *Mythography* (1986), Doty lists the various conventional definitions of myth that have been constructed by different fields of study.

1. In comparative religious studies, myth is often understood in contrast to theology: the former is associated with Indigenous cultures or 'primitive' peoples, and the latter with monotheistic systems of belief or philosophically inclined cultures.
2. In the study of poetry, drama, and fiction, myth is interpreted in relation to 'mythic elements' or 'legendary plots'.
3. In anthropology or ethnology, the phrase 'mythic period' is generally used to label, often negatively, periods in the history of a culture that resemble pre-modern ways of thinking and acting.
4. In political science, the appellation 'myth' is used to criticize ideologies such as democracy or socialism.
5. In sociology, the term is used vaguely for systems of beliefs and ritualized forms of behavior.[9]

---

[7] See Frye (1957). Of course, Frye's classification is not the only series of plot structures offering general categories for genres, but it is a helpful tool to begin analysis. To identify the kinds of plot structures manifest in Plato's dialogues, I fuse Frye's four 'master types' with more specific types of mythic plots. For an example of the influence of Frye's theory, see White (1973). In his introduction, White explains briefly the features of each mode and gives some examples of their application (pp. 8–11). For philosophical critique and development of Frye's mythographic work, see Lentricchia (1980).

[8] Propp draws attention to the problems associated with classifying and defining 'themes' or 'motifs'. He is correct in highlighting problems with dividing selected sections, ideas, or events from a narrative into strict classes. This approach, he argues, neglects inherent idiosyncratic qualities within those units and ignores the overlapping nature of different themes (Propp [1968] pp. 7–12). See Gerhart and Russell (2002) pp. 194–196, for examples of how themes influence political and scientific allegiances and how these allegiances characterize the way observation and research are narrated. The authors also explain how Gerald Holton incorporates methodological techniques from anthropology, art criticism and similar fields, and methods associated with thematic analysis and applies them to scientific writing with great success.

[9] Doty (1986) p. 6.

The way each discipline understands and uses the word 'myth' is contingent on a range of social, historical and political factors, and awareness of the disciplinary influences on mythography and its development is indispensable for multi-faceted interpretations of the term. Different cultures, eras, and systems of thought build up their own categories for situating mythic phenomena and including or excluding different elements according to basic and static definitions (monomythic definitions).[10] Knowing how to unite different perspectives involves deep consideration of evaluations produced by those perspectives. However, respecting each individual socially and culturally conditioned myth is a far more difficult task and a more vital and urgent interpretative matter (a polymythic hermeneutics).[11] I argue that the first step must be to move away from reductive approaches to myth and appreciate them in their different varieties and contexts.

Disciplinary nuances and developments particular to European and Anglo-American contexts have characterized readings of myth since the early phases of myth studies in the late seventeenth century. And social and political factors foregrounded a number of significant issues: the nature of religious truth; knowledge and interpretation of prehistory; the thoughts, ideas, and practices of Indigenous communities; the relationship between philosophy and myth framed within a debate about the relationship between science and religion; and the reinterpretation of imagination and artistic expression. These concerns and driving factors created the setting for movements in the middle of the eighteenth century; eventually myth became increasingly pivotal to intellectual and social life, ultimately influencing the Romantic Movement.[12]

Prior to the late seventeenth century, myth was generally equated with ancient Greek and Roman mythology.[13] It was rarely studied for itself and was considered unimportant. Particularly in the eighteenth century, scholarly studies of myth were fundamental to the formation of modern fields of study: anthropology, literary criticism, folkloristics, psychology,

---

[10] Doty (1986) p. 13 and pp. 174–182. Also, see Segal (2004) pp.4–6.
[11] Doty (1986) pp. 56–60.
[12] Eliade's forward to Feldman and Richardson (1972) pp. xx–xxi.
[13] One example of scholarship that indicates this partiality is Chance (1994).

# 1 Myth and Philosophy on Stage: Connections, Divisions,... 5

and the history of religion. By the middle of the nineteenth century, mythography had confirmed its place as a serious and respected area of research.[14] After the mid-twentieth century, interest in myth declined and it was no longer recognized and appreciated in the same way.

> ... from the Enlightenment down through the first half of the nineteenth century, myth was widely and increasingly thought of as a primary subject, even a synoptic one, a master field of the first importance. Myth was taken up because it was thought of as a key, variously, to history, to linguistics and philology, to religion, to art, to the primitive mind, and to the creative imagination.[15]

Examples of reductionism pervade the short academic history of myth studies. Some forms of reduction attempt to transcend the multifarious features of myth and determine its meaning and significance according to a dominant theoretical paradigm. Well-known examples include different forms of Christian theism, positivism, Romanticism, Euhemerism, psychoanalysis, structuralism, functionalism, and allegorical and historical determinist interpretations.[16] Reductive approaches attempt to find a certain factor—literary, historical, linguistic, cultural, and so on—and project it as the key to discovering the meaning of the story or the single most essential aspect of myth. According to these approaches, one element must be isolated for special consideration in order to understand the narrative; that is, one factor decodes the other major and minor features. Consideration of archetypes in relation to myth, for instance, is insightful and fascinating but does not address cross-cultural differences and the intricate narrative details of mythology; one approach is never sufficient for analyzing the many networks of meanings and significance.[17]

---

[14] Louis (2005).

[15] Eliade's forward to Feldman and Richardson (1972) p. xxi.

[16] Eliade's forward to Feldman and Richardson (1972) p. xix. Reduction should not always be interpreted as negative. Theories are reductive in that they discover similarities in a wide range of myths and present generalizations for analytic purposes. The type of reduction I criticize is one that enforces and perpetuates a simple dichotomy and limits or eliminates interpretative possibilities.

[17] For an application and criticism of Jung's views concerning archetypes in the study of myth, see Coupe (2006) pp. 139–146 and Gould (1981).

Similarly, reducing myth to certain structural features is limiting. Myth-creators summarize a range of events over a long period into a story, emplotting details to achieve logical coherence, and neglect temporal serialization.[18] The study of a myth's plot structure is necessary, but reducing the different meanings of a literary text to the plot leaves unaddressed many questions regarding the internal dynamics of a story.[19] Exclusive structuralist approaches often privilege the plot at the expense of content and tend to modify, adjust, ignore, attenuate, or amplify other parts of the text in order to preserve the imagined authority of the plot. Understanding a text according to structure—or more accurately, one perspective of structure—is equivalent to a 'theory of everything' which implies that the multifarious range of narratives can be interpreted by using one criterion.[20] One must also account for the interaction between the elements constituting the plot, such as characters (what they represent, how they represent, and who they address), dramatic setting, imaginary details evoked by the author/presenter, motifs or icons, and the interplay and transformation of these features throughout the course of the tale.[21]

Drawing boundaries between different discourses and deliberating principles essential for defining myth require interdisciplinary work; collaboration is necessary to disclose the most relevant elements in different cases. Narratives use particular plots to determine the selection and exclusion of available data, arrangement of information and the limits of interpretation.[22] The details used to construct, for instance, a historical narrative relate to reality through particular tropes and combine to

---

[18] For studies pertaining to myth, structure, and plot, see Frye (1957) and Cassirer (1946). Also, see Doty (1986) pp. 179–80.

[19] Segal (2004) p. 120.

[20] Schmitz (2007) p. 50.

[21] I interpret the place and significance of literary plot structures in different Platonic dialogues and explain how they integrate other important literary and philosophical components.

[22] White (1973) pp. 5–7. Also, Holton points out that in scientific writing, what he terms public science, the writer applies a similar kind of selectivity. He or she reports methods, data, and conclusions only after specific laboratory notes are taken and 'disembodied' from the historical context in which they are compiled. Public science supports a particular position or theory and guarantees further publication and reference (Gerhart and Russell [2002] pp. 194 and 204).

correspond with the imposed plot structure.[23] A certain amount of 'filling in' occurs when the selected data—at the expense of the excluded data—are arranged and matched with each other in order to satisfy the order and rhythm prescribed by the chosen story line. Labelling history as fiction is unfair and overexaggerated; however, historical accounts are not representations of events exactly as they occurred; they do not represent the only set of facts or the one correct story.[24] Consider depictions of recent historical events that reflect the creativity of the historian, novelist, filmmaker, or other kinds of artists. History and realist literature incorporate features and significant examples that are difficult to verify—but would never be considered myths.[25]

Criticizing the scholarly projects of prominent nineteenth-century myth scholars as forms of pseudoscience, Lincoln sheds light on the choices and modification made by theorists.[26] Dubious systems of knowledge production obsessed with pure origins—racial, linguistic, cultural, and geographic—plagued the systematic study of myth and religion during its most rigorous period:

> Within the anniversary discourses, Jones narrated his own quest for the origin of languages and the ancient center from which peoples dispersed. Still, as objects of experience and of 'scientific' knowledge, primordial origins and perfect centers remain notoriously elusive. They are constituted as objects of discourse, not knowledge, by bricoleurs who collect shards of information and prior narratives, from which they confect the fictions that satisfy their otherwise unattainable desires while doing their ideological work. When students of myth—even eminent ones, like Sir William Jones, Snori Sturluson, or Friedrich Max Müller—succumb to this temptation and engage in a discourse of origins and centers, the results are particularly ironic. In effect, they enter a recursive spiral, spinning their own myths while they sincerely believe themselves to be interpreting myths of others, others who may even be the product of their imagination and discourse.[27]

---

[23] White (1973) pp. 31–38.
[24] Carroll (2001).
[25] Consider White's interpretation of the way characters and events are represented in film and literature in White (2000) pp. 66–86.
[26] Lincoln (1999) Chap. 4.
[27] Lincoln (1999) p. 95.

Traditional standards for classifying myth are problematic; criteria are fluid and definitions of myth potentially divert to become myths themselves.[28] Myth studies and religious studies have advanced greatly since their inception less than two centuries ago, and today it would be naïve to assume, for instance, that the Indigenous Australian stories about the Dreaming and ancient Greek myths belong to one genre.[29] Kirk's analysis of the problems associated with choosing from available theories is enlightening: 'Each of these universal theories (and none of them is presented as stipulative, or as valid for only one particular kind of myth) can be negated by citing many obvious instances of myth that do not accord with the assigned origin or function. Indeed the looseness of the term "myth" itself, and its wide range of applications in common usage (even apart from vulgar meanings such as "fabrications"), together with the failure of specialists to offer acceptable definitions, suggest that it is a diverse phenomenon that is likely to have different motives and applications even within a single society—let alone in different cultures and at different periods'.[30] Fluidity and diversity characterize approaches to myth, and envisioning a pluralistic methodological strategy for selecting and using theories is necessary.[31] A more progressive method must involve sensitivity to historical developments, language, cultural factors and disciplinary

---

[28] Doty (2003).

[29] Influenced by Croce, Anglo-American New Criticism and Russian Formalism hold that artistic expressions are unique and incommensurable constructions and cannot be translated or explained according to another discourse without losing their original character. They do not deny the possibility of good translations or interpretations, only that they must insist on the value of the original. Theorists argue that generic theories destroy the idiosyncratic nature and quality of each text; the idea of genre must be replaced by close readings. Literary texts must be appreciated and understood according to their internal structure and the dynamic interrelation between their constituent units, not limited by overarching definitions reducing texts to vague categories or misrepresentations (Zima [1999] pp. 18–19).

[30] Kirk (1984) pp. 54–55. The notion of a universal theory that proposes a social or psychological origin and a basic function for myth is the product of the early period in the tradition of modern mythography. These earlier theories have continued to characterize theorizing and, indeed, Kirk was influenced by the prevailing structuralism of his time. Some of the most influential and prominent pioneers, particularly with respect to their impact on later philosophical perspectives, include Fontenelle, Bayle, and Vico. See Feldman and Richardson (1972) Part One.

[31] The views of eighteenth-century myth scholar Nicolas Fréret deserve particular mention in this regard. His complex and contextual approach to mythology opposes the common reductionist tendency of the time (Feldman and Richardson [1972] pp. 93–98).

# 1 Myth and Philosophy on Stage: Connections, Divisions,... 9

features in order to help decipher appropriate descriptions and functions of myth and introduce richer interpretations and analyses.[32]

When myth penetrates or influences our cultural and social fabric, it allows the existence of particular kinds of objects. Objects, whether they are physically possible, logically possible or actual, take a particular form and ascribe a certain meaning when incorporated into a worldview characterized by and aligned with the narrative framework of myth. Lévi-Strauss, in *Totemism* (1973), suggests that breaking the authority of myth to classify objects and experiences results in their vanishing or undergoing a transformation of meaning.[33] In this case, the oral stories and texts bundled together under the name myth disperse in search of new sets of categories. The very notion of myth must be scrutinized and deconstructed in order to move toward more refined readings of sacred narrative: Could many modern theories and ideologies be considered myths if we reconstruct the definition of myth in agreement with Lévi-Strauss's analysis?[34] A well-known quote by Lévi-Strauss gives reason to pause before agreeing to universal definitions or functions of myth:

> Of all the chapters of religious anthropology none has tarried to the same extent as studies in the field of mythology. From a theoretical point of view the situation remains very much the same as it was fifty years ago, namely, a picture of chaos. Myths are still widely interpreted in conflicting ways: collective dreams, the outcome of a kind of esthetic play, the foundation of ritual.... Mythological figures are considered as personified abstractions, divinized heroes or decayed gods. Whatever the hypothesis, the choice amounts to reducing mythology either to an idle play or to a coarse kind of speculation.[35]

---

[32] For a historical approach sensitive to the layers of influence in the construction of a myth, see Witzel (2012).

[33] Lévi-Strauss (1973) pp. 1–3. Lévi-Strauss's structuralist approach to the study of myth is significant for the way it influenced 'second-generation structuralists' (Doty [1986]) such as Detienne, Vernant, and Vidal-Naquet, who are critical of Lévi-Strauss and represent a poststructuralist and post-Freudian trajectory. For analysis of Vernant's contribution to structuralism and examples of his approach, see Csapo (2005) pp. 247–261.

[34] Cassirer (1961); Bottici (2007); Bottici and Challand (2010).

[35] Lévi-Strauss (1955) pp. 428–444, p. 428.

Lévi-Strauss's observation regarding the lack of consensus within myth studies, the difficulties faced by different positions, and the limits impacting resolution of those difficulties draws attention to the pitfalls associated with attempts to find an all-encompassing definition for myth. Many contemporary methodologies still

1. generally categorize myths as one genre
2. delineate common characteristics for all myths
3. determine the basic function of myths
4. and determine the epistemic status of myths.

I am critical of this framework for analyzing myth, and my approach addresses individual myths without assuming a general genre—a genre consisting of a set of predictable characteristics, a common function, and a standard epistemic role. Instead of enforcing the 'simple and easily memorized statements that suggest that myth does this… or that',[36] a less problematic and more constructive approach resists defining myth as a general category in opposition to other forms of explanation. I envision a horizon within which the context of different myths and their content determine interpretation—a horizon that allows previous definitions to exchange prominence and transform accordingly.[37] Myth is not a single story or a set of images originally intended for one purpose. The theoretical complexities and hermeneutical limits constraining approaches to mythology can be addressed constructively once one identifies and explores the most dominant reductive explanations of myth: a preliminary stage of scientific thought; an idealized representation of reality or a re-enactment of it (through ritual); an expression of a psychological state; a communication of yesterday's values; or one of the many different varieties of these grand mythographic explanations.[38] One of my aims is to search for an inclusive horizon that enables many kinds of myths to function according to their social, cultural, political, ideological, or literary settings.[39]

---

[36] Doty (1986) p. 10.
[37] See Colloud-Streit (2005) p. 15 regarding the problems associated with definitions of myth.
[38] Doty (1986) p. xiii.
[39] Consider Detienne's *L'Invention de la mythologie* (1981).

# 1 Myth and Philosophy on Stage: Connections, Divisions,... 11

The inextricable connections between the creation and rise of modern mythography, European colonial expansion and the history of racism[40] require more critical analysis and belong at the center of contemporary myth studies debates.[41] During the period when Western colonial powers were competing for geographic, political, and economic control of countries referred to as the Global South, particular schools of thought, concepts, categories, methods, and hierarchies were developed for interpreting the narratives that form the foundations for religious and sociocultural life of colonized peoples.[42] The intellectual and scholarly tools produced by Western scholars for interpreting mythology during this time, and the cultural and political trends determining their use, fashioned the short history of mythography and related fields. Scholarly projects developed out of a matrix constituted by invasion, domination, the popularity of deism and natural religion, pseudoscientific movements and the rise of a particularly aggressive form of rational inquiry; a peculiar logic connecting the desire to study, universalize, dominate and control.[43] Fundamental concerns, attitudes and approaches driving studies of non-European narratives and civilizations moved to the forefront of myth studies and contributed to characterizing and directing analysis of Greek and Roman mythology by positioning the religions and myths of colonized peoples in contrast to Western religious and cultural narratives.

Kirk identifies the lack of awareness regarding modern mythography among classicists and acknowledges the influential work in anthropology,

---

[40] Araújo and Maeso (2015); Maaka and Andersen (2006); Smith (1999); Weinbaum (2004); Buck-Morrs (Summer 2000); Jean-Marie (2013). See Bernal (1987, 2006, 2001) for analysis of these issues in the context of classical scholarship. For criticism of Bernal's work, see Lefkowitz and Rogers (1996); Marchand and Grafton (1997).

[41] For an example of scholarship that begins to address the extent to which colonialism and the politics of race characterize myth studies, see Csapo (2005) pp. 10–14, 19–22 and 45.

[42] Many of the authors who thrived during the Max Müller-inspired era of myth studies (nineteenth and early twentieth century) were prominent beneficiaries of the colonial period and driven by Müller's 'scientific' approach to the study of mythology (Eliade's introduction to Feldman and Richardson [1972] p. xiii; also, see Blok (1994) for analysis of Creuzer and K.O. Müller and scientific approach to mythology). One example of the pseudoscientific scholarship committed to studies of myth and advanced during this period is Müller's promotion and elaboration of the Turanism movement; see Lincoln (1999) p. 68. For the dynamic interrelation between colonialism, racism, and modernity, see Gilroy (1993); Wynter (2003); Weinbaum (2004); Mills (1997); Alcoff and Caputo (2011).

[43] Grosfoguel (2013); Quijano (2007); Saal (2013).

religious studies, and psychology. Although his critique also neglects the significance of colonialism and the history of racism, Kirk problematizes the privileging of Greek and Roman mythology in the context of classics, ancient history, and ancient philosophy: 'Moreover their views are often affected by the false assumption that Greek mythology affords a pattern for all other myths. Classicists have been able to contribute little in the way of control or caution, and indeed have remained largely unaware of work on myth in other fields'.[44]

Coloniality and racism receive little attention and remain on the periphery of modern myth scholarship.[45] A great deal of important research has been produced by academics on knowledge production in the context of colonialism, and a decolonial approach to myth studies deserves a prominent role in research.[46] Although the topic of colonialism has not been completely neglected in research on mythology and myth theory, more specialized work is necessary in order to draw clearer connections between the history of myth scholarship and European imperialist projects. Encouraging cross-disciplinary scholarly collaboration can contribute to reforming an area of study that once helped to support Western colonial expansion. New epistemologies reclaiming the problematic methods and concepts ingrained in myth studies are possible if decolonial forms of discourse are given prominence.[47] Decentering and dismantling dominant Enlightenment and Romantic perspectives are achievable only if institutional changes are implemented to foster genuine exchange between researchers working on myth and researchers from various schools of thought that critique the impact of colonialism and its afterlife.[48] Incorporation of non-Western epistemologies, particularly

---

[44] Kirk (1984) p. 54.

[45] Park (2013) indicates that critical awareness of coloniality and racism is also lacking in research into the history of philosophy and investigates the exclusion of non-European philosophy since the eighteenth century. He draws attention to important work in this area by Moellendorf (Summer 1992); Halbfass (1998); King (1999); Bernasconi (1997, Spring 1995, October 1995, 2000, 2002, 2003). Also, see Brennan (2014); Alcoff and Mendieta (2000).

[46] For examples of the decolonial approach in the humanities, see Mignolo (2011); Coleman et al. (March 2012); Nakata et al. (2012). And in social science, see Sillitoe (2005).

[47] Sillitoe (2005); Connell (2007); Arashiro and Barahona (2015); Bernal (1987, 1991, 2001); Cruikshank (1998); Anderson (2014).

[48] Coleman et al. (2012); Smith and Wobst (2005); Simmons (2013); Smith (1999).

Indigenous forms of knowledge and practice, is urgent and vital for future theories of myth.[49] Theories need to appreciate and interpret the complex role of myth in diverse histories and societies and the connections between mythology and different ways of being, knowing, and doing.[50]

## 1.2 The Study of Myth in Philosophy

Since the pre-Socratics, most philosophers have distanced themselves from myth as a valid form for representing reality. Much of the contemporary debate over the relationship between myth and philosophy puts the onus of proof on myth and veers toward the general *mythos/logos* dichotomy. The philosopher who wishes to prosecute myth and demands justification for its loitering among domains of rationality does so with legitimacy. But when some reduce the issue to a simple dichotomy, the analysis becomes superficial and has little import; the subsequent debate becomes almost inconsequential. One needs to consider deeper levels of communication between myth and philosophy even if one begins by simply comparing and contrasting styles of explanation and mapping shifts and developments in mythography. The crucial first step must be to critically analyze generally accepted definitions of myth, and this necessarily involves considering the history of the term and what it meant to different philosophers at different times.[51]

---

[49] Smith (1999); Nakata (1998, 2004, 2007); Denzin et al. (2008); Martin (2003, 2008); Rigney (2006); Sillitoe (2005); Hendry and Fitznor (2012); Grounds et al. (2003); Emeagwali and Sefa Dei (2014); Semali and Kincheloe (1999) p. 15; Jackson (2012); Kovach (2009).

[50] See Martin (2003); Buck-Morrs (Summer 2000) fn. 38; Jean-Marie (2013) pp. 249–255. Also, see de Sousa Santos (2014); Goody (2007) pp. 24, 46, 71, and 138.

[51] Hayden White's criticism of historicism is relevant in terms of illuminating the limits of evaluations of myth on the basis of particular views of history (such as positivist or Romantic). White contributes to the philosophy of history by blurring the boundaries between historiography and literary criticism highlighting the relevance and implications of the narrative structure in historical accounts and introducing the use of tropes. For White, historical writing and studies of history are subject to linguistic and cultural constraints. In addition, the moral and aesthetic preferences associated with historians' accounts influence the form of narrative selected to represent a series of events (Paul [2009] p. 56). These preferences determine particular forms of historical representation and influence content. The status and function of myth also need to be understood in terms of the interpreter's historical presuppositions and conditions. For a historical approach to modern theories of religion criticizing the different forms of historicism involved in understanding religion, see Capps (1995) Chap. 2.

Myth is usually a mix of different stories, carefully selected and modified, which in turn provide material for further appropriation. The heterogeneous basis of most myths—consisting of units influenced by different moments of history, different religions, cultures, and political ideas—reflects the multiple functions, possible interpretations, and uses of those myths.[52] The multifarious and competing interpretations of myth are the obvious outcome of networks of meaning and multiple messages constituting the nature of myths. The plot line, characters, themes, and motifs used to amalgamate the pieces of different stories constituting myths are closely associated with the identity of the writer and the philosophical milieu he or she operates in.[53] The most prominent meaning or meanings of myths must be deciphered without downplaying, ignoring, ridiculing, or attacking minor ideas and messages. Myth-makers include some material and exclude others under the influence of cultural and ideological paradigms. The exclusive social position or elitism pertaining to the one privileged with making and propagating myth is an important factor for interpreting Plato's writing; Plato's status and understanding of the intricacies associated with the myth-making process are significant for understanding his philosophical approach and critical for analyzing the interdependent relationship of myth and philosophy in the dialogues.[54]

Contemporary debates have started to address the complexity and controversy associated with reducing myth to one account. Some contemporary philosophers working on the issue acknowledge the importance of myth in various contexts and agree that simply invalidating or demoting myth as a fictional story or false account is naïve and hasty. Reducing *mythos* and *logos* to a basic dichotomy avoids more serious questions. Investigation of the status of myth in relation to philosophy gives rise to a variety of new approaches and evokes more compelling questions:

1. What reasons would a philosopher have for using myth as a technique?
2. Does or can myth symbolize anything expressed in philosophy?

---

[52] Consider Lévi-Strauss's explanation of the decomposition and recomposition of 'mythemes' and the description of the myth-maker as a *bricoleur*; for the concept of mythemes, see Lévi-Strauss (1955) pp. 428–444; for the concept of *bricoleur*, see Lévi-Strauss (1966).

[53] Gantz (1993) is an important resource for identifying themes, motifs, and characters from classical folklore and myths.

[54] Doty (1986) pp. 15, 17–18 and pp. 20–21.

# 1 Myth and Philosophy on Stage: Connections, Divisions,... 

3. What can myth contribute that philosophy cannot?
4. And the more central question for my analysis: what is the relationship between myth and philosophy when they appear in a philosophical text (in this case, the dialogues of Plato)?

I expand by exploring deeper questions:

1. What are the dynamics at play in a philosophical text when two genres are combined?
2. How and why would a philosopher need to look closer at the hybrid nature and structure of an argument?
3. What unconventional elements feature in arguments and how do they strengthen analysis?

Despite the multiplicity of theories toward the issue, critical approaches developed by philosophers, both ancient and modern, are molded out of the old debate we recognize as the 'quarrel between poetry and philosophy' (i.e., the traditional distinctions drawn between myth and philosophy).[55] Whether philosophers attack or defend particular aspects of myth, it seems the overbearing weight of the traditional distinction determines and limits attempts made to rethink the origins of the distinction and the development of ideas aimed at better understanding the difference.[56]

---

[55] Gould (1990) pp. 3–12 refers particularly to Socrates and Plato; also, see Rosen (1988) and Levin (2001). See Doty (1986) pp. 3–4 for a brief description of the origins of the separation that pays special attention to semantic shifts. The ancient quarrel between poets and philosophers is significant for analysis of modern myth theories and their relationship to philosophy. Most modern theories emerge from the social sciences, but some come from philosophy. The traditional poetry/philosophy distinction influenced modern philosophy in terms of its reading of the dichotomy paradigm promoted by modern myth theorists. Therefore, a common language and framework exist between philosophers and modern mythographers. Also, philosophy occupies an influential role in the emergence and development of social science disciplines, and there is a general agreement that poetry/narrative and philosophy/argument are in conflict, or at least divergent.

[56] Early Greek philosophers, particularly Plato, reject mytho-poetic truth claims, and many fundamental features of their arguments are valid. But outright rejection of all myths, including those presented in a philosophical context (such as Plato's myths), are based on or influenced by the general attack on myth and poetry prevalent among some early philosophers. I distinguish between different kinds of myth and argue that ultimately Plato, in his role as creator of myths, is distinct from Homer (Morgan [2000] 15–16).

The major perennial accusations against myth made by philosophers and explanations of myth in relation to philosophy are summed up here:

1. Myth is unfalsifiable; it is inaccessible to experience and reason. As a result, it is unavailable to rational demonstration.
2. Actors in myth engage in morally outrageous behavior, rendering myth morally inconsistent.
3. The same actors strive to define vice and social law, ordering mortals to practice moderation and adhere to order. However, the divine characters in myth are themselves unable to control their passions and desires or live according to their own rules.
4. Events in myth are bound together using rules of action and reaction rather than logical argument.
5. Myth appeals to the lower part of the soul influenced by passion.[57]

Even contemporary commentators who recognize myth as a legitimate form of philosophical expression ultimately arrive at the conclusion that myth and philosophy reside on opposite sides of an explanatory divide.[58] The assumption is that distinctions between the two modes of explanation operate within a structure framing them as two contrasting positions with two contrasting referents.[59]

Only a few contemporary philosophers and philosophical schools of thought pay serious attention to the relevance of myth in relation to philosophical issues. Kevin Schilbrack questions the negligence within modern philosophy and states that a rigorous philosophical project critically engaging with myth has not been undertaken with the exception of the writings

---

[57] Brisson (1998) pp. 9–10. In the introduction, under the heading 'Plato's Critique of *Muthos*', Brisson lists these five defects inherent in the nature of myth.

[58] For the influence of Hegel on literary theory and the history of visual art, which played a significant role in this form of modern interpretation of classical poetry and literature, see Zima (1999) pp. 6–8.

[59] Lévi-Strauss presents a model for structuralist approaches to narrative called the paradigmatic model. This theory involves establishing polar oppositions between phenomena in order to understand the deeper structure of a text. The model and associated methods are influential in many contemporary studies of myth that take dichotomy or independence of genres as a starting point. Lévi-Strauss relates the paradigms to other aspects of culture which influence the updated view of myth as model (Propp [1968] pp. xii–xiii; Lévi-Strauss [1955, 1963]). Also, see Csapo (2005) pp. 212–245.

# 1 Myth and Philosophy on Stage: Connections, Divisions,... 17

of some thinkers in the German Idealist tradition, Paul Ricoeur, Hans Blumenberg, and possibly a number of random philosophers of religion.[60] He also draws attention to the fact that until quite recently there has been very little interaction between philosophy and religious studies, anthropology, and the history of religion. He correctly argues that philosophy is significantly relevant to the social sciences, and vice versa—particularly concerning an issue as cross-cultural and cross-disciplinary as myth.

The more contentious issue, however, is how one discourse stands in relation to the other. Robert Segal classifies the different positions held by philosophers and non-philosophers: myth is part of philosophy; myth actually is philosophy; philosophy develops out of myth; myth and philosophy serve the same function but are independent; myth and philosophy function differently and are independent.[61] He identifies that these perspectives on the relationship are closely associated with the division made between religion and science. In many cases, the evaluation of the *mythos/logos* distinction has been predetermined by interpretations of the religion/science dichotomy. Scholars such as E.B. Tylor argue for the indispensable link between myth and religion.[62] He explains that myth supplements religion

---

[60] Schilbrack (2002b) p. 2. Schilbrack criticizes the overbearing influence of Christian theism on the philosophy of religion and argues that until philosophers from within that tradition—particularly philosophers in the English-speaking tradition—broaden the objects of their study, the questions that inspire and enhance the scope of inquiry will remain limited. For a comprehensive account of the history of religious studies that pays close attention to the significant influence of Christianity and Christian thought, see Sharpe (1975). For recent philosophical studies of political myth, see Bottici (2007); Bottici and Challand (2010).

Scanning through the enormous amount of scholarly literature written on religion and myth over the last couple of centuries, one notices an unequalled commitment to the use of continental philosophy or philosophers heavily influenced by continental schools of thought. The lineage is a long one and includes figures such as Friese, Hegel, Schleiermacher, Ritschel, Otto, and Nygren. More recent scholars in this field also express a debt to the tradition: notable figures include Müller, Eliade, Jung, Goodenough, Feurbach, Marx, Barth, Tillich, and Ricoeur. Among recent essays and books written on philosophical interpretations of myth and religion, the presence of continental philosophy is pervasive. (Consider many of the essays in Schilbrack (2002b), Hatab's use of Heidegger and Nietzsche [1990], and Capps's approach based on influence from Capps 1995).

[61] Segal (2002) p. 18 and (2004) p. 36.

[62] For classical theorists of religion and myth, such as Tylor, myth is explained in relation to cognition. Mythical explanations ascribe physical events to the personal will of a god or spirit, and scientific explanations involve postulating impersonal forces behind physical occurrences. The two are incompatible since there cannot be two different efficient causes for one event, but are methodologically connected in that they try to offer reasons for physical occurrences. For a concise account of Tylor's interpretation of myth, see Segal (2004) pp. 14–23.

by providing explanations and stories in which to situate religious belief.[63] Contemporary trends in myth studies veer away from this typically nineteenth-century interpretation and attempt to present less reductive explanations of myth/religion and philosophy/science interaction.[64]

An additional and plausible way of interpreting the relationship between myth and philosophy is one based on mutual interdependence: myth and philosophy function differently but are *interdependent*. Approaching Plato's myths in relation to arguments in this fashion avoids the burden of having to justify the relevance of the two discourses in the same way one would need to justify the relevance of religion to philosophy. By considering the two as interdependent, I show that a sound conclusion that involves dissociating interpretations of myth from the dichotomy paradigm can be inferred. My argument shows the interconnection between myth and philosophy without reducing the status of myth in Plato's dialogues to standard interpretations of the relation between religion and philosophy.

## 1.3 The Study of Myth in Plato

Historically, philosophers and philosophical traditions have been influential in the study of religion and myth, even though they remain on the periphery in contemporary myth studies. However, contemporary Plato studies does not necessarily benefit from the nuances and developments associated with the modern history of myth studies.[65] Mythography has

---

[63] For a summary of Tylor's theory of religion, including background information, see Sharpe (1975) pp. 53–58.

[64] Feminist philosopher Michele Le Doeuff identifies myth as a narrative that has always provided philosophy with imagery and a way to accommodate passion into rational deliberation (1989). She believes the two are inseparable and identifies the presence of myth in philosophical texts, thus rejecting the dichotomy paradigm. For Le Doeuff, myth and philosophy as combined renders a complete account of lived experience that must necessarily incorporate aspects of an embodied being such as sexual orientation, ethnicity, class, and political affiliation. Another feminist philosopher, Pamela Sue Anderson, argues that Le Doeuff's theory offers many important insights into the place of myth in philosophy that have remained unacknowledged by philosophers but have provided feminist theory with form and content (Anderson [2002]).

[65] However, the exceptions are significant; Barash (2011) reveals important insights in his contrast of Cassirer and Blumenberg.

far-reaching influences within the humanities and social sciences but does not have an explicit presence in research on Plato's myths. If Plato scholars consider myth theories, the tradition and its prominent figures and movements are not mentioned explicitly; criticism and development are missing in most cases.[66] Philosophical approaches to myth that ignore myth studies traditions and the debates that constitute their history overlook the ways myths have influenced intellectual history. Modern conceptions of myth are formed within a historically contingent intellectual and cultural milieu and myth scholars import intellectual developments from other fields and interests. Many problems arise, however, when analyzing the variety of myths belonging to very different historical and cultural contexts. Modern methodologies based on the dichotomy paradigm are limited—yet overemphasized—in their scope for interpreting ancient understandings of myth, and Plato studies requires an interdisciplinary approach to myth sensitive to more recent multidisciplinary theories of myth. 'Only an approach that flexibly combines formal criteria with features of content and that above all remains critically aware of its own inescapable anachronism can hope to do justice both to Plato's ancient texts and to our own modern ideas'.[67]

---

[66] One example of explicit connection and reference to one myth studies theory is the 'Cambridge School' or 'Cambridge Ritualists'. The work of Jane Ellen Harrison, Gilbert Murray, and F.M. Cornford is heavily influenced, and acknowledges their debt to, the myth-ritual school of William Robertson Smith and James Frazer (and to some extent K.O. Müller). See Louis (2005) pp. 351–354. Bremmer comments on the significance of Harrison in contrast to other prominent movements: '... Harrison's highly fertile idea had little effect on the wider classical world... moreover this period saw the rise of functionalism in anthropology, as personified by Bronislaw Malinowski, and functionalism had little interest in mythology. Meanwhile, in Germany, interest in mythology died with Usener and Robert, and the scholar who came to dominate the classical world was Ulrich von Wilamowitz-Mollendorff (1848–1931), who loathed the idea of "savages" in Greece, rejected the comparative approach, which indeed had overextended itself, and had little interest in mythology' (2011, p. 537). Wilamowitz is significant because a number of students from his 'Graeca' fled Germany for the United States in the twentieth century and helped shape the study of ancient philosophy and classics there (the study of myth and religion included). In particular, Gregory Vlastos's work reflects various forms of influence from Friedrich Solmsen. Vlastos's 1952 paper 'Theology and Philosophy in Early Greek Thought' makes reference to Solmsen's work, and Vlastos both collaborated with Solmsen and reviewed his scholarship. Vlastos also criticizes Cornford's *From Religion to Philosophy* for 'uncritical borrowings' from the then-fashionable school of French sociology—more likely earlier members from around the turn of the century, such as Comte, Durkheim, and Mauss. For further comments on Wilamowitz and his perspective and influence on the study of Greek mythology, see Bremmer (2010); and for his connections with right-wing politics, see Flaig (2003).

[67] Most (2012) p. 15.

Responses to fundamental questions concerning the topic of myth by modern scholars have explicitly or inadvertently shaped and directed modern Plato scholarship. The conceptual frameworks, debates, and sociocultural context determining theories of myth offer important insight into influential stages of development in the tradition. Regardless of its short history, myth studies functions in a network involving disciplines such as philosophy, anthropology, aesthetics, sociology, philology, and literature. The relevance of mythography reaches further than academia and pertains to coloniality and intercultural communication and informs study of contemporary popular culture.[68] A significant and influential tradition exists that occupies a special place in modern intellectual history. The emergence of modern mythography is relevant to philosophical investigations when one considers the following: the philosophers who posed central questions throughout the tradition; the philosophical context of significant topics and problems; and influential responses from philosophers. An interdisciplinary approach involving philosophy and myth studies projects a framework in which to create, criticize, and evaluate new research pertaining to Platonic dialogues. Historical and theoretical factors contribute to the study of Plato's myths and confirm the various forms of communication between the recent history of Plato studies and the modern mythography.

Kent Moors identifies the limits of scholarship pertaining to myth, offering a number of interesting critical observations. He encourages a contextual approach to the study of Plato's myths and highlights the interpretative obstacles created by scholars who isolate his myths for examination. For Moors, scholarship that dissects Plato's texts into myth and philosophy compromises the overall perspective of the dialogical context and replaces it with the scholar's own philosophical position.[69] Moors objects to detaching Platonic myth from the rest of the dialogue in which each one is framed. One must appreciate the distinct differences between both the mythical and logical features (along with a diverse range of other details) that move throughout each dialogue while identifying and interpreting different forms of interaction and fusion between discourses. There is a pleth-

---

[68] Scholarship on mythology and popular culture includes Coupe (2006); Fredericks (1980); Kovacs and Marshall (2011).
[69] A criticism also mentioned by Mattei (1988) p. 67.

# 1 Myth and Philosophy on Stage: Connections, Divisions,... 21

ora of intricate scenes, symbols, ideas, messages, and arguments conveyed in multi-layered fashion in Platonic dialogues, and, as Moors points out, assuming that the text as a whole must be the basis of study is naïve.[70]

Kathryn Morgan recognizes the importance of distinguishing between philosophical myths and other kinds of myths in Plato's dialogues. She acknowledges the potential of philosophical myths to elucidate one's inability to arrive at epistemic certainty and to expose the limits of language. As a point of clarification, she explains how philosophical myth does different things in different places. But Morgan emphasizes that one must never accept that it can be a satisfactory substitute for dialectic—a point that associates her analysis with some of the traditional dichotomy views.[71] She argues that, on its own, philosophical myth is insufficient for presenting unverifiable axioms. Myth must work in conjunction with dialectic to achieve this.[72] The existence of the transcendent realm of Forms and the incorporeal soul are two prominent themes in Plato's myths and justified in many dialogues by discursive argument. Echoing the position of classical myth theorists, Morgan describes philosophical myth as the 'metaphorical expression of the dialectical path' which supplements the discussion where argument cannot because of the constraints of time and the difficulties of comprehension experienced by the characters.[73] But she makes it clear that this category of myth can always be translated into logical argumentation differentiating it from educational and prophetic myth. Proposing the view that myth is not simply the 'other' of philosophy is a step toward multiple levels of understanding the many ties between the two genres. Attempts to find a link between myth and philosophy, such as Morgan's position, are progressive analyses. However, they tend to leave a number of explanatory gaps relating to the process connecting the two genres and the operational details between them. For instance, Morgan integrates myth and philosophy but does not clarify exactly how myth, inferior by nature, operates with philosophy. According to her analysis,

---

[70] Moors (1982) p. ix. This position reflects methods in classical structuralism. For the views of second-generation structuralists, see the works of Vernant and Vidal-Naquet (1990, 1991, 1992, 2000) and Detienne (1972, 1981, 2009).

[71] Compare Morgan's evaluation with Fowler (2011).

[72] Morgan (2000) p. 180.

[73] Morgan (2000) p. 180.

Plato's myths function in a system that does not contrast myth and philosophy on the basis of opposing qualities; they actually share qualities and myth supports many aspects of the overall project of philosophy. She argues that irrationality is not a normative feature of myth, but she does not elaborate on exactly how myth can be philosophical or the role played by philosophers in the construction of philosophical myth.[74] Morgan explains that since myth presents itself in the form of symbols it weakens itself in the presence of philosophy. However, she also points out that there is nothing innately wrong or nonsensical about symbolism. A gap emerges when one tries to work out the details that distinguish philosophical symbolism from the inspired use of symbols featured in poetry.

J.A. Stewart, in his book *The Myths of Plato* (1905), recognizes humankind's emotive and moral instincts, which he explains are fundamentally grounded in its dream-world consciousness, and he acknowledges their contribution to scientific and philosophical reasoning.[75] However, he does not explain the link between the two, or the process moving from symbolic representation to conceptual deliberation. A whole range of questions are left unanswered. Stewart is unclear about how the emotional state of dream-consciousness gives rise to notions of 'value'. There is no account of what role reason played prior to scientific thinking and why there was a shift in emphasis. More importantly, Stewart neglects rendering an epistemological explanation of the coordination between symbol and concept—myth and philosophy.[76]

Examples of religious studies and myth scholarship attempt to uncover the basic human capacity initially giving rise to religion and myth. Explanations of the creation of myth and religion as emerging from a basic human capacity have influenced Plato scholarship. According to this perspective, religion and myth are somehow evoked by a natural human tendency that motivates all humans from all eras and cultures.

---

[74] Morgan (2000) p. 31. Compare with Brisson (2006).

[75] See the opening chapter. Compare Stewart's mythopoeic theory with the views of Henri and Henriette Antonia Frankfort (Segal [2004] pp. 40–42) and many aspects of the earlier German Romantic (Schelling, Creuzer, Herder, Heyne, and the Schlegels) and English Romantic traditions. For a study of Romanticism and the rise of interest in myth, see Louis (2005).

[76] In his 1935 review of Frutiger's *Les Mythes de Platon* (1930), Hack contrasts Frutiger's book with Stewart's by stating that it is 'a refreshing contrast to the Kantian cloudiness of Stewart'.

# 1 Myth and Philosophy on Stage: Connections, Divisions,...

The predispositions most widely proposed by theorists for the creation of myth are divided into three categories:

1. Moral: myth is moral education.[77]
2. Aesthetic: myth expresses beauty.[78]
3. Rational: myth is a form of reasoning.[79]

---

[77] See Wetzel (2002). Rowe (2007) argues that myth motivates moral behavior (also, see Rowe [2012]). Like many other commentators, Most also acknowledges the emotionally appealing advantage of myth, which he calls the psychagogic effect, and details a particular kind of emotional appeal characteristic of myth and associated with duty. Most states that 'myth concludes an extended dialectical portion of the text, often so that the results that have already been obtained by logical means can now be repeated impressively in a mythical form' (Most [2012] p. 19). Also, see Edmonds (2012). Edmonds argues that myth is moral allegory and represents the interpretation of myth as persuasive and illustrative. See Rowe (2012) for an example of myth as persuasion while, in addition, introducing different terms and perspectives relating to punishment. The myth of the *Gorgias* is described as an explanation that is easy for Callicles to understand (i.e., watered-down philosophy). He explains that myth is an allegory about the suffering of the unjust which conveys a particular perspective on punishment. However, Rowe disagrees with the modern view that myth is an understandable way of communicating philosophy and explains that the myth of the *Gorgias* is a kind of allegorical extension of the arguments. For more examples of the moral allegory perspective, see Annas (1982) pp. 125 and 138; Sedley (1990); Collobert (2012). For ancient interpreters, see Diogenes Laertius (1925) (3.80).

[78] See Mattei (1988); Stewart (1905). For a description of the historical place and influence of the 'mystical experience' perspective of religion and a list of its major proponents, see Sharpe (1975) pp. 116–118.

[79] Tylor holds that myth was intended to explain not describe; cultures subscribing to myth attempt to tell us something about the causes of physical events. And the need to provide a theoretical scientific explanation, for Tylor, originates in the cognitive faculty or human mind. He contributed to the literal study of myth and developments in this field are reinforcements or reactions to his position. Segal lists a number of possible scientific reasons worth considering for why Tylor labels myth unscientific: first, the non-physical nature of personal causes; second, the inability to predict and test immaterial forces; third, the difficulty with generalizing mythical causes into a unity; and the final or teleological nature of personal causes (Segal [2002] pp. 21–22). All of these reasons presuppose that science is primarily concerned with the physical world and denounces or justifies a scientific theory based on the extent to which its premises can be empirically verified. Segal identifies the difficulties with applying this kind of scientific criteria since science is not necessarily physicalist and not all cultures that use myth as explanation are non-physicalist. Also, he argues that the criteria of predictability and generalization are not definitive standards—neither necessary nor sufficient conditions—with which to evaluate discourse as scientific or unscientific discourse. Also, compare Tylor with the views of evolutionary theorist Herbert Spencer. (For a summary of his approach to religion and his affinities with Tylor, see Capps [1995] pp. 74–83.)

Woloshyn bases his analysis of myth on Plato's comments regarding the status of image, and the 'divided line' analogy, in the *Republic*. He concludes that images fall short of knowledge and equates myth with analogy, both of which are designed to induce dianoetic understanding. For Woloshyn, myths can be only an indirect apperception of the Forms, implying that their relationship with *noesis* involves weaker epistemic understanding and never a mutual cooperation toward arriving at

Other theories pertaining to causation acknowledge myth as the epistemological foundation for our abstract accounts of the world.[80] Stewart describes the inception of science as closely linked with the 'mythopoeic' imagination of early humans.[81] He explains that, in order to account for the causes of the world of sense experience, humans refer to the images and events of their dream state. This form of early contemplation, Stewart argues, 'enlarged the mind' and eventually led to scientific understanding. Science is indebted to mythology for its rise and also for its limits. According to Stewart's position, reason is a part of humankind but not the whole, and it is in relation to this emotional, spiritual context that he believes we should aim to explain myth.[82] Stewart acknowledges that at a certain point in time myth was sufficient for satisfying one's scientific curiosity. More specifically, myth was the initial etiological account for the

---

knowledge (2008); also, for myth as an easier form of philosophy, see Partenie (2011) pp. 7–10. See Edmonds (2012) for myth as allegory for rational development through elenchus, and see Most (2012) (myth as discursive). Most recognizes *mythos* as access to truth complementary to *logos*. See Tarrant (2012) for comments on Plutarch spelling out Platonic philosophy through myth. See Collobert et al. (2012) for myth as grounded in knowledge and referring to philosophical propositions, argument, or form. Collobert et al. also refer to myth as rational complement to dialectic, a developed metaphor, and rational image—limited since it captures only a part and not the whole of the truth. For Collobert et al., myth is an image that cannot fully capture or represent knowledge (pp. 3–5).

[80] Cassirer (1955). Cassirer argues that underlying the creation of myth are a 'mythical *a priori*' and particular categories of mythic thought. He does not elaborate on the details of these features but deduces them from a unifying, harmony-inducing mythical 'tonality' that acts as a universal regulative force (p. 61). Cassirer conceives of the notion of 'wholeness' or 'unities' as an emotional impulse in contrast to Kant, who understands unities as logical or rational totalities. Cassirer believes that mythical thought grew out of an emotional drive and this proves that the *a priori* structure giving rise to myth and myths themselves are irrational, but that they appear to be logical. He explains in *Mythical Thought* that myth categorizes its material like science but instead of logical categories of genus it classifies them according to 'the law of concrescence' (p. 64). According to Cassirer, distinctly different elements can be unified under the principle of affect in which the elements both grow to relate to each other and become more alike. They are combined under one category by an irrational desire or need. It seems that logical force is at work in linking diverse mythical objects. But in mythical thinking, unlike a valid syllogism, one is simply unifying things by using an uncritical act of the will. Myth originates from the emotions and not from the intellect, so it is inferior to science, but using a Hegelian conception of the history of ideas, Cassirer argues that mythical thinking eventually led to scientific thought. Through his theory of myth, Cassirer tries to reconcile features of Romanticism with aspects of rationalism. He does not reduce the principle of unification and categorization of objects of mythical thought to the irrational but claims that the emotional source of mythical thinking, and therefore the content of myth, is irrational and false. For a concise analysis of Cassirer's views on myth, see Doty (1986) pp. 174–175; Segal (2004) pp. 38–40.

[81] A strong influence from the cultural positivism of Stewart's time is deeply embedded in his various explanations and use of vocabulary.

[82] Stewart (1905) pp. 4–6.

# 1 Myth and Philosophy on Stage: Connections, Divisions,...

creation of heaven and earth (cosmology), humans and their faculties, virtues, society, nations, cities, art, instruments, rituals, animals, and vegetation.[83] His historical account aside, Stewart's view is important because it is one of the only positions that does not subscribe to the inferior/superior paradigm of *mythos* and *logos* characteristic of other positions.[84] However, Stewart's analysis stops short in trying to integrate the two elements.

An approach that interprets the interrelation between *mythos* and *logos* with attention to the peculiarities of Plato's style of writing and his philosophical method must consider a number of salient questions. The methodology I use to analyze the use of myth in selected dialogues addresses questions that appreciate the following issues: (1) the literary and performative aspects, (2) structural authority, and (3) hermeneutical matters.[85]

Questions relating to 1:

(a) What are the literary and dramatic characteristics of myths?
(b) How is myth related to other, similar writing? Does myth have an equivalent in terms of style? Is it an anti-genre? Is it unique?
(c) What other texts may have influenced its formation and development?
(d) What are the dramatic or literary markers not found elsewhere in other examples of literature (including other Platonic dialogues), and why are they there?
(e) Are there indications in myth for the correct context for interpretation?

Questions relating to 2:

(a) What are the innate dynamics of myth and do they correspond to those found in the overall structure of the dialogue?

---

[83] Stewart (1905) p. 10. Also, consider comments related to etiology by Kirk (1984) p. 55.

[84] For other pre-twentieth century approaches that resist dichotomy or complicate and problematize the distinctions, consider Fontenelle, Vico, Fréret, Akenside, Lowth, Heyne, Herder, the Schlegel brothers, and Schelling. See Feldman and Richardson (1972).

[85] I am indebted to William Doty for listing some of these crucial questions and categorizing them in the way I have here (Doty [1986] pp. xvi–xvii). His methodology for understanding different kinds of myths shaped my approach to the study of Plato's myths; however, I apply only a select number of theories, functions, definitions, and interpretative techniques for my interdisciplinary reading of myth and philosophy in Platonic dialogues.

(b) To what extent does myth represent a class of similarly structured materials, and to what extent is it unique?
(c) How does myth fit into the dialogues' conceptual, aesthetic, and semiotic system? Is it shaped by other privileged codes or does it function as a master code governing other elements in the text?

Questions relating to 3:

(a) What symbolic and iconic traces of myth can be found in the rest of the text? Correspondingly, how can the place and function of certain symbols and icons be understood once they are identified as traces of myth?
(b) What relevance does the positioning of myths have in Plato's dialogues? How can we understand myth as a primary element rather than secondary or peripheral?
(c) How self-evident is the meaning of myth to the reader-listener? Does it require extensive exegesis?

In addition, one must not approach the relationship between *mythos* and *logos* in individual dialogues based solely on the general meaning of the terms for Plato's contemporaries or his use of the terms in other dialogues. Linguistic issues and use of terminology are important, but overemphasis on terms runs into problems when faced with Plato's notorious inconsistency in using the terms *mythos* and *logos*. At times, they are understood as alternatives (*Prot.* 320c); sometimes one follows the other, implying they express different perspectives of a single point (*Prot.* 324d). Other times a myth is actually *logos* (*Symp.* 193d and *Gorg.* 523a, 526d–527a).[86] To complicate matters, Plato does not elaborate conclusively on the criteria for evaluating the difference between the two—whether they are better or worse, true or false, accurate or misleading, primary or secondary, emotionally or rationally appealing. One cannot determine the relationship between the two on the basis of fixed normative categories. The relationship needs to be understood by focusing on Plato's use of the two in each text and, more specifically, in each individual instance illustrating a distinct set of problems and themes.

---

[86] Most (2012) pp. 14–15. Also, see Janka (2002).

Approaching the matter by trying to identify mythical form or mythical content does not clear up the confusion. The dialogues are narratives and therefore necessarily contain plots that share a structure similar to that of other Greek myths. In addition, many of the arguments in the dialogues import ideas and material from their corresponding myths or myths from other dialogues.[87] Simply searching for the appearance of the term myth or its derivatives in the dialogues does not necessarily provide justification that the passage represents mythology. One needs to consider the many parts of the dialogues that are examples of myth yet are not labelled as such (for instance, the end of the *Gorgias* and the Egyptian myth in the *Phaedrus*). If the passage under consideration is in fact a myth (regardless of whether the term *mythos* or its derivatives have been used), we must ask more penetrative and compelling interpretative questions: (1) What kind of myth is it? (2) Why was it used in that particular section? (3) What kinds of interpretations and meanings does it invite? (4) How does it pertain to the issue at hand? (5) How does it relate to the rest of the dialogue?

## 1.4 Methodology and Genre

Questions pertaining to the validity and veracity of narrative deserve further examination. Stressing myth's vicinity to philosophical truth risks neglecting the inherent ambiguity or the polysemantic character of myths that resist conceptual definition.[88] The semantic ambiguity of myth—a floating signifier according to Detienne—still conditions the reader epistemologically, guides one to truth, and makes subtle critical suggestions. I am not suggesting that these considerations replace approaches by past commentators of Plato's myths; the methods I suggest are not exclusive in illuminating fundamental features of Plato's thought. But the way scholars address the role of myth in the dialogues evolves out of a study of genre and other kinds of classification rather than the technical use of genres and themes in connection with each other; there is little

---

[87] Morgan (2000) p. 37. Also, see Brochard (1974).
[88] Flood (2002) pp. 183–186.

examination of the use of myth and philosophy in connection with each other. Attention to the notion of 'genre' should not restrict, misdirect, or cloud interpretation of a text that plays with and fuses different modes of explanation, and philosophical approaches need to exercise caution when using literary categories.[89]

Definitions of Plato's myths are also heavily determined by explanations of the origins of myth within the wider historical context influencing classical Greek oral and literary culture (the genetic fallacy). And Plato's own attitude toward poetry influences reception of his use of myth (the intentional fallacy). In addition, the reaction of readers impacts the study of the myths Plato either wrote or included in his dialogues (the affective fallacy).[90] In the context of Platonic dialogues, scholars begin evaluations of myth on the basis of one or a combination of the three sources of information and proceed to analyze the place of all the myths from the dialogues.[91] I propose an inversion of this method. I explicate the inherent logic or dialectic between myth and argument in the context of selected dialogues and only then attempt to develop an evaluation of Plato's myths, primarily and solely, as they are presented and used by Plato in a Platonic dialogue (leading to a polymythic hermeneutics).[92]

Reducing myth to an all-encompassing definition raises fundamental problems, and different forms of reductionism pervade interpretations of Plato's myths. Both defenders of myth and its prosecutors share problematic features. Divergent readings of Plato's application of myth interpret his stories by using general descriptions of mythology. Developing a multi-functional understanding and creating meaning based on a

---

[89] Croce is credited for introducing the criticism and mistrust of the notion of genre into literary theory.

[90] For an explanation of the denunciation of the three fallacies in the study of literature by the New Critics, see Zima (1999) p. 22.

[91] Edelstein makes the point that the questions about the significance of Platonic myth, according to modern commentators, are closely related to problems pertaining to the relationship between reason and imagination/philosophy and poetry ([1949] p. 464). Similar to the problems arising from a focus on genre when addressing myth in the dialogues, overemphasis on the role and significance of imagination and poetic expression can also distract one from the unique and central features of Plato's mythological project.

[92] Edelstein proposes a similar approach ([1949] p. 464). Doty uses the term 'polyphasic definition' to represent a view of myth that uses the many different 'schools' of modern myth studies to address the many different myths and their diverse contexts ([1986] p. 40).

# 1 Myth and Philosophy on Stage: Connections, Divisions,... 29

notion of mythic pluralism remain evasive without nuanced comparisons between different kinds of myth from Homer through the lyric and tragic poets to Plato.[93] Myth, I argue, is not reducible to a fixed definition, a basic set of rules, or a single structure.[94] Recognizing the dynamic nature and function of myth is essential to understanding where it stands in relationship to philosophy.[95]

Interpretations of myth as essentially allegorical, educative, persuasive, intuitive, and illustrative, for instance, have been held by thinkers before the modern era.[96] However, the particular character of traditional interpretations of myth, their intellectual basis, and the fundamental arguments supporting them are products of Enlightenment and post-Enlightenment thought.[97] Coinciding with the creation of religious stud-

---

[93] Different cultures, both transnationally and within the ancient Greek world, see myth in ways that do not correspond exactly to general views of myth debated by scholars working on the relation between *mythos* and *logos*. For an example of how a reductive view of 'Greek Myth' is used to understand Plato's myths, see Most (2012) pp. 15–17. For a critical discussion of the relationship between the presentation of myth and truth in Greek literature, see Kobusch (2002). For the changing significance of myth according to various stages of ancient Greek culture, see Hatab (1990).

[94] Thinkers such as Roland Barthes argue for a polysemantic interpretation of literary texts, including philosophical texts (Barthes [1975]). I share his anti-metaphysical or anti-logocentric position on literature which illuminates the multiple dimensions and the multiple functions of literary texts and encourages appreciation of diverse features. For a brief explanation of the background to Barthes's thought and similar thinkers, see Zima (1999) Chaps. 6 and 7. Also consider comments on universal approaches by Kirk (1984) pp. 59–60.

[95] Most commentators bundle all myths from Homer to Plato into one general genre with shared characteristics and as the target of one standard criticism (Edelstein [1949] p. 465). Plato's attack on the poets in parts of some dialogues confirms that there was a general view of poetry held by philosophers. But this does not establish that it was the only perspective on the vast range of poetry available at the time. Nor does the fluctuating dissatisfaction of philosophers like Plato signify anything substantial about the intricacies and complexities associated with different myths, poets, and audiences. In *Myth and Philosophy*, Hatab illuminates the diversity of meaning and significance of myth in the ancient world.

[96] As early as Diogenes Laertius, commentators have referred to the practical use of myth for educative and rehabilitative purposes (DL 3.80). However, the epistemological complexity associated with learning from myths or the inherent argumentative logic in myth has not been explored completely. According to many interpretations, myth seems, paradoxically, to be useful for teaching very sophisticated moral ideals, assisting agents to recognize the virtue in practicing ethical behavior, but elementary or insufficient as a method for acquiring knowledge.

[97] The influential 'myth and ritual' school championed by anthropologist Sir James Frazer and W. Robertson Smith is one of the best representatives of Enlightenment-influenced methods of interpretation. For a brief description and criticism of Frazer's approach to myth, see Coupe (2006) pp. 22–26. Also, see Capps (1995) pp. 71–74. And Chap. 3 in Doty (1986).

ies as a distinct academic discipline, mythography became a specialized discipline characterized by systematic interpretation. The methodological foundations of myth studies, like religious studies, continue to be tested, transformed, and supplemented. Since its inception, the study of myth has invited perspectives from various disciplines; transplanting and developing specific methods; appropriating and using techniques; selecting new examples; and asking a set of fundamental questions.[98] Scholars of myth engage in continuing dialogues over the knowledge produced about an increasing range of myths and related topics, themes, and issues. Myth studies has the advantage of reaping the benefits of advances in philosophy, theology, anthropology, sociology, history, classics, psychology, and literary theory and criticism among other disciplines. The vast amount of material to work with from many parts of the world, diverse cultures, and different periods are also significant factors contributing to the enhancement of the discipline. As a result, the study of myth in the modern era expresses a particularly active dynamism missing from prior approaches to myth.

Patterns, positions, and presuppositions are easy to identify when searching through the short but robust history of myth studies. Today, academics are in a position to approach myth in a variety of ways in order to support diverse theoretical concerns and intellectual projects. 'Scholars can engage in descriptive, comparative, isolative, and synthesizing intellectual activity, sometimes in order to defend the propriety of a subject, sometimes to demonstrate its utility, sometimes to verify it, or, conversely, to explain it away, sometimes to give it sanction, and sometimes to illustrate the attractiveness of a theory of their own'.[99] Regardless of the diversity of approaches and intentions in myth studies, the fundamental questions that modern commentators ask remain the same:

1. How does myth arise?

    (a) Which human capacity gives rise to it?
    (b) What kind of symbolic expression is it?

---

[98] Segal (2004) pp. 2–4.
[99] Capps (1995) p. xvi.

2. How can one describe it?

   (a) How can its truth be assessed?
   (b) What method of interpretation is valid?

3. What is its function or purpose?

   (a) What difference does it make to our lives?
   (b) How does it affect different kinds of thought?

Questions pertaining to causes, explanations, and essential and distinguishing characteristics have determined the third set of questions relating to function. The analysis and conclusions arrived at concerning description and cause shape and provide material for explaining the function of myth. Even though many theorists describe myth in one way, they accept that it can still have a number of functions. But ultimately, the function never steps beyond the limits drawn for it by the description of its essential meaning.[100]

Since interpretations of mythology by Presocratics, Western philosophers self-identify in contrast to myth, leading to a particular way of understanding and engaging with the genre. Philosophers communicate with myth by creating discourses that distinguish between philosophical and non-philosophical readings and applications of myth. Without recognition of the long history of this ambiguous medium, one easily stigmatizes all myths as the irrational 'other' in contrast to philosophy and falls back on the traditional *mythos/logos* distinction.[101] Morgan acknowledges that boundaries separating myth and philosophy exist but that these boundaries need to be redrawn in order to theorize regarding 'the permeation of one level by material from another'.[102] Myth considered in isolation from philosophy renders itself vulnerable to being categorized as decorative.

---

[100] Consider the methodology employed by Colloud-Streit (2005), which is sensitive to the problems associated with definition and function.
[101] Morgan (2000) p. 3. Also, see Schmitt (2002).
[102] Morgan (2000) p. 5.

Responses to the above set of questions shape the study of myth and determine the way Plato's myths are received. In order to understand the answers provided by modern scholars, one must acknowledge the conceptual philosophical framework developing or impacting theories of myth. The short history of myth studies consists of theories stemming from multidisciplinary concerns and interests, and the relevance of theories extends far beyond the subject of myth. But regardless of the origin of ideas or their consequences for other issues, there is nevertheless a tradition in modern intellectual history to draw upon.[103] Viewing the study of a subject within a particular time period, consisting of certain influential individuals and driven by central questions, helps establish a manageable research setting for critically evaluating interpretations and conclusions. Therefore, the dominant approaches in Plato studies must be identified as part of another narrative: the modern creation and development of myth studies.

---

[103] In his forward to Feldman and Richardson's *The Rise of Modern Mythology: 1680–1860* (1972), Eliade indicates the need for a comprehensive source book of the largely Max Müller-inspired era of mythography (i.e., the nineteenth/twentieth century). He states that most authors of this period are driven by a 'scientific' method in their study of myth (p. xii); also, see Blok (1994) and Bremmer (2011) pp. 533–538; and consider Fourmont's earlier contribution to the approach that combines philology with comparative mythology in Feldman and Richardson (1972) pp. 83–84; for the similarities between Max Müller's views of language and Heyne's notion of the 'disease of language', see Feldman and Richardson (1972) p. 217. For Müller's contribution to myth studies, see his foundational work *Introduction to the Science of Religion: four lectures delivered at the Royal Institution, February 19* (1882). For critical commentary of his work and influence, see Feldman and Richardson (1972) p. 481; Lincoln (1999) pp. 66–71; Capps (1995) pp. 86–71.

# 2

# Mutual Scaffolding: Unifying Myth and Philosophy

The distinction between definition and function is illuminating in relation to my analysis of myth. Rather than approaching the topic of myth with a general definition of genre, I concentrate on the function of myth in unique contexts; that is, the various functions of Platonic myths are determined by specific philosophical concerns and the thematic, discursive, and literary factors conditioning them. For many commentators, a particular definition of myth determines interpretation of its use and what it stands for in Plato's philosophy. In contrast, my position is sensitive to the complexities associated with the function of different myths as they appear in Plato's works.[1] I avoid rendering a general analysis of myth in Plato and strive to study the operation of particular myths in relation to exclusive philosophical arguments and the nuanced arrangements and interconnected dynamics between these aspects. I prioritize issues pertaining to function over definition; explanation and analysis of function coincide with Plato's references to his own myths and his suggestions about the distinctions between the different kinds of myths employed in

---

[1] Compare with Colloud-Streit (2005).

the dialogues. I avoid a generic perspective and conventional reductive notions and highlight specific kinds of philosophical myths.[2]

My analysis allows for an interdisciplinary and holistic look at Platonic dialectic through integration of myths and the arguments they partner with. I argue that little attention is focused on Plato as a writer of myth in isolation from other myth-makers. And since *mythos* and *logos* are too often dichotomized in Plato scholarship, the identification of influences by one on the other—or exchanges and appropriations of concepts, themes, and motifs—is underdeveloped; interpretations are still committed to the 'dichotomy' paradigm. By acknowledging the uncertainty and ambiguity associated with delineating the parameters of myth and philosophy, one relinquishes the search for an authoritative discourse. The content and delivery of myth are important but must be evaluated within the philosophical context in which they appear and the philosophical commentary Plato offers.

Luc Brisson's analysis of non-Platonic myth offers valuable insight into a worldview significantly influenced by literary culture, and his interpretation states that myth stands in contrast to philosophy in fundamental ways.[3] Brisson distinguishes and defines genres and gives less emphasis to Plato's individual technique. Over-concern with the *myth/logos* division neglects the substantial distinctions between Plato's myths and other myths; it limits evaluations of Plato as an author of myth and is insufficient in accounting for the multifunctional nature of myth.[4] Scott observes some of the confusion arising from analysis influenced by the dichotomy paradigm or the allegorical method:

> Some readers may be tempted to treat the dramatic element as mere packaging, or literary *joie de vivre* intended to draw us into the dialogue, which they then go on to ransack for philosophical arguments. But it is possible

---

[2] Consider the approach used by Manuwald (2002). See Droz's helpful classification of Plato's myths at the beginning of *Les Mythes platoniciens* (1992).
[3] Brisson (1998).
[4] In contrast to Brisson, Mattei states that Plato's criticism of myth bears only on the myths of his predecessors. However, both positions share the same problem of bundling a wide range of myths and literary figures into one category without considering the nuances and distinctions separating them (Mattei [1988] p. 67). For a study of Greek myth sensitive to the peculiarities and nuances of different writers and stages of myth literature, see Hatab (1990).

to go the opposite extreme, and to be so caught up by Plato's powers of characterization that one ends up reading a passage merely as an episode in an unfolding psychological drama, without asking what philosophical pay-off is involved.[5]

Plato's mythological project requires a method open to an interdependent relationship that aims at rethinking his interest and objectives concerning the traditionally non-philosophical genre. I examine a number of alternative ways to read Plato's use of myth and indicate the benefits of interpreting the relationship between myth and argument interdependently.

## 2.1 Mutual Scaffolding (A Dialectical Unity)

> Philosophical myth is tied to the rational arguments which surround it, draws its strength from that context, and can influence the progression and formulation of philosophical discussion.[6]

Plato wrote myths as integral parts of his dialogues, but methodological caution and historical awareness are necessary for comparing different Platonic myths and defining their functions.[7] My analysis describes the relationship between myth and argument in terms of a revolving dialectical circle or unity; I examine how Plato orchestrates a harmonious affair between philosophy and myth—an engagement conducted under

---

[5] Scott (2006) p. 5.
[6] Morgan (2000) p. 161.
[7] Edelstein (1949) gives a compelling explanation of Plato's myths that involves categorizing the most important myths into 'eschatological' and 'historical'. The eschatological myths, he says, take on a new and more sophisticated role after the *Gorgias* (p. 475), which feature an ethical dimension characteristic of Plato's epistemology but also detail the consequences of wisdom and ignorance. However, Edelstein does not clarify which myths have the more philosophical qualities and why. Also, he does not specify which characteristics distinguish philosophical myths form others. On page 478, he mentions that Plato did not intend his own philosophical myths to be used to educate children being raised for guardianship or to teach religion to the masses. This indicates that Edelstein saw Plato's myths as a heterogeneous form of explanation. However, he does not explore details concerning the different varieties of myth. Also, Edelstein's perspective accepts and confirms the bifurcation of myth and reason. He states that Plato reintegrated the two but holds that one pertains to the irrational aspects of the soul and the other to the rational. There is no analysis of the cooperation between the two types of explication (p. 476).

self-imposed regulations of reciprocity.[8] To disclose deeper connections between myth and philosophy, I use a new concept: 'mutual scaffolding'.[9] This trope is useful for analyzing situations in the dialogues when two distinct genres appear as equally valid and contingent on each other.[10] Interdependent exchanges between myth and argument do not occur with every use of myth; I identify myths that participate in this form of unification, their important function in this role, and what themes and ideas they introduce to the dialogue.

Ferrari proposes a similar approach to the *Gorgias*: '… announcing himself convinced of the truth of this narrative that he has heard, Socrates proceeds to "draw inferences" from it (524b). These inferences are not conclusions so much as they are statements of what is required by the story if it is to make sense. Death, he reasons, must involve the clean separation of the soul from the body; otherwise, Zeus's judges could not judge without prejudice, as the story requires. Furthermore, if the soul is to be judged naked, it must bear judgeable signs that are independent of the body it once wore'.[11]

Myths are fanciful stories but they must be regarded as equally important as the arguments in Plato's dialogues. Myths are an organic part of the Platonic drama and not an added ornament and far from an allegorical reproduction of argument.[12] Scholars such as Stewart recognize the inherent value of Plato's myths, which he feels deserve the same attention devoted to the discursive sections of the dialogues.[13] In pivotal places,

---

[8] Jean Piaget's perspective of structure is relevant to my approach: 'As a first approximation, we may say that a structure is a system of transformations. Inasmuch as it is a system and not a mere collection of elements and their properties, these transformations involve laws: the structure is preserved or enriched by the interplay of its transformation laws, which never yield results external to the system nor employ elements that are external to it. In short, the notion of structure is comprised of three key ideas: the idea of wholeness, the idea of transformation, and the idea of self-regulation' ([1970] p. 5).

[9] The definition of the term 'scaffold' suits the present argument both literally and metaphorically since 'scaffolding' means to provide or support an ascending construction with platforms often elevated high above the ground.

[10] Most (2002).

[11] Ferrari (2012) p. 70.

[12] Stewart (1905) pp. 1–3.

[13] The major contrast between my approach and Stewart's is that he isolates what he believes to be the most important myths—those of an eschatological nature—and interprets them apart from the rest of the dialogue.

## 2 Mutual Scaffolding: Unifying Myth and Philosophy

Plato's dialogues fluctuate between mythological material and discursive argument. The shifts occur mainly when prenatal existence and afterlife are considered. In certain dialogues, Socrates demands that we ask the moral question 'how ought one to live?'. Plato answers this question from two angles. At times he addresses the issue in relation to the afterlife and the consequences associated with one's way of living. Alternatively, he deals with the question as it pertains to worldly happiness and the harmony of the state.[14] Because Plato alternates between the two perspectives, he makes it difficult to identify whether he is using a myth or he is using argument (or both somehow). The interconnectedness of the two approaches adds to the complexity; deciphering the reasons for using myth alongside or in conjunction with philosophy requires an awareness of tropes suggesting hybridity and fusion.

There are many examples in Plato's works representing interdependence. For instance, the unconventional style of the *Phaedo* argument for transmigration of souls uses myth in philosophical ways rather than for rhetorical appeal or illustration. The literary style and techniques indicate a depth to the accounts that require a broader interpretative network of methods in order to penetrate. When responding to Socrates's description of the physical qualities acquired by inferior souls, apparitions, and the existence of Hades, Cebes states: 'It seems likely enough, Socrates' (81d). And when Socrates describes the transmigration of souls into animal or insect forms, Cebes replies: 'Yes, that is very likely' (82a) and 'Very likely' (82b). Plato ([1993a] p. xvi, fn. 12) mentions briefly the use of the term 'likely', indicating that what is implied is not the truth but an explanation that has some affinity with the truth. Also, at no point do any of Socrates's companions question or refer to the mythic quality of the eschatological account; that is, no influence from traditional folk tales, conventional Greek religion, or the mysteries is acknowledged, nor is there any hint at this point that Socrates is using allegory or playing on the prejudices of his audience.

Socrates changes the focus of the conversation from afterlife judgment to the care of the soul while embodied. At this point (82c), the dialogue

---

[14] For a study of the relationship between myth, perspective, distance, and truth, see Collobert (2012).

reconfirms the dualism characteristic of much of the *Phaedo*. Socrates prescribes a rigorously ascetic life solemnly devoted to philosophical investigation, avoiding the use of the senses 'unless it is necessary to do so' (83a). What clearly distinguishes this part of the dialogue from the previous section are Cebes's responses—bold, definitive, and unambiguously clear. Here Cebes answers with 'Quite so' (83c) and 'Yes, that is perfectly true, Socrates' (83e). And when he is questioned on whether he disagrees with the argued points he replies 'No, certainly not' (84a). Also, in a number of passages, Socrates highlights the fact that he is speaking metaphorically (83d) or clearly indicates reference to myth (84a). These literary tactics are employed in order to inform the reader of the status of the accounts, the comparisons and contrasts between the two accounts, and the importance of considering the character traits and expressions of the narrator and narratee. Also, more importantly, there is a guiding principle at work in the scenario which is represented in the myth at the end of the *Phaedo* and operating within the philosophical arguments.[15]

The manner in which Cebes replies in the *Phaedo*, corresponding with the two different referents of Socrates's arguments, presents us with an introduction on how Plato manages the relationship between myth and philosophy. In Socrates's account of the transmigration of souls, the events and objects are unfalsifiable (i.e., neither accessible to the senses nor the intellect).[16] And Socrates's instructions concerning the care of the soul in this world, and the reasons provided in support, engage with topics that can be verified empirically and rationally. Plato administers a reciprocal relationship between the two accounts. The argument for the care of the soul rests on the narrative account presented to illustrate the fate of the soul. Without the tale's description of the experiences of different disembodied souls, the moral justification for the soul's protection and maintenance loses efficacy. More importantly, without the myth, Plato's argument for the care of the soul lacks a governing principle or meaningful intention with which to build an argument. Certain truisms, or axioms, an ethical vision of the world, and a narrative framework (imbued with meaning and purpose) must be proposed in order for the argument

---

[15] I return to the *Phaedo* in Chap. 3.
[16] For these reasons, Cebes refers to Socrates's explanations as 'likely'. Also, see Burnyeat (2005) for criticism of interpretations of Timaeus's account in the *Timaeus* as a likely story.

## 2 Mutual Scaffolding: Unifying Myth and Philosophy

to form and develop.[17] And these emotive and normative features must correspond with, or ratify, the arguments in the passages regarding the care of the soul. According to the myth, one's actions ultimately lead to different degrees of damnation and salvation and, therefore, one must live a genuinely philosophical life even in the face of death. Plato's arguments are guided by this doctrine; he employs it to emphasize the ethical self-responsibility attached to human existence and promote a vision in which our actions are judged and either rewarded or punished according to a moral order.

These examples show that there is something important created out of myth and philosophy with profound connections to the philosophical questions and topics in the text. Categorizing particular literary and structural features assists in understanding my approach to individual dialogues and the internal dynamics interlacing these elements.[18] Philosophical myths are not completely open to the imagination; meaning is associated with support for philosophy. In the context of the dialogue, philosophical myths are unique and necessary creations; in Plato's literary work, they could not be replaced or be otherwise.[19] Morgan addresses the necessity for a reliable discourse to be unequivocal. One of the many criticisms aimed at myth by philosophers is that it comes in multiple versions, all of which are unavailable for verification but that philosophy provides inquirers with a stripped-down explanation committed to argument, completely open to verification, and available for scrutiny.[20] In relation to philosophical myths from Plato's dialogues, Morgan shows how they exhibit the same univocal quality found in the most rigorous philosophical treatise. Myths and arguments interrelate within

---

[17] There are significant parallels between my approach and Gould's theory in *Mythical Intentions in Modern Literature* (1981), in which he outlines the relevance of semiotics, interpretation theory, mythic expression, and the function of hypotheses in contemporary literature.

[18] For a study recognizing the profound relationship between literary analysis and myth criticism, see Doty (1986) Chap. 6. Also, consider Power's analysis of the literary structure of the 'Christian myth' ([2002] pp. 70–73). For other important interpretations from the modern history of mythography using literary criticism, consider interpretations by Andrew Ramsey (who also wrote on the *Phaedo* myth), Frye, Gould, and Propp.

[19] Plato uses different myths for some of the same topics. However, the perspective on the issue and the aspect addressed by the debate differ from dialogue to dialogue; varying contexts represent their own nuanced messages.

[20] Morgan (2000) p. 36.

the literary structure of a dialogue to create conditions for discourse and influence major themes and elements.

Plato constructs myths with a commitment to reason and restricts the subject matter accordingly. The plot structuring the myth becomes the regulating principle dictating Plato's selection, exclusion, and arrangement of literary elements and arguments. The myths that interrelate with arguments are unique and necessary, and modification of myths would alter the logical structure and efficacy of the rational parts of the dialogues.[21] Not all myths engage with arguments in this dialectical interplay. Illustrative or educational myths have different roles and functions in the dialogues.[22] My approach explores the possibilities in Plato's methodology and re-evaluates the distinctions that interpreters make between myth and philosophy in the dialogues. The systematic approach I take to the literary and philosophical components of specific dialogues proves the viability of mutual scaffolding. My primary concern is to understand Plato's administration of myth and argument, set up in the form of a philosophical drama, in which both are indispensable components of an intellectual and cultural message. The mutual scaffolding approach is aided by an appreciation and careful philosophical use of specific literary techniques. The interdependent connection between myth and argument requires systematic analysis of the literary and philosophical components. My reading examines the intricacies of form and content in selected dialogues and orders the details into a series of integrated thematic steps. I outline the analytical stages of my interpretation and the interrelated movements in my argument below. However, each of my five case studies of dialogue analysis integrates one example of modern myth theory which I employ to illuminate the important philosophical advances made possible by interdisciplinary work in this field. Introducing selected theories of myth to the study of Plato's myths is particularly useful for disclosing the interdependence of narrative and argument in the dialogues. My application of modern myth theories is heuristic and suggestive of the potential methodological and philosophical insights available to cross-disciplinary endeavors combining investigations of philosophy and myth. In his book

---

[21] Ferrari (2009).
[22] See Pender (2000).

## 2 Mutual Scaffolding: Unifying Myth and Philosophy

*Myth: A Very Short Introduction* (2004), Robert Segal promotes the use of theories of myth and offers critical suggestions for moving forward:

> Being skeptical of the universality of any theory is one thing. Being able to sidestep theorizing altogether is another.
> Theories need myths as much as myths need theories. If theories illuminate myths, myths confirm theories. True, the sheer applicability of a myth does not itself confirm the theory, the tenets of which must be established in their own right. For example, to show that Jung's theory, when applied, elucidates the myth of Adonis would not itself establish the existence of a collective unconscious, which, on the contrary, would be presupposed. But one, albeit indirect, way of confirming a theory is to show how well it works *when* its tenets are assumed—this on the grounds that the theory must be either false or limited if it turns out not to work (p. 10).

I employ a distinct theory of myth for each of the dialogues I have selected; however, the applicability of the individual theories is not exclusive to the philosophical myth I match it with. The analytical interpretations of sacred narratives I use for discussing specific dialogues are not mutually exclusive; theories are interchangeable and have the potential to illuminate unique aspects and meanings depending on the dialogue and the function of each particular myth.[23] The important move for my analysis is how I apply the theory to access features of the myth and elucidate the multilayered and interconnected structural, stylistic, mythical, and discursive elements of Plato's philosophy:

1. I begin by concentrating on the way Plato introduces the central theme of the dialogue—how the philosophical questions and problems arise, who raises them, who responds, and how they perform speech acts. In addition, I explore the setting of the dialogue, the

---

[23] For instance, the trickster trope or the concept of liminality that I integrate into my analysis of the *Meno* has the potential to operate in important ways in many other dialogues. (I also employ factors such as liminal time in my reading of the *Phaedo* and liminal space in relation to the *Phaedrus*.) A theory of myth focusing on liminality discloses unique elements in different works and indicates the versatility of theories of myth. However, myth theorists themselves claim that their approaches are theories of myth per se and can be applied universally. My analysis is more pragmatic; rather than attempting to justify one theory over others, I incorporate theories as part of my investigation of the myth/philosophy interdependence in Platonic dialogues.

potent themes and motifs portrayed, and their significance in relation to the other major elements of the text. My focus on introduction and setting also involves consideration of narrative mode (i.e., the role of the explicit or implicit narrator(s) and narratee(s)); I am concerned with Plato's choice of narrator(s) and narratee(s) and what this choice tells us about the presentation of important issues in the text.[24]

2. I analyze the major myth and the philosophical arguments in selected dialogues, followed by a description of how Plato orchestrated the intricate interplay between the two.
3. I clarify some of the most important literary motifs at work in the reciprocal relation between myth and argument by concentrating on plot structure and character selection.[25]

The first dialogue I analyze is the *Meno* and I focus on its important instructional value. The *Meno* does not contain a myth but makes strong reference to myths. The argument develops from a belief system introduced by Socrates's interpretation of religion and myth. The dialogue is a compelling introductory example of how *mythos* and *logos* cooperate (i.e., how a belief is justified by its intellectual and social consequences). I describe the *Meno* as a 'meta' dialogue in which Plato shows us a more complex way of doing philosophy. It provides an accessible example for introducing my methodology and justifies the structure of my analysis of how Plato orchestrates and intertwines theme introduction, setting, narrative mode, myth, philosophical arguments, plot structure, and characters. Although the other texts I analyze—*Protagoras*, *Phaedrus*, and *Phaedo* and the Atlantis myth in *Timaeus* and *Critias*—have more complex philosophical messages and structures than the *Meno*, my study remains methodologically and structurally consistent. The uniformity of my approach aims to strengthen the justification for the mutual

---

[24] For a comparison and contrast between dramatic dialogues and narrative dialogues and their use of literary devices such as setting, narrators, and narratees, see Morgan (2004).

[25] For the use of literary motifs in historiography and the transformation of a chronicle of events into a story, see White (1973) pp. 5–7. White discusses the significance of 'inaugural motifs', 'terminating motifs', and 'transitional motifs' in characterizing certain events in a chronicle. Considering themes and motifs from the dialogues in similar ways opens new interpretative possibilities. I expand on these three motifs by searching for examples in Plato's texts that reflect or strengthen structural themes from the plot, characters, and events.

## 2 Mutual Scaffolding: Unifying Myth and Philosophy

scaffolding method. I replicate the same framework in each study, and my interdisciplinary reading of the relationship between *mythos* and *logos* uses different multidisciplinary techniques and trans-disciplinary ideas; however, the structure positions the diverse theories and reinforces my methodology.

I limit my analysis of the six dialogues to a set of issues that encompass major themes and concerns: (1) theme introduction, setting and narrative mode, (2) myth analysis, (3) the philosophical arguments, (4) mutual scaffolding, (5) plot structure, and (6) character selection. Using these particular topics to approach *mythos/logos* interdependence (a) identifies the most significant literary features and amplifies the potency of the mythical and philosophical content and (b) best assists my arguments for elucidating the kind of interaction that exists between them. Social, cultural, and literary concepts and theories are important to the study of philosophical texts, and I make use of different techniques and ideas from a range of disciplines.[26] The emergence of modern approaches to literature coincides with the development of philosophical methods and supports my integrative reading of myth.[27] Historical and multidisciplinary methodological issues are important especially for interdisciplinary style research of Plato's dialogues.[28]

My analysis of plot involves interpretation of the structural patterns shared by the major myth in each dialogue and corresponding philosophical components. Plato's dialogues are governed by plot structures aimed at achieving multiple purposes, one of which is to introduce complex arguments. As examples of embedded narratives, myth in Plato's works is also controlled by plots employed to arrange the sequence of events and convey a meaning consistent with the context of the dialogue. Comparing the structure of myths and arguments helps disclose the way *mythos* functions as a guiding principle and illuminates the significance of many themes and motifs constitutive of the text. Plot structures characterize myth and argument and determine the communication

---

[26] See my outline for dialogue analysis and other references in the introduction.

[27] See Zima (1999), particularly Chap. 1, 'The Philosophical and Aesthetic Foundations of Literary Theories', pp. 1–16.

[28] Eckstein (1968) pp. 16–17 also promotes an interdisciplinary approach to the dialogues and explains how Plato reveals his meanings through what the characters *do* (active judgments), *make* (exhibitive judgments), and *say* (assertive judgments).

between them.[29] The deeper structure or plot orders various elements of the dialogues such as literary symbols or steps in an inference. The narrative structure determines the setting, standpoint, and purpose of the dialogue and assists in interpreting the nuances of the text.[30] An approach that focuses on literary plot draws attention to features such as setting, introduction, narrator(s) and narratee(s), characters, and motifs and their important relationship with the arguments and their premises.[31]

The speech acts in Plato's modes of presentation display complex dramatic elements and require interpretation to elucidate the importance of characters and their temperaments, delivery, the different scenes, and the issues interlocutors investigate together. I focus on specific speech acts and draw attention to the connection between the nuances of what is said at particular moments, the personal features of the speaking character, the context in which the utterances are made, and the recipient and reception of the speech act. Important details worth considering include the reputation of the protagonists; their way of speaking; narrative mode and manner of narrating; attitudes toward ideas and positions; and the actions, reactions, and occurrences that take place while someone is speaking, including interruptions and diversions of different sorts.[32] 'By imitating language mimetically, by reproducing its phonetic particularities and oddities, the narrator conveys a vivid impression of

---

[29] Mythic narratives also play a crucial role in the development of knowledge in other disciplines such as science. See Gerhart and Russell (2002) pp. 192–193. For the influence of myth in relation to politics and culture, see Bottici (2007); Bottici and Challand (2010).

[30] Roland Barthes's distinction between the syntagmatic level and the paradigmatic level is useful for understanding the 'grammar' of narratives. (For a brief account of the origins and details associated with this distinction in structuralist approaches, see Propp (1968) pp. xi–xii; Csapo (2005) Chap. 5.) The syntagmatic level is characterized by core functions, or essential events that cannot be omitted from the story, and catalysts, which absorb the core functions and shape them. The paradigmatic level is made up of informants, which are usually unalterable facts about people, places, and situations, and indices, which depict the atmosphere in which the facts acquire meaning and influence our judgment of the events and actions (Barthes [1996]; also, see Schmitz [2007] p. 51). In my study of the dialogues, I concentrate on the plot as a paradigmatic feature that governs the units of information in the text and projects a particular environment in which the units take form. I consider the myth to be an indication of the kind of plot that pervades different dimensions of the dialogue; the plot also structures the myth itself. Also, see comments on plot by Doty (1986) p. 16. See Gould (1981) for the relationship between logic, myth, and plot and the extent to which an author's system of logic is constrained by modes of mythic thought.

[31] For a similar approach used to study fairy tales, see Propp (1968).

[32] See Bondell (2002).

## 2 Mutual Scaffolding: Unifying Myth and Philosophy 45

people's psyche, their social status, their problems.... what counts is the *how*: the way of saying and the narrative technique'.[33]

I distinguish between the act of narrating or the produced narrative action, the narrative text (the signifier), and the story or content (the signified).[34] Following Genette's theory, once narrative mode is respected as a distinct feature of the dialogues, worthy of specialized research, a number of insights can be gleaned.[35] An approach that is sensitive to the narrator—explicit or implied narrator(s)—is essential, particularly in dialogues in which narrative voice shifts.[36] Also, the perception of the narrator in relation to the story at the time of narration must be accounted for along with reception by characters in the story (narratees).[37] In addition to these important issues, some temporal factors need to be acknowledged and integrated into a study of narrative mode. For instance, the distance between the narration and the story is critical, and the events that took place during the interval need to be considered when determining the levels of meaning expressed by a text. And in cases in which no narrator is mentioned or implied, the issue is complicated even further.[38]

---

[33] Zima (1999) p. 30. Also, consider the insights of Virginia Woolf on Plato's literary and philosophical style: 'All this flows over the arguments of Plato—laughter and movement; people getting up and going out; the hour changing; tempers being lost; jokes cracked; the dawn rising. Truth, it seems, is various; Truth is to be pursued with all our faculties. Are we to rule out the amusements, the tenderness, the frivolities of friendship because we love truth? Will truth be quicker found because we stop our ears to music and drink no wine, and sleep instead of talking through the long winter's night? So in these dialogues we are made to seek truth with every part of us. For Plato, of course, had the dramatic genius. It is by means of that, by an art which conveys in a sentence or two the setting and the atmosphere, and then with perfect adroitness insinuates itself into the coils of the argument without losing its liveliness and grace, and then contracts to bare statement, and then, mounting, expands and soars in that higher air which is generally reached only by the more extreme measures of poetry—it is this art which plays upon us in so many ways at once and brings us to an exultation of mind which can only be reached when all the powers are called upon to contribute their energy to the whole' (Woolf, *On Not Knowing Greek* [1925]).

[34] I am indebted to Gerard Genette's theory regarding the act of narrating in a story for this distinction. His work is indispensable to the study of narratology in general and narrative mode in particular (Genette [1980]; [1982]; [1988]; [1992]). 'Genette's narratological system is arguably the most important one today because even narratologists who do not simply accept and follow it often take it as a starting point of their own approaches' (Schmitz [2007] p. 56). For Genette's influence on Plato studies, see Morgan (2004). In addition, consider the work of Mieke Bal in relation to the most salient aspects of narratology (1997).

[35] See comments by Larivée (2012) pp. 236–237.

[36] de Jong (2004b) pp. 1–10. Also, see Bondell (2002).

[37] de Jong (2004b) pp. 1–10.

[38] See Genette's interesting view of 'zero focalization' ([1988] p. 73).

Other compelling issues regarding narrative voice include instances in which narrators are influenced by the point of view of other characters in the story, which is the case in many Platonic dialogues: 'the narrator-text does not consist of a succession of events only, but is interspersed with short 'peeps' into the minds of the characters participating in those events'.[39] Considering these narrative aspects raises more interesting question about the aim and message of the text, the subtle suggestions made by the author indicating how to engage with the exchanges, and the extent to which one must interpret the encounters and outcomes as representations of the view of the author.[40]

A re-evaluation of the description and function of myth must be understood in the context of modern myth studies and critically assessed upon identifying the problems associated with theories of myth. The chasm between myth and reason expanded further in the nineteenth century, and many dominant narratives aggrandizing the advancement of Western civilization predominantly support the myth/philosophy dichotomy by arguing for the victory of reason, history, science, and liberation over unreason, myth, dreams, and religious speculation.[41] Philosophers such as Horkheimer, Adorno, and Foucault criticize this view of Western history. They argue that interpreting the two sides of the dichotomy as polar opposites and striving to eliminate the weaker side is misguided since both sides need to be harmonized for a truly human approach to the world and oneself. Hayden White reinforces their critique by explaining that both sides must be taken seriously. In *Metahistory* (1973), he aims to illuminate the continuity between reason and fantasy and their partnership in assisting the discovery of truth.[42] To understand the place of myth in history and its relationship to reason, one must avoid using

---

[39] de Jong (2004, originally published 1987) p.113. Larivée (2012) pp. 236–237 discusses the significance of narrative voice when Socrates presents the myth of Er.

[40] Different forms of narrative mode and their possible relationships to authorship are areas of study central to philosophy, literature, cinema, and other forms of media. For insightful studies of these issues looking at literature and cinema, see Wilson (2006) and Currie (2006) pp. 185–210. Also, see the helpful introductory comments by Carroll (2006) pp. 175–184.

[41] Paul (2009) p. 62. Critical essays in Wians (2009) question the narrative that describes the emergence of ancient Greek philosophy out of, and in conflict with, mythology. Also, see Buxton (1999).

[42] White (1973) p. 51.

## 2 Mutual Scaffolding: Unifying Myth and Philosophy

the modality of opposition and introduce continuity and interchange instead. Myth and philosophy must not be seen as binary opposites but as parts of a whole, similar to the way philosophers such as Nietzsche, Hegel, Herder, Vico, Leibniz, and Le Doeuff interpret the relationship between the two.[43]

White argues that Western Enlightenment theorists, such as Kant, are convinced that a metonymical relation exists between myth and philosophy—one which operates in the mode of severance or extrinsic opposition. In accounts of the place of myth in history, Enlightenment historiography eliminates the possibility of recognizing symmetrical part-whole interaction and assumes that truth developed out of fantasy. Kant conceived of human nature as acting either rationally or irrationally and understood these functions as contradictory.[44] This perspective delineates the description and function of non-rational phenomena such as myth in contrast to an Enlightenment conception of rational discourse. And it represents individuals whose lives are not ordered and governed by those principles of reason, or who live according to the structures and schemata derived from cultural narratives or myths, as underdeveloped, capricious, disorderly, and epistemologically inferior (i.e., far removed from reality and human potential). Myth and reason need to be recognized as interacting in a symmetrical relationship—rather than evaluated and contrasted on the basis of modern scientific or modern philosophical principles—in order to reflect a more complete picture of human experience and thought. Kant criticized Herder by exposing his view regarding a human soteriological need for the reunion of science and myth, arguing that the notion is itself a myth.[45] My critique and approach avoid grand claims and are essentially heuristic: I challenge and rethink the artificial borders separating myth and philosophy, the cognitive consequences of maintaining these borders, and the cognitive and methodological possibilities that arise once we deconstruct them.[46] I show that an interdependent,

---

[43] Paul (2009) p. 63; Coupe (2006) pp. 118–121; Le Doeuff (1989).
[44] Kant (2002).
[45] Paul (2009) p. 64.
[46] Benitez describes Plato's reduction of *mythos* and *logos* as a contrast between story and arguments. He points out the problems associated with understanding this distinction in terms of a dichotomy ([2007] p. 226).

symmetrical harmony through mutual scaffolding is closer to what we find in Plato's use of philosophical myth—a way of thinking about the two in terms of creative interdependence or as integral parts of a totality. This approach to Plato's myths helps deconstruct the traditional binary interpretations and dichotomies—such as positivist and Romantic readings—that constitute the foundation for most modern theories of myth.

Interpreting myth and argument in the dialogues using this approach entails that Plato has full control and authority over the construction, the meaning, and the interactive structure of the two elements. Readdressing the philosophical myths and arguments in terms of their participation in a unity helps illuminate the variety of significant features in the dialogues; in particular, one begins to recognize how themes and motifs contained in the myths have a more enhanced meaning and occupy a more central place in the text. A mutual scaffolding approach interprets discursive arguments as indispensably bound to aesthetic representation. However, combining myth with philosophical arguments does not suggest demythologizing them. I argue that Plato respects the value of both forms for what they can contribute to the dialogues, which avoids the limitations imposed by modern categories or rigid notions of genre. Both myth and philosophy are specially selected and carefully combined to construct Plato's literary-philosophical work. The myths are symbolic, fictional (but not necessarily unreal), extravagant, and unfalsifiable. And Plato's philosophical components are dialectic, factual, logical, and demonstrative. What they are not is independent of each other, and I demonstrate that interpreting each in isolation compromises the significance of salient philosophical features.

The centrality of myth in Plato is informed by clarification of his critique and application of myth. Plato is 'critical' of myth; however, he simultaneously applies myths.[47] By 'critical', I mean Plato's analysis and evaluation of myth reflected in examples of his definitive descriptions of what it is, and prescription for why and how it should be used. The term 'applied' refers to the way myth is appropriated, manipulated, or implemented by

---

[47] Strenski uses these two terms to refer, on the one hand, to the theoretical analysis of myth by writers such as Cassirer, Eliade, Lévi-Strauss, and Malinowski and, on the other hand, to cultural and practical exploitation of myth by people such as Joyce, Rosenburg, and Bultmann (Strenski [1987] p. 2).

## 2 Mutual Scaffolding: Unifying Myth and Philosophy

Plato without providing explicit explanation directly related to the way he uses it in each instance.[48] A study of the relationship between myth and argument in Plato must show awareness of when Plato approaches myth critically and when he applies myth for his own purposes.

In some dialogues, Plato does not entertain the possibility of seeing myth in different ways and reduces it to one explanation. In other instances, he tolerates myth and recognizes the fact that it is more complex than one theory can accommodate.[49] Plato includes myths in some dialogues without reservation and in others he has Socrates provide commentary on myth or suggests a particular interpretation of myth (*Meno* 86b–c). Plato is not addressing one and the same discourse when he is being critical of myth and when he is applying myth. I distinguish between different kinds of myth in order to help understand Plato's ambivalence. The allegory of the cave, for instance, represents a narrative that is presented as neither fiction nor a real event. It is connected with argument through metaphor and not in the kind of symmetrical interdependent relationship characteristic of philosophical myths. In contrast to metaphor or allegory, philosophical myths participate in a unity, a display of mutual scaffolding. Myths that interact with arguments in this way are only applied and never criticized. In dialogues in which Plato is critical of myth and makes a distinct contrast with argument, he often chooses to employ myths for rhetorical purposes: illustration, education, or persuasion.

A key byproduct of my approach is to draw attention to a recurring 'liminal' theme in the dialogues. Liminality, 'outsiderhood', and 'lowermost status' are represented and implemented differently by Plato depending on the myth in question and the context of the dialogue. Liminality and associated entities and themes represent the marginal, the interstices, the outcast, underground or rejected elements in relation to structure.[50] Liminal phases in ritual are those moments coinciding with

---

[48] In addition to the critical/applied modes, also consider the detailed account of the modern distinction between mythology and mythography in the preface to Doty (1986).

[49] Examples include the *Protagoras* and *Timaeus*.

[50] Turner (1969) pp. 110–111 and (1974) pp. 233–237. As examples of despised or outlawed people who represent universal human values or 'open morality', Turner refers to the good Samaritan, the Jewish fiddler Rothschild in *Rothschild's Fiddle*, Jim in *Adventures of Huckleberry*

social structure, sometimes as an anti-structure, in which an individual or group breaks free and explores expressions of creativity made impossible or not tolerated within the standard structure or system. 'It is especially in the freedom of liminality that new metaphors are born, revisions of the social structure are first attempted, and creative insights are developed and nurtured'.[51] The 'outsiders' often represented in literature and oral histories who have the potential to express this kind of creative freedom in phases of liminality include shamans,[52] diviners, mediums, priests, monastic ascetics, hippies, hoboes, tricksters (the mythological character),[53] and Romani peoples.[54]

Liminality is a term first used by Arnold van Gennep referring to the phase in a rite of passage or transition ritual when change occurs in relation to place, state, social position, and age.[55] The use of the concept was made popular by Victor Turner, who realized the applicability of liminal themes to a wide range of sociological and anthropological topics. According to Turner, a liminal phase is an intervening period in the sequence of a ritual when the subject's status and qualities are ambiguous. The initiate does not possess the attributes of the exited state of being or the upcoming state; social status is temporarily suspended; and the stability characteristic of mundane social structures is shattered. Liminality is contrasted with structure (i.e., the hierarchy-based social system (political-legal-economic) that governs everyday life).

---

*Finn*, the fool in *King Lear*, and Sonya in *Crime and Punishment*. Turner also makes reference to Hume's view of the 'inferior' or 'outsider' who symbolizes the 'sentiment for humanity'. In relation to political philosophy, Turner uses the images of Rousseau's noble savage, Marx's proletariat, and Gandhi's untouchables (Turner [1974] p. 265). I do not examine Turner's notion of 'communitas' and its relation to liminality, marginality, and inferiority here. See Turner (1969) Chaps. 3, 4 and 5 for description and analysis of communitas.

[51] Doty (1986) pp. 91–92.
[52] Bertens (1995) pp. 74–75.
[53] Doty (1986) pp. 91; Hynes and Doty (1993). For a contemporary example that uses the trickster as a literary device, see Emily Wroe's analysis of Diran Adebayo's novel *My Once Upon a Time*: 'Towards a 'non-ghettocentric Black Brit vibe': A Trickster Inspired Approach to Storytelling in Diran Adebayo's *My Once Upon a Time*' (2005). Also, see Henry Louis Gates Jr., *The Signifying Monkey* (1988). For a cross-cultural and cross-historical study of the trickster character, see Helen Lock, 'Transformations of the Trickster', www.southerncrossreview.org/18/trickster.htm (visited 2008).
[54] Turner (1974) p. 233.
[55] Turner (1969) p. 94.

> The attributes of liminality or of liminal personae ("threshold people") are necessarily ambiguous, since this condition and these persons elude or slip through the network of classifications that normally locate states and positions in cultural space. Liminal entities are neither here nor there; they are betwixt and between the positions assigned and arrayed by law, custom, convention, and ceremonial.[56]

Turner explains that the ambiguity associated with liminality propagates a spectrum of profound symbols. These symbols often represent death, imprisonment, pre-natal or pre-birth states, invisibility, darkness, bisexuality, timelessness, wilderness, and the eclipsed sun or moon. Liminal individuals may be symbolically represented as, likened to, or equated with monsters, ascetics, certain animals, and special mythological and divine figures.[57] Familiar character traits of liminal figures are passivity, humility, and a willingness to accept punishment. These features play a crucial role in empowering the liminal person, people or other entity, and provide possibilities for surviving the liminal phase and successfully re-entering the social structure—a structure which is disrupted and transformed after interaction with an example of liminality.

Turner explores how liminal figures and phases allow original hypotheses to emerge. When a particular structure is disconcerted by an example of liminality, a free rearrangement of elements and factors is made possible and the newly constructed systems are tested according to reconsidered and re-evaluated criteria. Plato makes use of this motif primarily through liminal figures (*Meno*), liminal time (*Phaedo*), and liminal space (*Phaedrus*).[58] In my study of the dialogues, I indicate where and how liminal features are used and the reasons for introducing them.

---

[56] Turner (1969) p. 95.

[57] Turner (1974) p. 253.

[58] For a narrative that combines liminal time and liminal space, consider the myth of Er in the *Republic*. Also, see Gonzales (2012), who, in addition to dealing with spacio-temporal peculiarities associated with the narrative, discusses the way the tale blurs certain dichotomies—a characteristic of liminality. And see Ferrari (2009), Larivée (2012), and De Luise (2007) on relevant interpretations of the myth of Er. Other themes from the dialogues worthy of study in respect to liminality are the use of the twilight motif in the *Crito* and the initiation ritual in the *Symposium*.

Liminality, marginality, and structural inferiority are conditions in which are frequently generated myths, symbols, rituals, philosophical systems, and works of art. These cultural forms provide men with a set of templates or models which are, at one level, periodical reclassifications of reality and man's relationship to society, nature, and culture.[59]

---

[59] Turner (1969) pp. 128–129.

# Dialogue Analysis

# 3
# Myth and Instruction: *Meno*

## 3.1 Introducing the Trickster

Trickery as a strategy is integral to many myths and mythic traditions, and related practices such as deception, foils, mischief, play, mockery, and laughter help maneuver thought and emotion through layers of cultural meaning. They help convey the ambiguity and paradox associated with aspirations for wisdom and the fragility underlying the search for truth. Sacred stories employ trickery not as a simple form of embellished entertainment but to overturn or invert the structures governing thought, action, and custom and allow creativity and critical faculties to explore new possibilities. Myths that feature trickster characters or themes recondition and renew the structures determining thought, action, and custom. Humor functions as a subversive technique in these narratives; examples of complacency, conservativism, arrogance, and unconstrained and unquestioned power in myth are exposed when diminutive or weaker characters use tricks to gain the upper hand. 'Their stories provide a fertile source of cultural reflection and critical reflexivity that leaves one thoughtful yet laughing; and what a culture does with laughter reflects its

© The Editor(s) (if applicable) and The Author(s) 2016
O. Tofighian, *Myth and Philosophy in Platonic Dialogues*,
DOI 10.1057/978-1-137-58044-3_3

vitality, flexibility and creativity'.[1] Trickster tales represent the many manifestations of this subversive approach by instigating irreverent questioning, disrupting authority, and reframing social order and cultural custom. The trickster character is often portrayed in narratives as a religious and social critic and, simultaneously, both sacred individual and fool. These stories evoke a heightened expectation of immanent dissolution or disconcertion. The figure assigned the role of trickster—or the one who assumes the position—disrupts social and moral norms and embarrasses those who benefit from the preservation of the status quo.

Various forms of transformation take place in trickster myths, but the characters guided through the stages of change experience ambiguity about their development and destination. The trickster is both deviant and savior and other characters in the narrative experience his or her presence and instruction differently. 'Transformation is an important aspect of the story: a change of some kind is being experienced or described, whether a rite of passage or a move to a new society. In most stories, the trickster is not present as a trickster; he shadows the change that is being described'.[2]

Paul Radin's landmark work *The Trickster* was published in 1956 and included contributions by eminent myth scholars Karl Kerényi and Carl Jung. Radin's detailed inquiry introduced scholars to specialized study of the trickster, encouraged further investigation of the mythological character, and initiated new debates.[3] Academics from different disciplinary backgrounds disagree on whether, or to what extent, the trickster figure is universal; some argue that tricksters are so different across cultures and periods that a single category is unhelpful. However, an interpretation that acknowledges the trickster as a cross-cultural device is necessary for identifying and understanding profound similarities between myths from different societies. This must, of course, be tempered with concerns expressed by comparative mythographers from the social sciences who highlight the sociocultural specificity of divergent narratives.[4]

---

[1] Hynes and Doty (1993) p. 4. Also, see Russell (1991).
[2] Scheub (2012) p. 24.
[3] Babcock-Abrahams (1975) pp. 163–164. For examples of different approaches, see essays in Hynes and Doty (1993).
[4] Hynes and Doty (1993).

## 3 Myth and Instruction: *Meno*

In different tales expressing liminality, social variables and cultural indicators such as marginality, fringe, deviant, and outcast have either negative or positive connotations.[5] The trickster motif adopts many of these characteristics with the same kind of fluidity. Scheub clarifies how tricksters are distinguished from other phenomena with similar qualities by the far-reaching consequences of their actions, misgivings, and achievements. He defines the malleability associated with the character by explicating how tricksters maneuver easily between different experiences and shift form accordingly. They are conditioned and guided by their environment and interactions rather than actively defining experiences and encounters; their situations subsequently become the basis for ritualistic and artistic experience.[6]

> And there's a very special property in the trickster: he always breaks in, just as the unconscious does, to trip up the rational situation. He's both a fool and someone who's beyond the system. And the trickster hero represents all those possibilities of life that your mind hasn't decided it wants to deal with. The mind structures a lifestyle, and the fool or trickster represents another whole range of possibilities. He doesn't respect the values that you've set up for yourself, and smashes them.[7]

Liminal characters and other 'threshold' or 'border' phenomena from diverse oral and literary traditions function similarly; research in comparative mythology has produced a wealth of studies illustrating social, psychological, literary, religious, and performative comparisons. Therefore, searching for trickster themes and motifs in various traditions is valuable and helps disclose profound literary and philosophical messages. Investigation into the significance of the trickster also helps elucidate the phenomenal and emotive aspects associated with transition and transformation in sociocultural experiences and knowledge acquisition. In particular, the prevalence of liminal themes and subjects in Plato's dialogues deserves serious interdisciplinary analysis, and the use of trickster devices

---

[5] Babcock-Abrahams (1975) pp. 147–158.
[6] Scheub (2012) pp. 10–11.
[7] Campbell in Maher and Briggs (1988) p. 39.

in the *Meno* is one of a number of significant examples.[8] This chapter approaches the *Meno* with the range of analytical tools developed for understanding the trickster trope in comparative mythology. I demonstrate a hermeneutical sensibility that comes from acknowledging and engaging important literary, historical, and cultural contexts that situate the mythical character. Exploring the role of Socrates in the dialogue, I select and combine the relevant features that elucidate Plato's views in the text and position them within a liminal context. My approach situates the *Meno* in a framework that foregrounds liminality and projects related cross-cultural mythic elements (dualism, ritual transformation, and renewal), including the trickster figure.

Plato has Socrates refute many positions in the different dialogues, but a definitive theoretical position attributable to Plato hardly comes across.[9] Considering the range of situations and approaches across the dialogues, defining Plato's philosophy in terms of a definite metaphysical position may be too hasty.[10] In different dialogues, Plato guides the reader to see the world in a particular way and then reveals the spiritual, ethical, intellectual, and aesthetic value in seeing it in that way; he readjusts the perspective and method to expose any one of the many topics he feels requires critical attention.[11] Evidence for a definitive theory is scattered and if certain theoretical positions feature in a dialogue, description and commentary are incomplete. But this is no reason to reject the presence of a systematic theory of some form—a consistent theoretical perspective derived from discursive and literary features, structural factors, and intertextual examination.[12]

---

[8] I examine liminality as it pertains to the *Phaedo* and *Phaedrus* in Chapters 5 and 6. Socrates is depicted more as a rebel than a trickster in most of Plato's dialogues (consider the dual characteristics displayed by Prometheus or Hermes); however, in the *Meno*, trickster characteristics such as playfulness, jest, and deception are more pronounced.
[9] Crombie (1971) pp. 521–522.
[10] Sternfeld and Zyskind (1978) pp. 30–34.
[11] Bluck (1964) pp. 75–108.
[12] Ionescu states that the *Meno* represents Plato's first attempt at blending epistemology, ethics, and the Socratic form of argument (elenchus) with a hypothetical method of investigation. She argues that in this text Plato is not concerned simply with the essence of virtue but also aims to justify the search for the essence of virtue ([2007] p. xii). In addition, Ionescu explains how the *Meno* functions as transition by introducing theories and ideas revisited with more sophistication in later

## 3 Myth and Instruction: *Meno*

Hypothesis for Plato is not an abstract or purely theoretical proposition simply waiting to be proven. Perspectives and propositions introduced in the dialogues reflect serious social and political concerns contemporary with Plato and drive the intellectual debates prevalent among the various groups and individuals he encountered. The dialogues frame these sociocultural issues and analyze them by using Plato's philosophical method and literary style; in particular, they express the difficulties with finding working definitions and theories for explicating physical, moral, and aesthetic phenomena.[13] Plato's systematic use of the hypothetical method functions to create conditions limiting the scope of investigation, maintaining clarity, and sustaining rigorous methods as the inquiry proceeds.[14] As Bluck ([1964] p. 76) explains:

> So far as Socrates' immediate purpose in the *Meno* is concerned, he is using this method as an expedient to get over, or to get around, the difficulty that what virtue is has not been decided. But he is not simply making a random assumption, any more than the imaginary geometrician is making a random assumption about his figure...if these conditions [suggested in the hypothesis] are not satisfied, his answer will be No. The conditions are limiting conditions, and seeing whether or not they are satisfied will make possible a definite answer to the original question.

For Plato, a philosophically successful hypothesis renders a set of conditions from which to infer outcomes that correspond with the Good. This chapter interprets the success of myth in creating limiting conditions to determine the responses to epistemological questions. I argue that the myth interweaves with arguments to imply satisfactory consequences and conclusions. The role of myth in the *Meno* also informs the dialogue setting, character formation, tropes, and other literary techniques used to characterize the exchanges between interlocutors.

---

dialogues. (For further comments on the *Meno* as a transition dialogue, see Scott [2006] pp. 6–7 and Thomas [1980] pp. 10–16.)

[13] See Thomas's concerns regarding the problems associated with basing a theory of truth on coherence and hypothesis (Thomas [1980] pp. 155–156).

[14] In the *Republic*, hypothesis is used as a technical term and the *Phaedo* provides further elaboration of its use and significance. Crombie (1971) p. 528 also discusses the important place of hypothesis in the *Meno* and its relation to other dialogues.

I analyze the references made to myth and the mythic content imbued in certain passages of the *Meno* by examining how they introduce conditions for knowing and how those conditions impact the philosophical arguments. I test my theory of mutual scaffolding by analyzing the harmonious association between the discursive parts of the dialogue and the epistemic conditions introduced by the mythic passages—or references to myth by Socrates early in the *Meno*. I demonstrate how arguments following the myth refer back to, and draw their validity from, the myth (i.e., how all elements participate in an inference). A perspective concerning the structure and limits of knowledge is communicated by the myth, and by intertwining this view in the story line of the dialogue Plato both animates and constrains the literary features and philosophical sections. I also investigate how the mythic content referred to by Socrates provides the reader with a horizon for understanding the dialogue's plot, the place of the characters in the narrative, and the significance of particular themes and motifs in Plato's literary construction.

## 3.2 Theme Introduction, Setting, and Narrative Mode

The stylistic characteristics and narrative techniques employed in the *Meno* support the intellectual aims and philosophical purpose of the text. First, the dialogue begins abruptly.[15] There is no background to the story and no introduction explaining why and how the question is raised. Second, there is no setting for the dialogue.[16] Unlike in many other dialogues, the details concerning the location of the discussion and the sociocultural context are not even referred to.[17] Finally, Plato does not give any clues pertaining to the narrator in the text. These issues

---

[15] Meno begins by brashly asking a question and expects a quick, concise, and precise answer, reflecting his previous training under the influence of the sophists. This characteristic is indicative of his attitude in the first half of the dialogue (Eckstein [1968] p. 19 and Klein [1989] pp. 38–39).

[16] Sternfeld and Zyskind (1978) p. 20.

[17] For a study of some of the elements and possible presuppositions about the opening scene, see Ionescu (2007) pp. 1–10. Scott also makes important observations concerning the opening scene and the character of Meno (2006) pp. 11–13.

are important for a reading of the dialogue that appreciates the author's literary strategy; the points help inform a fuller analysis of structure and philosophical method. The narrative is detached from a scene; that is, no imaginative space is created by Plato. There is a 'meta' quality to the text, meaning that by using the analysis of virtue as a pretext Plato is actually presenting a didactic manual on how to begin doing philosophy.[18] This involves demonstrating the correct and incorrect; successful and unsuccessful; easy and difficult ways to evaluate definitions.[19] The dialogue also conveys a normative account of philosophical practice. Plato elucidates the relevance of philosophical inquiry for individuals aspiring to live a good life and the philosophical method most conductive for knowledge acquisition.

The lack of setting is a literary device that defines the philosophical messages of the text, and by neglecting this dramatic aspect Plato signals key points about interpreting the *Meno*. Plato's audience must wait until the demonstration involving the slave for the slightest evidence regarding environment (the experiment uses merely the sand on the ground); without a sense of location in any scene, the dialogue indicates abstraction, a general didactic quality, or purely theoretical principles.[20] Many intellectual Athenians at the time of Plato recognized the relevance of questions pertaining to the nature and teaching of *arête*; these issues had become commonplace within Greek moral thought.[21] The dialogue poses questions about the nature and teaching of virtue as pretext for an examination of epistemological issues.[22] Plato uses myth to frame the debate and

---

[18] Thompson explains that hardly any dialogue 'is so clear-cut and simple in its construction as the *Meno*' ([1901] pp. xxvi–xxvii).

[19] Tarrant argues that the *Meno* offers the reader a concise explanation of the key elements of Plato's philosophy and methodology. In particular, he explains how the text is a convenient introduction to Plato's ethics and epistemology. 'The kind of introduction that was then required would include material on Socratic definition, the link between virtue and knowledge, and the rules and importance of co-operative inquiry; the *Meno* fulfilled these requirements' (Tarrant [2005] p. 4). I add to Tarrant's interpretation by demonstrating how forms of narrative like myth provide a philosophically satisfactory and aesthetically rich framework for intellectual investigation.

[20] I use the term 'slave' rather than the commonly used compound noun 'slave boy'. Justification for removing 'boy' is provided by Benetiz (2016).

[21] Tarrant (2005) pp. 22–23.

[22] Other scholars share the view that questions pertaining to virtue were essentially a pretext for other concerns: 'But the drama of the episode consists in the fact that Socrates gives virtue a

in the absence of physical setting he relies only on conversation, rhetorical exchange, and the literary movements throughout the dialogue to animate the philosophical discussion. Interpreting the dialogue beyond the question of virtue and whether it can be taught requires interdisciplinary engagement with the mythic references and how they situate Plato's philosophical investigation. Also, the dialogue's structure shares features with the myth and informs the interaction between interlocutors and the knowledge produced through dialectic exchange; the *Meno* misses the dramatic embroidery found in other dialogues, but myth and narrative structure provide sufficient replacement.

Klein analyzes the dialogue in terms of its likeness to the hypothetical method used by geometers.[23] Plato renders a form of abstract analysis using models from geometry to support basic instruction of philosophical method. The interaction between these analytic concerns and the religious dimension of the dialogue offers more than the myth/philosophy dichotomy allows, and careful examination of structural features reveals narrative models administering both the discursive and mythic. An evaluation of structure as it pertains to both the dramatic scenes and philosophical inferences is necessary for interpreting consistent themes and motifs and their combined messages. The range of cultural and emotive elements enriching the *Meno* interweave with other dimensions of the inquiry and demand approaches that recognize their integration; overemphasis of the geometrical or mathematical (purely abstract) aspects of the dialogue risks neglecting the other forms of philosophical thinking on offer.[24] Plato is concerned with providing basic instruction rather than theorizing, and investigating the interaction between myth and philosophy grants insight into the delivery of his instructions. The critique of Meno, the inquiry into virtue, the

---

treatment as laudatory (and logically faulty) as anything Gorgias can produce … The principal point is that to find virtue to be knowledge or wisdom (hence teachable) is the wholly laudatory thing to say, and to sing virtue's praises is undoubtedly the object in the fine speeches Gorgias prepared Meno to make. To construe the hypothetical deductive section dramatically in the way that we have—as saying what Meno finds most satisfying—is more plausible than to consider it the locus of Socrates's real opinion about virtue, since he subsequently upsets it' (Sternfeld and Zyskind [1978] p. 14).

[23] Klein (1989) pp. 206–222.
[24] Klein (1989) pp. 206–222.

demonstration with the slave, and other dynamics in the text all comply with the conditions introduced by Socrates's discussion of his religious beliefs. His references frame the topic, pose the problems, and guide the questioning; myth constructs conditions for inquiry and meaning in the *Meno*.

The text begins by Meno posing a question to Socrates. By the time of the *Meno*, Socrates had established a reputation as *the* quintessential questioner in Plato's works.[25] The dialogue begins with Socrates under investigation rather than being the investigator; the scenario is unusual because it reverses many of the conventions of interaction between interlocutors preceding the *Meno*. Early in the dialogue, Plato implies that Meno will not complete his 'learning' experience or have time to be 'initiated'; Plato informs us that he must leave before the mysteries (76e). Education and philosophical instruction are key themes in the *Meno*, and in the early part of the dialogue Plato prepares the reader for the example of an individual who arrives at knowledge through the dialectic method. He introduces myth to create a context for inquiry.[26] Tarrant points out how ancient commentators saw the dialogue as an instructional manual to be used for philosophical practice. 'The work is an initial close encounter with philosophy, driven more by the interests of the potential recruit than by the philosopher's own agenda'.[27] Chronologically, the *Meno* comes after dialogues that are primarily concerned with definition and end in *aporia*, and recognizing its placement as a pedagogical contribution is important.

## 3.3 Myth Analysis

After being perplexed by Socrates, Meno presents an argument regarding learning; more accurately, he attempts to expose a paradox he sees in the activity of learning (80d). 'But how will you look for something when you don't in the least know what it is?'; alternatively, 'To put it another

---
[25] Tarrant (2005) p. 18.
[26] Day (1988) pp. 16–17. For a discussion of the link between dialectic and myth in philosophical education, see Most (2002).
[27] Tarrant (2005) p. 5.

way, even if you come right up against it, how will you know that what you have found is the thing you didn't know?'[28] Meno does not explain the theory of knowledge he holds in relation to this argument against learning but states the paradox immediately after he has been bewildered and humbled by Socrates (i.e., after a dialectic exchange has left Meno intellectually 'numb' and he cannot even begin to explain anything about virtue). Historically, Meno had a reputation for being an opportunist and for conducting an inquiry simply for the sake of winning a debate; he did not necessarily devise strong arguments for the sake of contributing to knowledge. His role in the dialogue is not far removed from this description except, in the privacy of a conversation with Socrates, he begins to reveal an openness to criticism and admits his misgivings.

In response to the paradox, Socrates endeavors to show Meno that his position on learning is misguided and that he ultimately fails at epistemology. Meno's learning is taken seriously and Socrates uses his paradox to mount a well-thought-out counter-theory. The points of reference he uses to explain why Meno's perspective is problematic are priests and priestesses who understand the truths of religion (81a). Socrates also acknowledges the significance of Pindar and other divinely inspired poets in his account and refutation of Meno's paradox. The views of these religious figures are true by virtue of inspiration. On the basis of two religious ideas, the immortality of the soul and reincarnation, Socrates deduces the theory of recollection.[29] By acknowledging the salience of the moral insight evoked by religion, Plato permits emotion and cultural concerns to resonate and enter the conceptual debates and rhetorical procedures implemented in philosophy.[30] He does not present his response with any argumentative rigor but explains, based on the religious beliefs he recalls, that his account is actually what everyone describes as 'seeking and learning'. Therefore, at this stage of the dialogue, the foundations for what he later demonstrates and argues, *anamnesis* or the theory of recollection, are religious beliefs and myths

---

[28] Weiss describes how the paradox is an objection to elenchus, thus marking, in dramatic terms, the correct time to step up to a more advanced method ([2001] p. 52).

[29] Bluck provides an important study of the place of earlier ideas and beliefs and their influence on Plato's theory of recollection ([1964] pp. 61–75).

[30] Tarrant (2005) p. 6.

about the transmigration of the immortal soul attributed to Pindar and other poets.[31] Plato's theory of recollection is based on claims derived from myths and religious beliefs,[32] and Socrates's attitude toward the 'truth' of the theory represents the indispensable function of myth in the arguments that follow.[33]

Plato counters Meno with a theory traced back to what priests, priestesses, Pindar, and other inspired poets tell. He quotes Pindar and presents the theory of recollection as an interpretation of Pindar's poem. Plato draws from the Orphic and Pythagorean traditions that share his interpretation of reincarnation, the basis of a righteous way of life, and possibilities for good and bad incarnations and salvation.[34] Socrates's comments following Pindar's poem endorse particular features of an Orphic and Pythagorean understanding of the poem, and Plato incorporates significant elements from these religious traditions into his theory of recollection. Orphic and Pythagorean features are appropriated and fused and, therefore, need to be understood in accordance with Plato's

---

[31] Ionescu gives three reasons for the use of myth in the *Meno*: first, Meno's lack of intelligence and its appeal to the emotions and the imagination; second, cultural familiarity and rhetorical appeal; third, as an introduction or basic facilitator (i.e., a mediator which assists one in moving from a simple story to a sophisticated philosophical theory) ([2007] pp. xviii and 47–49). Compare Ionescu's view of myth to what I describe in the first chapter as the dichotomy paradigm, or evaluation of myth using an inferior/superior framework to contrast with rational discourse.

[32] Later dialogues provide the necessary arguments required for removing the label myth from the theory of recollection (especially the *Phaedo*) but as it is represented in the *Meno* it features in a story without convincing rational justification. One must be careful not to import doctrinal peculiarities associated with Plato's later works and respect the text for its unique dramatic, structural, and philosophical arrangement and message (Tarrant [2005] p. 8). For an overview of the different perspectives of Plato's initial hypothesis in the *Meno*, see Ionescu (2007): 'Appendix II—The Initial Hypothesis in the *Meno*'.

For an analysis of the connection between recollection and mythical narratives or themes, see Klein (1989): Chap. V. He also discusses the significant role of the theory in some dialogues and Plato's reluctance to use it in others.

[33] Tarrant argues that it is absurd to suppose Plato introduces the theory primarily to combat Meno's eristic argument (Tarrant [2005] p. 37). I agree that it is implausible to assume the theory was developed *only* to respond, ad hoc, to Meno's paradox. However, the way the theory is presented is peculiar to the dialogue, is characterized by the myth, and is profoundly bound to the scenario in which it takes place. My interpretation sees the myth as sharing philosophical and literary affinities with *anamnesis* and provides inquirers with a better predisposition for learning. The myth's literary and stylistic qualities inform the structure of the text reflected in the plot, the characters, and dominant themes and motifs. I elaborate on these issues later in this chapter.

[34] Morgan (1992) p. 237; Bluck (1964) pp. 274–283.

metaphysical, epistemological, and ethical framework.[35] Although the dialogue does not present a myth in a formal sense, it does more than imply or suggests a myth. In the context of the discussion between Meno and Socrates, mythic content stratifies and combines pivotal elements in the text, such as (1) the proposition 'that it is worthwhile inquiring into what one does not know', (2) prenatal existence and afterlife, and (3) recollection.[36] Therefore, Socrates's philosophical response to Meno's paradox is characterized by a mythical narrative and system of belief based on an esoteric myth. The literary, religious, and philosophical networks operating in the text combine to construct meaning, and interpretation requires unpacking the diversity of themes and elements.

After the myth, Socrates compares his response with Meno's paradox. Socrates states, 'We ought not then to be led astray by the contentious argument you quoted. It would make us idle, and is pleasing to the indolent ear' (82d).[37] Socrates refutes Meno on pragmatic grounds and argues initially that the view derived from the poem aligns with the human tendency to seek and learn, is conducive to a personal drive and social atmosphere of knowledge acquisition, and is intellectually more sustainable than Meno's argument. When contrasted with Socrates's response, Meno's paradox is represented as intellectually dangerous and destructive. Socrates does not proceed to offer a systematic counter-argument in support of his position but, instead, conducts an experiment to prove why his position is superior to Meno's argument. The belief in recollection is more conducive to philosophical investigation, whereas the paradox ends the search before it begins. Meno's view hinders any attempt at inquiry since it holds that learning is impossible. The strength of Socrates's alternative rests on the fact that it is heuristic; that is, it 'produces energetic seekers after knowledge' (81e).

---

[35] Klein discusses the unique notion of soul represented in the myth and its special relationship to learning, knowledge, and the world as a whole ([1989] pp. 95–96). Also, see Weiss (2001) p. 67 for comments on the distinction between Plato's notion of recollection and a similar view implied by Pythagorean thought.

[36] For a comparison and contrast of the idea and use of recollection in other dialogues, see Bluck (1964) pp. 47–61.

[37] See Scott (2006) pp. 60–62 for a comparison between Meno's intellectual laziness and his earlier three definitions of virtue.

...neither the recollection thesis, as a general account of how knowledge is acquired, nor the metaphysical notions that undergird it are Socrates' own beliefs, but that his development of, first, the myth and, then, the slave-boy-demonstration constitutes his fight 'in word and deed' (*M.* 86c2-3) for the value of moral inquiry. As Socrates makes clear, what recommends the view that all knowledge comes by recollection is that it makes good men of its adherents, whereas the alternative view, Meno's paradox, makes bad men of those who subscribe to it.[38]

Once the recollection thesis and the demonstration prove that inquiry is worthwhile (i.e., learning is possible) and the two interlocutors decide to begin a new search into the nature of virtue, Socrates holds back from committing wholeheartedly to the truth of the myth and is devoted only to promoting the myth's consequences (86b–c). Both the proposition that it is worthwhile searching for what one does not know and the conclusions drawn from the experiment justify Socrates's position in response to the paradox. The combination of these factors, as opposed to a fixed systematic metaphysics and epistemology, makes up the theoretical basis of the dialogue.[39] One of Socrates's critiques of Meno's view is based on its inevitable consequences: that it leads to laziness. In contrast, Socrates's thesis has the potential to lead to truth.[40] It is only now, after justifying the myth in this way, that Meno asks for arguments in support of whether virtue can be taught; they decide to avoid the problem about the nature of virtue.[41]

I avoid subscribing to the view that the epistemological position and methodology proposed by the text are exclusively hypothetical or

---

[38] Weiss (2001) p. 64. Also, see p. 66.
[39] Weiss (2001) p. 69.
[40] See Sternfeld and Zyskind (1978) pp. 13–14. The authors discuss how the hypothesis functions as a point from which to make reasonable inferences but may, in fact, be logically faulty. For a description of various demythologizing interpretations of the myth, see Thomas (1980) pp. 127–146. My interpretation, presented here and elaborated below, allows the myth to remain what it is as a narrative and does not require rationalizing. The potency of the myth, therefore, lies in the literary structural features it introduces and how these function in conjunction with the arguments.
[41] One of my intentions for giving primacy to the dramatic details of the myth and the literary dynamics of the dialogue is to offer a compelling interpretation of the *Meno* that counters notions that myth in Plato is irony.

experimental, that they exist simply for an intellectual exercise. Reducing the meaning of the text to a mathematical-style analysis is extreme and marginalizes the literary, cultural, and religious dimensions of the dialogue. The model may be mathematical but the conclusions about ethics and its relation to epistemology deserve deeper multidimensional consideration. There are some dramatic features that condition the exchanges between the interlocutors and make the scenarios impossible to reduce to mathematical- and geometrical-style investigations. In fact, Socrates does not introduce the theory of recollection as his own theory and does not express complete commitment to it but sees it as indispensable for the point he wants to make.[42] The multidimensional elements of the dialogue operate together to reflect Plato's preference for a hypothetical method, inform the conditions for using hypothesis to unpack the topics in the *Meno*, and help arrive at the desired outcomes.[43]

## 3.4 The Philosophical Arguments

Socrates introduces beliefs such as immortality and recollection to convince Meno that it is 'right to inquire into something that one does not know' (86c). Socrates wants to analyze the nature of virtue but, on Meno's request, must clarify the notions of immortality and recollection.[44] The experiment involving the slave is a compelling technique for justifying Plato's statement that knowledge is recollection; evidence involves discursive argument and a demonstration. Both immortality and recollection are expressed to compete with Meno's paradox. The dialogue contrasts these two views of learning (Socrates's and Meno's) by considering their consequences in order to demonstrate and instruct rather than debate the truth and relevance of the myth. In fact, the earlier references to myth and religion do not play the same significant role in the second half of the

---

[42] Tarrant (2005) p. 8.
[43] Landry (2012).
[44] One must be careful not to label recollection a theory in the strict sense; that is, it does not occupy an unambiguous systematic position found in other dialogues and used to address different topics or situations. The description and use of the 'theory' in the *Meno* differ considerably from its appearance in the *Phaedo* or the *Phaedrus*, for instance (Tarrant [2005] p. 35).

dialogue (after the experiment and Meno's acceptance of the hypothesis that learning is recollection).

The experiment with the slave is a pivotal literary and philosophical device in the dialogue and deserves close examination in order to link its features and structure to the myth. Socrates tries to convince Meno of the value in searching for knowledge by demonstrating how a slave, who is guided correctly, arrives at knowledge. Socrates commits to the notion of an immortal soul (a belief derived from the wisdom of priests, priestesses, and poets) and uses this belief to construct the theory of recollection and supporting arguments. The belief in an indestructible soul, a constituent part of the myth, is necessary for engaging with and understanding the demonstration and is instrumental in Plato's critique of Meno's disavowal of learning. Meno's paradox renders philosophy a pointless pursuit and by proving that learning is actually recollection Socrates promotes philosophy as a worthwhile endeavor and essential for living a good life. Socrates establishes that knowledge is worth searching for by justifying the theory of recollection, and his position is based on both religious traditions (81b–d) and argument. In this context, myth is not referred to by Socrates as a *mythos* but as 'something true' (81a)—a story in response to an unacceptable epistemological claim that induces intellectual inertia and is attractive to the 'indolent ear'. Socrates's religious views not only promote 'energetic seekers of knowledge' (81e) but also form an indispensable connection between the soul, learning, and human destiny.[45] The myth fulfills its function until the pair move on to the next question. But what remains is the value of inquiry—the moral built into the design of the myth.

> In the ensuing interview with the slave boy, we shall observe him seeking to show: (a) that in a qualified sense one can pursue meaningfully what one does not know, and, (b) that there is a sense of 'know' in which it is not superfluous to seek what one already knows. These lessons come out in conjunction with the doctrine of anamnesis.[46]

---

[45] 'As has been abundantly illustrated in the present century, the evaluation of myth goes together with a specific understanding of religion and, accordingly, with a specific conception of man' (Eliade, forward in Feldman and Richardson [1972] p. xiv). See Vico's views on myth and a 'true human science' (Vico [1999]).

[46] Thomas (1980) p. 123.

My concern here is to discuss theories regarding liminal characters particularly in relation to Socrates as trickster. The use of a slave for his demonstration, a timeless liminal individual, has important interpretative potential. As trickster, Socrates selects another liminal individual to demonstrate the truth value of recollection—a slave whose personality and appearance are represented in almost completely dull terms. Socrates and the slave share an affinity that goes beyond their roles as figures on the fringes or in the interstices of society. Socrates is dependent on the slave to facilitate Meno's learning process and it is likely that the inclusion of the slave is a statement about social justice and a universal statement about a human capacity for philosophic inquiry. The function of the slave, for a brief moment in the text, creates an anti-hierarchical and non-abusive milieu needed in order to combine the argument, the myth, characters, and the dramatic setting. Consistent with the liminal phase—the moment when the two liminal characters combine and the conventional social structures and taboos breakdown—the characters display a heightened sense of awareness and the *Meno* portrays a new form of creative and critical pedagogy.

As an example of the positive consequences of trickster activity, Socrates achieves his aim of convincing Meno. Tricksters usually disrupt the norm and confuse the situation before encouraging and establishing new meaningful possibilities. Alternative forms of knowledge and identity are made available by constructing and testing unconsidered hypotheses often introduced through ritual or other kinds of transformative practice. The perplexity that tricksters drive toward must be understood as a means to an end—a technique that persuades one to shift perspective, re-evaluate and dissolve structure, and create new horizons for knowing, being, and morality.

## 3.5 Mutual Scaffolding

A mutual scaffolding approach illuminates the dialectic between myth and argument in the *Meno*. Plato incorporates myth and facilitates a harmonious exchange between two genres that enables myth to operate and function in multifaceted ways. Justifying a number of arguments supporting recollection, Meno confesses that Socrates must be right. But Socrates is uncertain of the truth of the myth: 'I think I am [right]. I shouldn't like to take my oath on the whole story' (86b). This attitude is unbecoming of one with strong religious convictions. The use of irony is eliminated by the comments that follow: 'but one thing I am ready to fight for as long as I can, in word and act—that is, that we shall be better, braver, and more active men if we believe it right to look for what we don't know than if we believe there is no point in looking because what we don't know we can never discover' (86c). The function of myth in the *Meno* is not exclusively illustrative, educative, allegorical, or mystical.[47] Socrates provides a deeper and more personal understanding of learning with qualities that correspond with his religious views. The point that Plato makes in these passages is that one's beliefs, whether religious or otherwise, characterize the degree of virtue one displays.[48] Scott argues that the function of arguing for the theory of recollection in the *Meno* is not to offer a solution to the problem of teaching virtue. He explains that the debate concerning virtue and recollection discloses compelling and penetrative observations about important meta-philosophical issues:

> In short, recollection should not be seen as the philosophical solution to the dilemma. First, the theory is not actually relevant to solving it... Second, in his explicit dealings with Meno, Socrates ignores any epistemological problems the dilemma might raise, and instead focuses on Meno's psychology: his motives for deploying the argument and the incentives he needs to restart the inquiry. Third, Socrates' own statement of the challenge that faces him at the end of the passage suggests he is concerned with the possibility of successful inquiry, rather than inquiry *per se*.[49]

On one side of my mutual scaffolding interpretation are a myth and associated religious beliefs. The *Meno* presents a quote from Pindar along

---

[47] For an interpretation that reduces the mythic elements to metaphor for the purposes of communication and convincing non-philosophers, see Ionescu (2007) pp. 49–64.
[48] Tarrant (2005) p. 55.
[49] Scott (2006) p. 82.

with extra interpretative comments by Socrates (81b–d). The major constitutive components of Socrates's reading of the poem are the following:

1. immortality
2. prenatal existence and reincarnation
3. cognitive perfection during disembodied state[50]
4. connection between knowledge and happiness/salvation.

On the other side are a demonstration and a series of arguments. One function of the demonstration is to illustrate how the theory of recollection can be learnt without teaching in the traditional sense; teaching, as opposed to recollecting, Socrates explains, is not possible (81e–82a).[51] The experiment guides the slave to recollect geometrical knowledge and Meno to understand that learning is recollecting. In fact, by witnessing Socrates conduct the demonstration, Meno gains knowledge of more than recollection. He comprehends what a philosophical inquiry involves: an understanding of what a hypothesis is; correct use of a hypothesis; consideration of consequences; how to incorporate argument and empirical data into one's investigation; arrangement and correlation between hypothesis and argument; valid inference; and the interdependence of myth and philosophy.

The experiment with the slave ends when Socrates returns to the myth. Prenatal existence and knowledge, an immortal soul, and *anamnesis* are essential to the conclusions drawn from the demonstration (85c–86c). The aim of the myth is not to promote and justify a set of religious beliefs but to function in a mutual exchange with the demonstration and arguments. The speculative mythical premises I listed above must

---

[50] It is not specified whether an ignorant individual has the same disembodied cognitive state as an enlightened individual. Also, how prenatal states differ from post-death states is not a consideration, and the dialogue does not address transition phases that may occur between the time a soul leaves a body and enters a new one. These ambiguities and Plato's uninterest in clarifying their details suggest that recollection and immortality are constitutive of the conditions introduced by the myth and serve a particular function within those limits. These metaphysical issues are more important for a dialogue such as the *Phaedo* but have little relevance, if any, in the *Meno*.

[51] Thomas contrasts the type of instruction Socrates gives Meno (i.e., a shared inquiry leading to personal insight) with the sophistic-style instructions Meno was used to (i.e., listening to a speech about the truth from another) ([1980] p. 123).

be interpreted in the context of the myth/philosophy interaction and how the new framework informs Plato's views on teaching and learning.[52] My analysis of the role of myth in the *Meno* explicates how an interdependent form of interaction unfolds between the religious views derived from the myth and the subsequent philosophical arguments. The method of mutual scaffolding illuminates this connection and informs other important parts of the dialogue. The myth prepares the reader to understand how the slave experiment and the arguments extending from the demonstration provide exegesis of the myth and assist in interpreting Socrates's religious commitments and literary style in relation to his philosophical thinking.

## 3.6 Plot Structure

The plot structure of the *Meno* is syncretic and manifests traces of traditional themes such as the notion of 'ideal origins' and transmigration of the soul. This is represented in the account pertaining to the source of the human soul—a pure non-physical state. Also, the plot incorporates the esoteric idea of dualism by interpreting soul and body as essentially distinct ontological entities corresponding with knowledge and ignorance. These potent mythic themes are integral parts of transcultural and transhistorical plots representing the idea that soul, being distinct from the body and eternal, needs to return to its ideal origins in order to find salvation. In this narrative, redemption or deliverance is achieved through acquisition of a special form of esoteric knowledge available to one initiated in the mysteries. Both the plot structure and the epistemology of the *Meno* are determined by the 'two-worlds' view which characterizes the distinctions between soul and body and their relationship with knowledge and ignorance.[53]

The dualism theme also plays a metaphysical/ethical role in the narrative and the plot represents this trope in a form of the 'life-death-rebirth' structure. The narrative moves through Meno's arrogant certainty and

---

[52] Tarrant (2005) p. 37.
[53] Sharples's introduction to Plato (1985) p. 7.

challenge by Socrates, Meno's *aporia*, and finally Meno's understanding and acceptance of recollection. Meno arrives at knowledge but not without undergoing a crisis during the process; Socrates's response to the paradox—a construction that combined myth and rational argument—compelled Meno to re-evaluate completely his original presuppositions. Without rationalizing the mythic plot structure or interpreting the scenes involving Meno's cognitive development as an allegory representing successful inquiry, I argue that Plato's complex and dynamic use of narrative structure involves incorporation of a philosophical myth as one of the dialogue's integral dimensions. The plot functions in multiple ways and harnesses the fluidity of the myth; it is instrumental in its structural influence and unifies divergent elements. As a character in the dialogue, Meno exemplifies the seeker who goes through an intellectual life-death-rebirth ritual.[54] This character role occupies a particularly salient place in a plot committed to mytho-religious dualism and incorporates the ritual initiation trope as a device for shaping and directing both the narrative and arguments. The plot structure of the *Meno* resembles a mosaic of symbols and themes from esoteric traditions familiar to Plato, as opposed to one clear archetypal religious story line, and fuses a number of mythic traditions and ideas into a process that unfolds in literary, religious, and philosophical terms: the cycle of life-death-rebirth.

When the universe is dichotomized in this way, humans are on either one side or the other, enlightened/unenlightened, good/bad (Meno represents one side of the dichotomy, but since Socrates admits that he does not know, the other side remains a goal or ideal). However, this vision of the world allows for one other role: the trickster, who dwells on the threshold.[55] The place, significance, and communication between the characters in the dialogue introduce important details and qualities for interpreting the trickster motif. They also inform and justify the inextricable connection between plot, myth, and philosophical argument. In the next section, I examine aspects of the three characters: Meno, Socrates, and the slave. My approach is sensitive to peculiarities that correspond

---

[54] Scott (2006) pp. 69–70.

[55] For symbolic representation of the trickster, see 79e–80d and Socrates's use of a slave to enlighten Meno. I discuss both of these 'trickster' features below.

with the interpretation of the plot introduced above, a reading that addresses the combination of literary features and philosophical discourse. Therefore, I interpret the interlocutors in terms of their roles in Plato's delivery of argument and as literary figures guided and conditioned by the plot.

## 3.7 Character Selection

### 3.7.1 Meno

> Throughout, Meno's own personality and his reaction to philosophical cross-examination are vividly portrayed. At a number of points Socrates makes explicit reference to his character, even calling him bullying, spoilt and arrogant.[56]

The 'rejuvenation' plot (life-death-rebirth) in the context of cosmic dualism requires a figure that traverses the whole journey. In the dialogue, and historically,[57] Meno is an opportunist interested in winning arguments and securing social status.[58] He is introduced in the early part of the text as being pretentious and sure that he has knowledge about the nature of virtue. Through an exchange of question and answer, Socrates brings Meno to *aporia*; Meno arrives at a state from which he cannot even say what virtue is, let alone whether it can be taught. But he is dissuaded by Socrates from choosing the path to intellectual lethargy and by the end of the scene can recognize the practice of philosophical inquiry and its merits. Meno's engagement with Socrates during the demonstration is a form of philosophical preliminary, and the process influences Meno to disavow the earlier position he held regarding the impossibility of learning. Meno arrives at the conclusion that knowledge acquisition is not learning but recollection, and he develops an awareness for the value of

---

[56] Scott (2006) p. 5. Also, see Day (1988) pp. 14–15. Bluck suggests that Plato intended to present Meno as a 'type' of person rather than an actual person ([1964] pp. 125–126).

[57] For details, see Thompson (1901) pp. xii–xx.

[58] See Scott (2006) pp. 11–13 for an interesting comparison between Meno's character and the literary elements of the opening scene.

philosophical endeavor. These objectives are achieved even though he is still unsure what virtue is and whether it can be taught.[59]

Meno is represented as the character that moves from self-assurance to confusion, to re-evaluation, to knowledge. In addition to a study of the nature of virtue, whether virtue can be taught, and an introduction to the recollection theory, there exist other literary and philosophical aspects of the text that deserve equal measure. For instance, the plot creates the conditions for a character who proceeds through stages of self-critical evaluation and traverses through the life-death-rebirth plot. The implications of this narrative structure resonate with the arguments, symbolism, and the dynamics between myth and philosophy.[60] The issue under debate is virtue and the metaphysical/epistemological context used to explain that learning is *anamnesis*, but it is Meno's recognition of philosophical inquiry and the correct interpretation of, and engagement with, myth that have the closest affinities and structural relationship with the transformation plot.[61]

### 3.7.2 Socrates

Dualist mythologies incorporate special roles for intermediaries who facilitate communication between the two realms. In different cultures and mythologies, this figure is represented by shamans, priests or priestesses,

---

[59] In addition to being lazy, Meno has been described as shallow and unsophisticated. Socrates deceives Meno by giving him the impression that the discussion is based on his own lead and interests (Ionescu [2007] pp. xiii–xiv). Socrates debates with the Meno as characterized in the text, and by employing the rejuvenation plot Plato accommodates the two personalities in the way they are introduced in the dialogue and tailors the conversation to suit.

[60] In contrast to Klein, Sternfeld and Zyskind argue that Plato is less concerned with who Meno is and more interested in illustrating what happens to him ([1978] p. 7). They compare the plot to Sophocles's *Oedipus Rex* because both Oedipus and Meno are transformed by the realization of their true identities (see p. 13 for other parallels). And see pp. 8–18 for a step-by-step analysis of Meno's transformations in the dialogue which reflects, to some extent, the plot structure I postulate here. Sternfeld and Zyskind also compare briefly the role of Meno and Anytos, who is not willing to journey through the course of development that Meno goes through (pp. 8–9).

[61] There are many other important features of Meno's character that I do not explore here. For instance, Scott discusses the influence of Gorgias on Meno's personality and his arguments ([2006] pp. 23–25). In addition, Scott alludes to the significant differences between Plato's Meno and Xenophon's account of Meno that extends until his punishment and death (pp. 64–65).

wizards, or witches. These personalities exist on the fringe of society; they disrupt what is commonplace; they break down barriers between levels of society or boundaries of thought; they shatter previous hypotheses and allow new hypotheses to emerge and assist in establishing them as valid.[62] In many instances, they are the connection between this world and the next. As a literary device, this character is traditionally known as the trickster and has its origins in all ancient mythologies but is also revived in more recent legends, folk culture, and popular culture. The plot used by Plato for the *Meno* implements a trickster figure to function as intermediary between metaphysical and epistemological binaries.

> Trickster is constantly tricking and being tricked. The purpose of such tales is to bring about psychotherapeutic change in the individuals who hear the tales. As Trickster changes from an amoral, instinctual, amorphous, desocialized, subhuman being to a character who has the right to govern an earth of his own, the students of the tale are expected to see their own behavior in the Trickster and to desire such a transformation in themselves.[63]

There are many features associated with Socrates's role in the dialogue that support his role as trickster. First, he admits to knowing nothing but leads his interlocutor to an advanced position of knowledge. Trickster characters are never simply 'fools' but help others to access knowledge through their antics. Second, he drives Meno to perplexity; tricksters are recognized as people who disconcert by challenging traditional perspectives and common assumptions. Socrates sets up a dualist framework of the cosmos and makes reference to traditions well known for their connection to mystery, initiation rituals, and esoteric knowledge (i.e., Orphism and Pythagoreanism). In the context of a cosmic dualist framework, Meno acknowledges Socrates as the mediator between ignorance associated with this world and knowledge associated with the beyond.

In the passages before Socrates's references to the priests, priestesses, and Pindar, the dialogue incorporates unique symbolism representative of liminality. Meno's attitude toward learning early in the dialogue,

---

[62] Thomas (1980) p. 23.
[63] Lundquist (1991) p. x.

which culminates in the paradox, is anti-intellectual, and he is willing to terminate his inquiry and withdraw from critical thinking as soon as he is confronted with an obstacle or anomaly. For Meno, the debate ends with his paradox of learning. Meno's submission follows a series of questions and answers about the definition of virtue after which Socrates leaves Meno in a state of *aporia*. Meno credits Socrates for perplexing him and uses metaphors such as 'magic' and 'witchcraft' to describe Socrates's technique and the sting of a stingray or torpedo fish to express how he feels after debating with Socrates. Meno also mentions that Socrates's physical appearance resembles a stingray and that his behavior will be labeled wizardry if he did the same thing in other cities. Plato selected these symbols carefully and injected them into the dialogue for special literary and cultural effect. These symbols foster a particularly important understanding of the subsequent discussion. The metaphors and mythic symbols all appear in the same passage after Socrates confuses Meno, and the use of terms such as magic and witchcraft to characterize Socrates's actions, together with the feeling evoked in Meno, are traits and activities evoked in recurring tropes used in mythology to represent the trickster figure.

### 3.7.3 The Slave

The use of a slave to illustrate that learning is recollection operates as a literary and philosophical device that impacts the trajectory of the arguments. The conditions for its place in the dialogue are also determined by the myth. The role of the slave is not limited to the experiment but is instrumental for interpreting the structure of the dialogue.[64] A quintessentially liminal figure, the slave gains geometrical knowledge by following instructions from Socrates, and his participation in the experiment contributes to Meno's learning—Meno's 'rebirth'. The guidance Socrates provides is student-focused and leads the slave to recollect what he knows

---

[64] Thompson, following Fritzsche's suggestions, describes the slave as an abstraction and not a real character—he argues that the slave represents an example of a blank mind ([1901] p. xxiv). I argue that his social status, his relation to Meno, Socrates's style of communication with him, and the effect of his participation prove he is more than a conceptual tool. Thomas also criticizes the view that the slave is an abstraction ([1980] p. 24).

intuitively; witnessing this encounter ignites an intellectual spark in Meno that results in an understanding of *anamnesis*, the acceptance that inquiry is worthwhile, and a realization of what philosophical learning entails.[65] There is evidence to suggest that the slave is an extension of one of Socrates's literary functions in the text: his role as agent employed to revitalize Meno. The slave's lack of physical and personal attributes is a curious technique and Plato's introduction of such a character is unprecedented. Socrates needs the slave for his argument/demonstration and the slave depends on Socrates's assistance in order to recollect. The identities of the pair interweave and the liminal status of both characters is reinforced. In partnership, Socrates and the slave occupy an intermediary function in the dialogue for the purposes of introducing *anamnesis* to both the reader and Meno.

## 3.8 Conclusion

The *Meno* constructs a debate between Meno and Socrates beginning with questions about virtue. The subject of discussion shifts to epistemology, and the flow of the exchange gradually falls apart as Meno realizes he has insufficient intellectual capabilities and Socrates explains that his views are in fact intellectually damaging. The two inquirers occupy specific roles in order for Meno to proceed through stages of 'initiation'. The dialogue employs myth in combination with liminal techniques to create a drama demonstrating Meno's transformation—an activity that replicates ritual initiation. Plato's uses trickery as a strategy and depicts Socrates as a trickster figure who plays with Meno by fooling and indirectly mocking him; Meno is left perplexed and stunned into re-evaluating his presuppositions, attitude, and the consequences of his ideas. Meno realizes he is part of a game or thought experiment created to replace the dialogue's non-existent social environment—a context consistent with the abstract and theoretical nature of the text. Socrates practices elenchus to maneuver Meno's thinking and feeling through experiences reflecting the stages

---

[65] By the end of the dialogue, the slave is not inferior to Meno or Anytus. In fact, Socrates is promoting a kind of epistemological egalitarianism unique to the *Meno* (Scott [2006] pp. 106–108).

of the life-death-rebirth process indicative of mystery rites and other initiation rituals.

Myth operates with philosophy to accentuate paradox in a dialogue structured by a strict form of religious and cosmic dualism. Plato uses *anamnesis* and belief in the transmigration of souls to facilitate an analysis of learning that promotes philosophical endeavor and respect for knowledge. As trickster, Socrates helps challenge and invert Meno's paradox and by using myth to structure his response he offers commentary on how thought, action, and custom are governed by our accepted sociocultural and religious conditions. The trickster disrupts the assumptions and complacencies associated with established social structures and creates spaces for reconditioning and replacing those dominant structures. The *Meno* demonstrates how that occurs and the need for liminality in the process; certain individuals or groups residing in between or on the margins of structure are both outsiders and insiders and best placed to bridge the two perspectives and enact renewal and reform.

Trickery functions to subvert complacency, pride, and power, and the *Meno* provides a general lesson or guide in practicing philosophy for the purposes of genuine transformation. The dialogue also gives cause for reflection about the conditions for knowledge and the roles of belief, truth, and justification. The myth and Socrates's faith in recollection and the immortality of the soul are justified by their consequences and their role in combating Meno's paradox. The truth of the myth is not an urgent matter for Socrates; the mutual cooperation or unity of myth and philosophy and their ability to transform Meno take priority. Trickster myths are characteristically subversive and this same approach to revered or prominent figures, social taboos, hierarchies, and tradition is indicative of Socrates's character. As both sacred individual and fool, the trickster embodies liminality and operates within dualist frameworks; Socrates maintains the separation but through deception blurs the boundaries for a limited time.

Liminal themes and subjects are prevalent in the *Meno* and interdisciplinary analysis is necessary for unpacking how they manifest in the plot, literary features, and arguments. Approaches from comparative mythology reveal significant examples of liminality in my study of the *Meno*, including the instrumental role of trickster motifs. Situating the mythical character within the dialogue's plot helps define the importance of dualism, reincarnation, and ritual performance as literary and philosophical techniques. These structural and thematic elements elucidate how myth contributes to constructing the conditions for the philosophical inquiry and assists in interpreting pivotal themes and topics such as belief in the immortality of the soul, reincarnation of the soul, *anamnesis*, the notion of pure origins, the life-death-rebirth ritual pattern, and the partnership between Socrates and the slave.

# 4

# Myth and Partnership: *Protagoras*

## 4.1 Radical Typology

Whether or not there is a realm of the "supernatural," there are *words* for it. And in this state of linguistic affairs there is a paradox. For whereas the words for the "supernatural" realm are necessarily borrowed from the realm of our everyday experiences, out of which our familiarity with language arises, once a terminology has been developed for special theological purposes the order can be reversed. We can borrow back the terms from the borrower, again secularizing to varying degrees the originally secular terms that had been given "supernatural" connotations.[1]

Expressions, practices, and exegesis of the sacred are conditioned by language and display, according to Kenneth Burke, the rhetoric of religion.[2] Drawing on the theories and ideas of Burke and Don Cupitt, Laurence Coupe explains the need to challenge the notion that our invented systems have independent validity and to resist the hierarchies they construct and

---

[1] Burke (1970) p. 7.
[2] Burke (1970); also, see Burke (1966), Chap. 5.

perfection they aspire toward.[3] Emphasizing the indispensable connection between language and myth, Coupe argues that, like language, myth is never final; he celebrates the perpetual and 'endless self-generating power of myth' and its potential to reformulate and reanimate itself in the process.[4]

Myths have a past and a future that operate in their structures, ideas, and aesthetic features. The dialectic that takes place between history and possibility exists in the foundations of every myth and informs cultural, aesthetic, and philosophical content. Interdisciplinary approaches are necessary for unpacking the dialectic between the past and future that shape myths and for raising awareness of their relevance for exegesis.[5] Coupe argues that language and history are the basic elements of myth-making and that suppression of either one stifles the possibilities inherent in sacred narratives. But he cautions against imposing an absolute and self-validating truth removed from the historical and temporal context out of which myth emerges.[6] Coupe draws on an important distinction made by Cupitt between 'realism' and 'non-realism' to examine allegorical readings of myth that aim to extract meaning 'beyond' or 'beneath' language and symbols.[7] He explains realism in this context:

> In the philosophical sense, then, 'realism' is the belief that there exists a reality beyond or beneath the universe we articulate through language. This belief in turn may be further considered as moving through two main phases, in line with the words 'beyond' and 'beneath' in our definition. Traditional realism assumes this reality to exist 'beyond' language, in the form of some ultimate and absolute essence; this might be called the Good, or God, or the Word. Modern realism assumes this reality to exist 'beneath' language, as when Marxists take literally Marx's architectural metaphor of 'real foundations' (economic 'base' as opposed to cultural 'superstructure').[8]

---

[3] Coupe (2006) p. 58.
[4] Coupe (2006) p. 58.
[5] Coupe's reading is influenced by Ricoeur's theory that myth is 'social imagination'. Coupe explains how Ricoeur denied the notion of a future totality but incorporates hope in his reading of myth as a necessary principle (Coupe [2006] p. 58; Ricoeur [1965] pp. 190–191). For Ricoeur, the function of myth is best understood as the dialectic between 'ideology' and 'utopia'.
[6] Coupe (2006) p. 60.
[7] For essays by Cupitt on non-realist philosophy of religion, see Cupitt (2002).
[8] Coupe (2006) p. 60.

## 4  Myth and Partnership: *Protagoras*

A realist allegory (traditional or modern) searches for meaning either beyond the chain of images and sequence of events or beneath the tale, hidden under the symbols, characters, and scenes.[9] It attempts to demythologize through rationalizing narrative, devaluing the medium, and rendering it arbitrary. This method assumes that meaning transcends the story or that intended messages are immanent, buried within the basic structure. Examples of this approach include attempts to interpret myths and other stories in terms of, for instance, the medieval fourfold interpretation: text as literally or historically accurate and stating a factual description of events; text as allegorical narrative elucidating philosophical, theological, or spiritual theory; text as moral prescription, tropological lesson, or ethical awareness-raising; and text as analogical instruction for mystical ascent, initiation, or foretelling eschatological events. 'Allegory is domesticated myth', according to Coupe.[10] In many allegorical readings of this kind, interpreters search for a removed essence, and the mechanics and components constituting the myth are simply instrumental; they exist to communicate the meaning beyond or beneath.

A non-realist allegory, on the other hand, derives meaning by engaging with the medium: the style of language used in the myth; historical, political, and cultural context; the modes of communication; expressions and behaviors; environment and backdrop; tropes and allusions; and personality traits. These factors, and numerous others, operate in networks of meaning, contribute to creating layers of narrative language, and are essential for interpreting messages in myth. The messages emerge out of the interaction between characters, objects, and particular events, eliminating the need to use a realist form of allegory; non-realist allegorical readings counter attempts to find meaning outside the myth or lying underneath the dramatic and symbolic components and instruments.[11] The dramatic and symbolic elements function as language and myths project their messages only through that language; therefore, understanding the myth demands deep investigation of the medium of communication and the nuances of its material.

---

[9] Coupe describes Eliade as a traditional realist.
[10] Coupe (2006) pp. 64–66.
[11] Tofighian (2013) pp. 105–106. My analysis of non-realist allegory in this paper engages with the Iranian film *Baran* (2001) by Majid Majidi.

Since the particulars of a story transmit a more immediate and untranslated meaning—rather than meaning as transcendent or immanent—interpreting narrative as theory ignores the possibilities inherent in the story. Non-realist interpretations demonstrate a commitment to the language and material particulars of the myth rather than risk imposing desires, beliefs, agendas, and systems of knowledge. Radical typology 'sees myth as a matter of permanent possibility, trusting in the ongoing power of *mythos* itself'.[12] Instead of interpreting myth as a realist allegory, one can open a horizon for rereading and refiguring the elements of sacred stories with the aim of perpetuating new meanings. Unconstrained by an essential meaning that assumes 'the perspective of perfection', non-realist allegory or radical typology 'has a perpetual sense of horizon, involving an ongoing dialectic of the sacred and the profane'.[13]

Elements from earlier versions of the Prometheus myth are prefigured in Protagoras's version; the older elements prefigure as types.[14] Prominent features displayed in the *Protagoras* myth and the dialogue's themes, symbols, and plot structure become the antitypes; they prefigure antecedent examples and fulfill them as antitypes. The dialogue represents new forms anticipated in previous versions of the story and its exegetical history. The interaction between types and antitypes is fluid, and radical typology reads myths in ways that are forever present and encourages interpretations that speak to contemporary situations. Radical typology gives Protagoras's myth the opportunity to speak and enables the medium to indicate and instruct regarding its interaction with arguments; there is no need to search for an imagined essence from the past, no need to frame one's interpretation according to different theories and sociocultural contexts, and speculation regarding the psychology of the author is unnecessary.

The same process of prefiguration and fulfillment continues into the future to spawn new and relevant narrative meanings.[15] The older myths

---

[12] Coupe (2006) p. 61.

[13] Coupe (2006) p. 61. In addition to Coupe, consider the theories and methods of Vico, Benjamin, Auerbach, and White.

[14] Consider Coupe's criticism of rational demythologizing of Greek myth (Coupe [2006] pp. 62–64). However, his evaluation of Plato differs from my interpretation and analysis here. Also, see pp. 65–66.

[15] Compare with McGrath (2009).

are necessary and in retrospect become preludes to Plato's dialogue; the myth in the *Protagoras* has acquired new meaning and significance for a different audience and set of questions. In this sense, radical typology is a remythologizing process rather than an act of demythologizing past mythic accounts. This understanding distances Protagoras's myth from traditional allegorical readings and allows myth to retain the richness and far-reaching cultural impact of a sacred narrative, while determining the rules of engagement.

> If orthodox typology involves a thorough rewriting of scripture, radical typology involves a shift of emphasis from the sacred to the profane. While it may appear to be arrogant appropriation, similar to that by which one set of scripture becomes a foil to another, its effect is to liberate the imagination.[16]

The *Protagoras* also prefigures traditional narratives to draw awareness to philosophical concerns and criticisms pertaining to definitions, sophists, and the significance of partnership in inquiry. By appropriating and transcending traditional plots and redirecting attention to the literary and social nuances of the dialogue, Plato reveals the profound potential in mythopoeic activity. The reinvigoration of characters, objects, and themes in the context of a philosophical text reflects the permanent possibilities inherent in mythic discourse and promotes analysis of the exoteric rather than the esoteric; the *Protagoras* encourages radical typology rather than traditional allegory.

## 4.2 Theme Introduction, Setting, and Narrative Mode

Major themes appearing throughout the *Protagoras* are fellowship, cooperation, and how particular forms of collaboration foster knowledge acquisition. Partnership tropes are demonstrated and repeated in different scenes and represented in the structure, literary elements, and arguments

---

[16] Coupe (2006) p. 67.

of the dialogue.[17] The dialogue introduces Socrates as a first-person narrator who relates the events of the morning to an unidentified friend.[18] Socrates agrees to explain the details of the earlier discussion. The morning's dialogue between Socrates and Protagoras—the embedded story—occupies the majority of the dialogue and is recalled and described by using binaries: a conversation between a philosopher and a sophist, an Athenian citizen and a foreigner, a young man and an old man, an invited guest who has come to teach and an uninvited guest who has come to learn. These literary features introduced in the frame dialogue have far-reaching impacts and deserve further analysis; they are reflected in the philosophical developments throughout the text and share an important structural role with the myth.[19]

Socrates's function as explicit narrator and the details pertaining to the delivery of the narrative imbue both the literary and analytical features of the dialogue. Issues of narrative voice add nuance to interpretations of critical scenes and elements. In my analysis of the *Meno*, I examined the absence of an explicit narrator and its impact on the meaning of significant aspects of the dialogue, including literary structure, character choice, and arguments. Also, the absence of both introduction and setting in the *Meno* has dramatic and theoretical consequences for the construction and delivery of philosophical and cultural messages. The *Protagoras*, on the other hand, contains a great deal of material to interpret even before the major sections of the dialogue begin.[20] The introduction to the dialogue (the frame dialogue) and the beginning of Socrates's narration of events (the emphasized dialogue) contain elements that complement important scenes and ideas

---

[17] The Prometheus and Epimetheus myth is pivotal for understanding the theme of partnership pervading the dialogue. Partnership is significant for interpreting the literary structure and the arguments in the text as I discuss in the section on plot structure.

[18] Bartlett draws attention to Plato's use of the term *hetairos* rather than *philos* (Plato [2004] p. viii). The ambiguity of the word *hetairos* introduces a complexity into the relationship that cannot be recognized in the word 'friend'. I explain how the distinction between advantages, disadvantages, and pragmatic concerns characterizes the way the theme of partnership is portrayed in the dialogue. A more formal and conditional relationship between two parties is presented as opposed to the intimacy associated with friendship.

[19] Ebert (2003) also identifies the importance of the frame dialogue. However, his interpretation arrives at conclusions different from mine.

[20] Ebert (2003) pp. 9–11. Ebert refers to three different kinds of poetry outlined in the *Republic* to assist his classification of the formal style exhibited by the *Protagoras*.

## 4  Myth and Partnership: *Protagoras*

expressed later as the dialogue develops.[21] Socrates is in control of the story line, demanding that we concentrate on what he says about himself, how he expresses it, and his depiction of the conversation.[22] Plato recreates Socrates for each dialogue and his standpoint in different scenes represents perspectives contingent on setting, situation, and interlocutors. Comparative interpretations of the Socrates character are complex, particularly since he is the narrative voice in some instances. In the *Protagoras*, Plato incorporates a frame dialogue or story, in which Socrates depicts himself in an emphasized story. Plato, therefore, establishes a certain distance from the Socrates actually communicating with the reader as the narrative voice; as a result, he is twice removed in most scenes. A somewhat challenged and sometimes unconvincing Socrates is presented in the *Protagoras* and it is plausible that his intentions may differ from most other dialogues in which the Socrates character is heroic and authoritative. Could Plato be attempting to portray a less idealized Socrates who finds himself in difficult situations and unable to employ the Socratic method at will? Could the text be a case of 'historical fiction'? I do not want to speculate on this possibility; it is enough to mention the issue of narrative mode and the contrast between author and narrator and raise awareness of the significance of the frame dialogue. I return to discuss issues pertaining to the personalities of Socrates and Protagoras in further detail when I address character selection.

Before meeting with Protagoras, Socrates perplexes Hippocrates by using the Socratic method as they search for a definition: in this instance, they search for the definition of 'sophist'. The discussion ends in *aporia* and at that stage the impression is that Socrates has the upper hand in the

---

[21] In an introduction to the *Protagoras*, Frede points out that the slave closes the door on Socrates and Hippocrates (Plato [1992] p. xiv). The scene indicates, for Frede, that generally people cannot distinguish between a philosopher and a sophist and connects this confusion to Socrates's trial and execution (in contrast, Protagoras led a successful life as a teacher and political ideologue). Through the dramatic setting of the dialogue, Plato conflates or overlaps categories, personalities, and stereotypes. I argue that a fusion of these different aspects is one of the most fascinating features of the text and a concomitant to plot structure.

[22] There are eight dialogues in which the main dialogue is reported by an explicit narrator (Ebert [2003] pp. 11–20). These are the *Phaedo* (Phaedo), *Parmenides* (Cephalus), *Symposium* (Apollodorus and Aristodemus), *Charmides* (Socrates), *Lysis* (Socrates), *Euthydemus* (Socrates), *Protagoras* (Socrates), and *The Republic* (Socrates). In addition, there are two spurious dialogues that are narrated: *Erastai* (Socrates) and *Eryxias* (Socrates). In all cases, the personality of the narrator, as he is presented in the particular dialogue, has a profound impact on many of the philosophical and dramatic features of the text.

exchange. The introduction to the emphasized story or main narrative sets a particular mood and attitude and positions Socrates favorably. One might anticipate the subsequent dialogue with a sophist to replicate the process and possibly the outcome—a Socratic debate not unlike that already experienced with Hippocrates. A Socratic victory indicative of the Socratic dialogues? The *Protagoras* surprises us. Upon entering Callias's house, Socrates identifies the attendees after briefly observing the interaction between the various individuals. The details pertaining to the topics under discussion are passed over and Socrates describes where certain people are placed and admires the manner in which some speakers and listeners order themselves in the arrangement (315b–316a). Socrates expresses interest in conversing with Protagoras and is welcomed by those managing the proceedings.

## 4.3 Myth Analysis

In conversation with Socrates, Protagoras suggests presenting a myth that explains why the art of politics and good citizenship can be taught. Both interlocutors understand them as practices associated with virtue, and Protagoras's position, or his mythic account, responds to Socrates's earlier argument; Socrates's position is that they cannot be taught (319a–320c).[23] Socrates bases his argument on his own observations of Athenian practice rather than define virtue and how it relates to civic life; he claims that inquiry into the different ways humans practice politics helps answer the question of whether virtue can be taught. He justifies this view with a number of examples. Socrates notices that the Athenians do not consult experts when they deal with political and civic issues—something they certainly do when it comes to other technical matters such as building. Combined with the fact that no teacher is ever referred to as the source of relevant theories, Socrates concludes that subjects pertaining to politics and good citizenship cannot be taught.[24]

---

[23] Van Riel points out that Socrates presents Protagoras with a dilemma: if he agrees with Socrates he jeopardizes his occupation as a teacher and if he disagrees with him he criticizes the democratic constitution that enables him to work as a teacher ([2012] p. 149). Protagoras's myth renders Socrates's problem irrelevant by placing the details and data within a new framework.

[24] Van Riel attributes the failure of the conversation between the two interlocutors to the fact that they are using two different conceptions of *arête* (Van Riel [2012] pp. 147–148).

## 4 Myth and Partnership: *Protagoras*

Socrates continues by citing the example of Pericles to describe how great political leaders and virtuous citizens could not teach their children how to be good citizens. Socrates's argument is inductive; he selects certain examples from Athenian society and history and, based on his evaluation, he constructs an account of things that can be taught and those that cannot. Socrates's argument does not offer an explanation for the connection between virtue and the art of politics and good citizenship. Actually, Socrates begins by discussing why political practice and good citizenship cannot be taught and only in his conclusion raises the issue of virtue (320b). What is missing is an explanation for how the combination of the two civic practices, a 'special kind of wisdom', is one and the same thing as virtue. However, Socrates ends his argument by praising Protagoras's wisdom and experience and accepts, without irony it seems, that he can demonstrate that virtue can be taught in his response.

> …myth is often ready to become the field of final causes. It steps in where no explanation in terms of efficient or formal causality seems to be available. In terms of both time and space, it furnishes the means to describe a wholeness. It tells how the immortal soul should behave because of the judgment. It describes the structure the cosmos was given because of the similarity to its model. In the *Protagoras*, the teleology operates within the political context.[25]

In response to Socrates, Protagoras tells a myth.[26] Whereas Socrates begins with empirical data and moves on to a proposition, Protagoras begins by explaining a myth involving the origins of human nature. The narrative consists of an explanation for how political practice and the values of citizenship are indispensably connected to virtue.[27] After the myth, Protagoras shifts strategy to provide arguments against Socrates; he draws on the principles established in the myth in order to justify that

---

[25] Thein (2003) p. 61.
[26] Tarrant describes the social dynamics associated with seniority, interpretation, and storytelling and how these factors influence the presentation and status of myths in Plato's dialogues (Tarrant [2012] pp. 50–53). Also, see Manuwald (2002).
[27] Zilioli (2007) pp. 96–98. Zilioli connects the theory proposed in the myth to the fragments of Protagoras.

virtue can be taught, and his account includes empirical evidence.[28] The way Plato structures Protagoras's myth, his selection of elements from different versions of the myth, and his emphasis on particular features all prepare the foundation to construct arguments and assist in interpreting the philosophical potency of the dialogue's literary structure and constitutive aesthetic features. I examine these elements of the myth and their relationship with other parts of the dialogue later in this chapter. After explicating the details of the myth, I clarify the connection between the art of politics/good citizenship and virtue.

The myth tells of the creation of humans and animals out a mixture of two elements: earth and fire. The gods assigned the job of equipping humans and animals with their distinctive powers to the titan twins: Prometheus and Epimetheus. After Epimetheus failed to assign humans with powers, Prometheus steals the gift of skill in the arts and fire from the gods and gives them to humans to aid their survival. As a result, humans could create religion, language, and the things required for basic subsistence. But because they did not possess political skill and civic expertise, they were in danger of extinction at the hands of beasts and themselves. Hermes was sent by Zeus to equip humans with virtue, which the myth equates with political skill or 'qualities of respect for others and a sense of justice, so as to bring order into our cities and create a bond of friendship and union' (322c).[29] These gifts are distributed to all and constitute their nature, but Protagoras clarifies that they must be acquired by each individual or the individuals risk becoming unjust and, ultimately, face capital punishment. Therefore, Protagoras makes a distinction between political wisdom, which necessarily involves justice and moderation, and skill in other arts (a distinction that Socrates does not make). Because all men have this potential, everyone acknowledges the opinions of their fellow citizens. The myth explains why political skill and good citizenship

---

[28] In his introduction to the *Protagoras*, Taylor argues that Socrates's style of argumentation, which subjects an opponent's hypothesis to critical questioning with the aim of exposing its contradictions, was first pioneered by the Sophists. The difference, he explains, between Plato's use of the method and the sophists' is that Plato's aim is not victory by one party but healthy cooperation between two parties to arrive at truth (Plato [1996] p. xi).

[29] 'The myth has supplied a framework within which excellence might be considered; the myth is used for such purposes by those with a fatherly point to make' (Tarrant [2012] p. 6).

## 4 Myth and Partnership: *Protagoras*

are conduits for acquiring virtue and the consequences for humans when they are missing or underdeveloped. It follows that, since each individual must acquire virtue by enhancing their natural predisposition for political activity and it is unanimously desirable to acquire virtue, virtue can be taught; in fact, virtue must be taught for the survival of humanity.[30] Subsequently, Protagoras presents Socrates with empirical examples for why virtue, shown to be expressed through political activity and a productive life as citizen, can and must be taught. Protagoras's position is more convincing in contrast to Socrates's account because it considers a variety of consequences in cross-reference to the myth and incorporates them in constructing the arguments.

> The concept of technique that was historically predominant in the fifth century BC helps us understand that for those Greeks living at that time, such as Protagoras, the employment of a technique just meant following some codified procedures; no assumption was ever made about the objectivity of the result obtained through the application of those codified procedures...The account of the birth and development of human society that Protagoras gives in the Myth combines the divine origin of the *technai* with their role for improving human life.[31]

To recapitulate, Protagoras's myth explains the important connection between virtue and political activity and good citizenship. In contrast to Protagoras, Socrates begins by stating that the art of politics and good citizenship cannot be taught because of certain examples indicating the failure of men who try to teach it. Socrates does not explain (1) what politics is, (2) what a good citizen is, (3) what virtue is, and (4) the relationship of (3) with (1) and (2). On the other hand, Protagoras covers all points and I argue in this chapter how a mutual scaffolding approach illuminates the dynamic interplay between (a) Protagoras's arguments and their structure, (b) his references back to the main ideas expressed in the myth, and (c) the inferential steps and conclusion reached.

---

[30] For a critical reading of Protagoras's myth arguing that it ignores individual value, see Bartlett's comments in Plato (2004) pp. 73–74.
[31] Zilioli (2007) pp. 101–102.

## 4.4 The Philosophical Arguments

The myth introduces conditions sufficient for defining and analyzing our innate ability to sustain ourselves and communicate in the context of a structured society. Protagoras's myth explains our natural potential to organize politically and live as productive citizens. It affirms that the general state of being intended for humans is one of 'friendship and union' (322c).[32] The myth describes how all humans came to have a predisposition for virtue and the imperative to make use of that predisposition; citizens must participate in politics if they wish to guarantee justice. After telling his myth, Protagoras presents Socrates with a number of examples to argue that political skill, good citizenship, and virtue are linked and justify the proposition that virtue can be taught. He distinguishes virtue from other skills by first explaining that Athenians listen to everyone on matters of politics but consult experts regarding all other crafts. Protagoras reasons that all humans have the ability to contribute to political life and that if learning to use that potential were not possible the state would not permit citizenship to so many; individuals would be excluded from participation in political and civic matters; and increased punishment would ensue. Socrates stated earlier that virtue could not be taught because experts were not consulted in running the state. The fact that Athenians ask everyone's opinion regarding politics means, for him, that everyone recognizes education of individuals in political skill and citizenship as unachievable. The examples of Pericles's sons and Clinias represent failed attempts to teach virtue and are interpreted by Socrates to explain why all citizens (including non-experts or amateurs) are consulted in political matters.

Protagoras's myth establishes conditions for another view regarding the acquisition of virtue and its place in human development. The myth defines principles that determine selection of empirical data to support Protagoras's view and how best to deliver the examples when constructing arguments. The moral and intellectual conclusions of his position are clear and well supported and correspond with a vision of a good state. Protagoras continues by referring to the Athenian custom of punishment in targeting the unjust and irreligious rather than those who suffer from physical

---

[32] This is a significant recurring theme in the dialogue and integral to the plot, the character roles, and the arguments.

## 4 Myth and Partnership: *Protagoras*

disadvantage. Individuals are punished for immoral or criminal practices and behavior rather than an action that is the consequence of physical or cognitive impairment. Protagoras deduces that virtue can be taught: otherwise, a spectrum of punishment for degrees of ethical transgression would not exist. Recognition that mental and physical disadvantage can impact behavior, and must be factored in when judging habits and actions, indicates belief that all humans have the potential to be virtuous regardless of the level of demonstrated skill or the consistency when practiced (323b). Also, Protagoras acknowledges that states have a consequentialist view of punishment; that is, they administer it for moral education and to prevent crime, which he sees as proof that citizens believe virtue can be taught. For Protagoras, humans are predisposed to being virtuous and one ultimately becomes virtuous through forms of education; lessons pertaining to civic virtue enhance one's potential for embodying good citizenship (324b). Protagoras also responds to Socrates's description of virtuous men failing to teach their children about political skill and good citizenship.

In response to Socrates's account of good men failing to teach virtue, Protagoras again builds on the view narrated in the myth that virtue is integral to political practice and good citizenship. A state exists and for Protagoras this very fact proves that all men partake of virtue (324d). He also gives examples from the state education system and how different subjects are taught with the vision and intention of creating good citizens (325d–326e). As for the sons of good men who go wayward, Protagoras does not see this as a dilemma for his account. Once again, he describes how the potential to learn virtue is connected to the existence of the state and explains that natural talent is not determined only by one's family ties and influences; this point contributes significantly to weakening Socrates's argument (327a).

> [Socrates] draws on the same questionable following of young men as the sophists; and he, like Protagoras, questions the adequacy of their traditional upbringing and envisages a rational art or discipline to guide one's life, private or public. But, unlike Protagoras, Socrates uncompromisingly insists on the idea of a special expertise, in spite of its obvious consequences for our attitude both towards traditional values and democratic tenets.[33]

---

[33] See Frede's introduction to Plato (1992) p. xiv.

For Protagoras, Socrates's argument makes an invalid inference from bad sons of good men to the inability to teach virtue. Protagoras draws an analogy with language and points out that there are no specialized teachers of language but that no one would state that language could not be taught. And the same with virtue: all humans are taught because, being able to set up and live in a state, they have the natural capacity to learn about virtue as concomitant to functioning in the city.[34]

## 4.5 Mutual Scaffolding

This section considers the connections between arguments and the myth by using mutual scaffolding in order to illuminate how the two complement each other; I examine both elements of the dialogue as active and essential parts in a dialectical unity.[35] The myth provides a schemata for understanding the relationship of virtue to the practice of politics and good citizenship within a narrative framework; the story establishes sufficient conditions for interpreting how political skill and good citizenship are essentially linked to virtue and, by extension, that virtue can be taught. The myth creates a possible system of reference where virtue is ingrained in civic life and is indispensable for successful application of politics and functioning as a good citizen. The understanding of virtue developed in the myth is not a contingent notion; it is a necessary definition for positioning humans in society. The definition of virtue establishes a meaningful place for individuals in a state that depends on deliberative participation of citizens for its identity, maintenance, and flourishing. The narrative institutionalizes indispensable political, metaphysical, and sociocultural links between virtue and Athenian citizenship and attempts to universalize them. Virtue is expressed when one fulfills their political responsibility as a good citizen under the assumption that the general

---

[34] I give Protagoras's arguments more credit than some scholars have attributed to them (for criticisms of Protagoras's arguments, see Taylor's introduction to Plato [1996] pp. xv–xvi). As a unity, the myth and the arguments have far more rhetorical weight and more compelling insight into the issue than Socrates's arguments.

[35] For an interpretation that recognizes the interdependent relation between the myth and the arguments, see Tarrant (2012) pp. 50–53.

character, development, and practice of civic virtue can be delineated and deliberated using the Athenian context. The myth makes it very clear that virtue is a natural predisposition and citizens are obliged to enhance their inherent potential and endeavor to educate others. Protagoras renders the proposition that virtue can be taught, and all of his arguments support the principles and suggestions represented in the myth.

The mutual exchange between myth and philosophy is achieved by symbols and premises partnering to promote a vision of humans as natural citizens of the state. Citizens imbibe the structures and habits of political and civic life and maintain political and civic harmony through virtue. The features of the myth appear in the arguments to support premises and the story incorporates, or rather anticipates, examples brought up in the arguments. Protagoras's arguments enforce the idea that virtue is realized through the art of politics as recognized by the state and practiced with the intention of becoming a good citizen. The arguments build on this view of virtue proposed in the myth. The narrative presented by Protagoras describes how all have 'the qualities of respect for others and a sense of justice' (322c) as a natural predisposition—qualities that are essential for creating bonds. Humans were given the capacity for these attributes as a consequence of receiving fire and artistic skill. These divine powers foster ingenuity and dexterity in almost all aspects of civic life but mean very little without another element; an additional skill is required if one is to administer their use with success and influence. Founding cities was a natural consequence of receiving fire and skill in the arts, but without political skill humans were unsuccessful in maintaining their newfound social cohesion. Political skill is significant in directing and controlling all other skills and assets successfully because it gives rise to virtue. One exists in a community where one learns artistic skills and one also learns how to use them correctly for the benefit of the community. This leads to the acquisition and application of political skill; an asset that translates into the establishment and development of good citizenship. Therefore, in line with the view presented in the myth, good citizenship is equated with virtue. Clarification of this equation is crucial for interpreting the relationship between myth and philosophy in the *Protagoras*; a mutual scaffolding approach illustrates how literary and discursive elements operate in conjunction to solidify and sustain the position that virtue can be taught. The contribution of the myth is not limited to a mere literary or educative device but is significant in the way it functions in a symmetrical relationship with the arguments.

The myth represents and interweaves an influential view of human nature into the dialogue: Protagoras devises a narrative that accounts for our tendency to create language, provide sustainable living conditions for ourselves, and gather in communities on different scales.[36] This account of human nature projected through the myth occupies the backdrop for the arguments, and there is a tacit acceptance that the tale confirms the human capacities necessary for survival and conviviality. Therefore, Protagoras does not elaborate how and why these human tendencies exist—or whether they are accurate descriptions of human capacities— and does not feel the need to investigate their status and meaning.[37] Since the issue under investigation is the nature of virtue and whether it can be taught, Protagoras feels that his earlier mythic account regarding the origins of certain human capacities—one that best incorporates the view that we all share a sense of justice—is sufficient. The myth anticipates the arguments, dictates the arrangement and content of the arguments, and contributes to proving that virtue can be taught. The central features exhibited in the myth impact one's perception of human nature, and the reader is led to accept the following arguments as viable if human nature is seen from that perspective. Therefore, many of the Greek practices Protagoras references are presented as proofs for the sociopolitical account stated in the myth, and one of the reasons he cannot accept or accommodate Socrates's interpretation of civic practices is that the views do not align with the earlier narrative. Protagoras analyzes civic life and habit to correspond with his myth and avoids interpreting political practice and civic engagement in ways that conflict with his story.

Protagoras's position and his manner of delivery are more conducive to intellectual inquiry and the pursuit of moral perfection than Socrates's contribution. At this stage of the dialogue, Protagoras appears to be the more 'Socratic' of the two. Protagoras identifies political life with

---

[36] Zilioli presents an anti-objectivist interpretation of the myth that incorporates modern debates concerning cultural relativism ([2007] pp. 105–112).

[37] Van Riel argues that the myth promotes the Platonic view that we all possess certain basic human capacities ([2012] p. 158).

the pursuit of virtue—values for which an education system must be designed. Also, punishment must be administered with the intention of cultivating virtue within the perpetrator and the community at large. The myth introduces a definition of virtue reinforced and replicated in the arguments and it also provides interpretative tools allowing systematic engagement with issues and experiences pertaining to politics, education, and retributive justice. Protagoras's myth illustrates a literary and cultural sphere that promotes the notion of an active and enthusiastic citizen dedicated to fostering virtue in oneself and the community. The development of one's natural capacities to benefit the state is one aspect of that imagined sphere; this vision flows into the arguments and subsequently contributes to the reality of political and civic life. Protagoras's myth/philosophy dialectic encourages more than a search for knowledge and offers specific pathways for forging partnerships in society. The rest of the dialogue describes Socrates in opposition to Protagoras, disrupting the dialogue between them; he pedantically picks on particular details and it is uncertain whether his line of questioning advances the inquiry, clarifies stages of the investigation, or leads to desirable conclusions or consequences. Socrates's persistent demand for definition (329c–331e) is questionable and his subsequent approach to the debate seems unconducive to constructive and informative discussion; here, the Socratic method becomes dismissive and obstructionist (331a–335c). The most significant difference between Socrates and Protagoras is the systematic development and unity of Protagoras's myth/philosophy approach as opposed to the unclear direction of Socrates's question-and-answer method and the sometimes ad hoc style of shifting the focus of investigation. Protagoras's myth and arguments operate together in a relationship I interpret by using my mutual scaffolding method. The implications of Protagoras's philosophical contribution are projected by the myth and his conclusions prescribe a situated, accessible, and practical understanding of human nature and its connection to the state. Protagoras's methodology, as presented by Plato in this particular dialogue, deserves an interdisciplinary and generous evaluation; he overshadows the representation of Socrates and his mode of delivery, objectives, and conclusions. The Socrates/Protagoras contrast is reflected and reframed in the Prometheus/Epimetheus partnership. The myth conveys the idea that successful cooperation depends on the style of engagement and level of knowledge exercised by each party. Frede comments on the responsibility we have in both rationalizing and imagining a competent human being and what might be the most desirable human capacities and competencies. He considers the consequences of our envisioning on contemporary society and future generations—considerations that illuminate the qualities exhibited by Protagoras's vision and account.

> It does make a difference to our lives what, in the end, we want to have succeeded in; it makes a difference what we think it takes on our part to succeed, what abilities and kinds of competence we think we need in order to be, as we say nowadays, competent human beings; we want to know what it would take to be the kind of person one would, on reflection, like to be, if that were possible; whether and how one could acquire this ability and competence, and what roles natural endowment, upbringing, and reflection play in this.[38]

The dialogue ends with Socrates expressing uncertainty about whether the two interlocutors agree or disagree on whether virtue can be taught. However, the dialogue is clear about the details of Protagoras's contribution: the *Protagoras* begins with a myth that structures and reverberates through the arguments and provides a clear indication of Protagoras's position on political skill, the qualities of good citizenship, and the essential role of virtue in the account.

Similar to my analysis of the *Meno*, in the *Protagoras* a myth leads to and determines the subsequent arguments and characterizes the literary dimensions of the text. In both dialogues, the analyses that proceed using myth result in successful and compelling arguments. The myths in the *Meno* and *Protagoras* correspond with arguments in order to constitute a whole; the myth/philosophy nexus is a fusion of narrative structure, religious symbolism, narrative voice and character interplay, premises, empirical data, and logical consequences that combine as part of a dialectical whole. The conflation constructs interpretative conditions for defining cogent and comprehensive perspectives on ethics, education,

---

[38] Frede's Introduction to Plato (1992) pp. vii–viii.

government, and other social and philosophical phenomena. The standard by which we judge a theory to be acceptable shifts from logical inference to a more profound and inclusive criterion that accommodates historical, social, cultural, and emotional factors.

## 4.6 Plot Structure

The plot structuring Protagoras's myth is characterized by partnership; this theme pervades the literary and philosophical elements of the *Protagoras* and has significant formal influences on exchanges between characters and their arguments. In the context of a philosophical work, the myth is peculiar in that its plot structure extends to the internal dynamics of the text and, in particular, induces a selective reading of discursive content. The plot also directs the narrative force of symbols and impacts the cadence of the scenes. The structural investment endorsed by the myth is unique and adds a dimension to the philosophical dialogue much richer than if Plato were only to incorporate hypotheses. A hypothesis does not create the same effect and does not have the same qualities or deliver the same import. Plot structure is constructed and emphasized in the text through the different literary techniques; it is artificial but not arbitrary and this means that the myth is encountered through reading the text but functions as though it were the reality out of which the dialogue was conceived. Introduced into a philosophical investigation, the plot acts as an epistemological condition for approaching the issues. It determines what data one uses to support the claim or view, which arguments are most relevant, who one refers to as sympathetic or antagonistic to the view, what theory complements which views, and how one arranges and interprets the material.

The plot structure controlling the myth in the *Protagoras* displays a combination of familiar themes from the plots framing similar myths and narratives. Comparisons with other stories place Protagoras's myth in a historical and cultural context, and the shared themes and motifs assist in interpreting the social and emotive paradigms informing the dialogue. The most important literary compositions to consider for deciphering the relevant themes from the *Protagoras* are 'paradise lost' or the 'fall of man' and different myths featuring the theme of friendship or partnership.[39]

> After all, it is Socrates who suggests that he and Hippocrates make their way to Protagoras and the other Sophists (314b6-c2), just after he has issued a stinging rebuke to Hippocrates for his uninformed desire to do so, and at an important juncture in the dialogue Socrates assures Protagoras that his cross-examinations have as their goal the discovery of the truth about virtue, about a question that perplexes Socrates himself. His conversation with Protagoras is intended to make certain one or more of Socrates' own thoughts, as only conversation with or 'testing' of another can do (347c5-349a6; consider also, e.g., 328d8-e1, as well as 357e2-8: Socrates is not consistently concerned with harming the business prospects of the sophists, Protagoras included).[40]

The dialogue is consistent in presenting examples in which confrontation transforms into a mutually beneficial partnership—situations in which each party provides an individual contribution or component essential to the development of the discussion. The myth features two brothers, titans, who have been given a task by the gods to assign all animals, including humans, with certain powers to ensure their survival. Epimetheus fails to complete the task adequately, causing Prometheus to sin against the gods when trying to repair the damage. Owing to Prometheus's blasphemy, humans find themselves in a situation in which they require intervention by the gods in order to survive. Zeus's grace rescues humans from extinction but also puts humans at an existential crossroads far removed from their original state. Humans must now endeavor to gain happiness and salvation and this requires developing their gift from the gods: Zeus ensures that all humans have a predisposition for respect and justice. This, of course, must be perfected to the best of one's ability in the context of a community or state. The myth portrays the original state of

---

[39] Zilioli suggests another kind of structure that begins with an inferior stage of human society (the Epimetheus stage) and progresses to another stage where survival is ensured (the Prometheus stage) before entering a more advanced level of community dynamics (the Zeus stage) ([2007] pp. 98–100). There is clearly a prominent 'progressive' historical theme running through the story that deserves priority when interpreting the *Protagoras* and requires interdisciplinary investigation.
[40] Bartlett's comments in Plato (2004) p. 68. For the original ideas and contribution of Protagoras to the Greek intellectual tradition, see van Ophuijsen et al. (2013).

humans as lacking autonomy, not dissimilar to the situation of other animals. As a result of a botched-up effort by the brothers, the result of bad teamwork, humans now find themselves having to deal with morality; therefore, humans have to grapple with the dilemmas of free will.

Comparison between central features of Protagoras's myth and myths describing the 'fall of man' is plausible given the cross-cultural parallels between them. Scholars have interpreted the Prometheus story as a prototype of the Biblical tale and many similar stories found in other cultures. The overlapping themes worth considering include the following:

1) The myth presumes there was a natural tranquility that has now been lost forever. (For Plato, the emphasis on the original state is more about the non-existence of social and cultural norms, particularly morality, rather than a utopia.)
2) A partnership involving two characters; the actions of one cause the other to commit sin.
3) The sin affected human destiny.
4) Humans are no longer in their original state of being and now find themselves in a more complex and structured social and cultural setting where they must develop virtue for salvation.
5) God(s) spared humans; humanity was not left to exterminate itself. God(s) blessed humankind by giving them a last chance in the form of a gift, but with certain conditions.

The partnership paradigm employed in Protagoras's myth is necessary for interpreting the structural, literary, and philosophical issues and relationships in the dialogue and many of the symbols incorporated into the different scenes. For instance, the theme of partnership between contrasting pairs is exemplified from the beginning. The symbolism that reflects this theme includes the introduction to the emphasized dialogue featuring Socrates (a known figure) and an unknown companion, the transition from darkness to daylight, and movement from outdoor setting to indoor setting. A crucial partnership that deserves special consideration in the text, and is not merely symbolic, is the relationship between Socrates and Protagoras. This combination does not adhere to the binary oppositions familiar to us from other dialogues: philosopher and sophist; inquirer and teacher; Athenian and foreigner; young man and elder; uninvited and invited. The dialogue reflects the myth in representing and discussing partnership and the perils each party may encounter if the working relationship is not attended carefully. But the dialogue transcends the portrayal in the myth and adds subsequent 'scenes': situations that indicate the possibility of coordination and harmony. The dialogue departs from the limited framework of Protagoras's myth and adds a form of addendum or sequel—a reworking of the plot present in Protagoras's myth.[41]

The two main interlocutors begin an exchange at 329b focused on finding a definition for virtue.[42] Socrates switches his line of argument at 332a when he feels that Protagoras is annoyed and the inquiry is not going the way he had hoped; in fact, the debate is in danger of being relinquished by Socrates because Protagoras does not provide succinct answers, the way Socrates demands (334e–335a). But before the conversation breaks down, the group of witnesses (Protagoras's audience) are successful in reconciling the two and encourage them to continue by way of 'discussion, not a dispute' (337b). The partnership struggles to find common ground on various levels. Socrates demands brief answers (335a), but immediately after he demands this condition he responds to Protagoras's question on poetry with the longest answer in the dialogue (342a–347a). When Socrates continues to question Protagoras, he focuses on the issue of definition once again.

> The Protagoras gives us a vivid picture of the practice of dialectic, of how the respondent can be fair or unfair, cooperative or uncooperative, of how the questioner can conceal the aim of his questioning, of the role the audience plays, of the possible need for an umpire (cf. 338a8). But our dialogue also allows Protagoras, the main character besides Socrates, repeatedly to break this scheme; for example, to exchange roles with Socrates (338e6 ff.), or to hold forth in long speeches.[43]

Frede's interpretation provides critical commentary of Socratic elenchus and raises problems regarding an inquirer's fixation on establishing a

---

[41] Van Riel (2012) pp. 159–62.
[42] Also, see 331a–b and 333a–b.
[43] Frede's introduction to Plato (1992) p. xvi.

definition in order to proceed with an investigation. Socrates bases his argument solely on the notion that 'if knowledge, then it can be taught'. Throughout this section, the narrator, Socrates, is presenting himself positively, but one is suspicious as to whether the narrator is misleading the listener/reader regarding the description and evaluation of his own performance in the story.[44] The story ends when both agree to come together for a future exchange, and before the end of the dialogue Socrates recalls the myth (361c–d).

## 4.7 Character Selection

### 4.7.1 Socrates

The narrator in the *Protagoras* is clear in contrast to the narrative mode of the *Meno* explored in the previous chapter: Socrates is assigned the role of explicit narrator. Very few details are provided about Socrates's personality in the opening scene as he engages in conversation with the unknown interlocutor. After he begins to recall the story, the dialogue offers fewer (if any) indications regarding the narrator. However, the frame dialogue involving Socrates's communication with the unknown companion reveals some telling features about Socrates's character as narrator. The distinctions between narrator and the depicted character of Socrates are clear upon considering mise-en-scène. The conversation of Socrates, as narrator, has no setting, and the personality of the unnamed interlocutor is difficult to decode.[45] The little background to the frame narrative we have is the reference to Socrates's physical relationship with Alcibiades. Almost everything about this introductory conversation, from the casual tone with which they discuss Socrates's attraction to Alcibiades to the use of Homer as an authority,[46] gives a very conservative or traditional

---

[44] Frede's introduction to Plato (1992) pp. xvii–xviii.
[45] Ebert (2003) pp. 15–16. On page 16, Ebert states: 'Since he remains an anonymous interlocutor, he is, as it were, anybody from Athens. Thus, his anonymity makes him a perfect representative of the *polloi*'.
[46] The discussion involving the admiration of Alcibiades's beauty is at 316a, and reference to Homer regarding the most handsome age for a male is at 309a.

impression of the personalities involved or at least signals that what is going on is commonplace among the status quo.[47] Also, the setting of the main conversation consists of spectators including foreigners and citizens, some of whom are sophists.[48] But there is no definite distinction or judgment made of them in the text.[49] In fact, the dialogue does not judge whether being a sophist is good or bad; at times, it only seeks a definition for what a sophist does or what he teaches. Socrates is not represented here as a critic of conventional, commonplace practices and ideas. Although he is distinguished from the Sophists, his social status in the *Protagoras* is obvious: Socrates is a 'member of the club'.

### 4.7.2 Protagoras

Sophists are not attributed the same characteristics in the *Protagoras* as other dialogues, and the occupation does not have negative connotations.[50] The historical Protagoras played a salient role in the democratic constitution of one of Athens's colonies and the myth he tells in the dialogue defends democratic ideals.[51] Dualism is not used to influence the plot, and instead a theme of partnership heavily influences the story. Consistent with the partnership theme, Socrates is not pitted against a 'foe' in this dialogue; there is no hero/enemy dichotomy. There are no victors, no one relinquishes their position, and the meeting promises to continue on amicable terms. The plot structure and the strong

---

[47] My critical reading of this aspect of the opening scenes is not shared by some interpreters. See Frede's introduction in Plato (1992) p. x.

[48] The man attending the door is unable to distinguish between the two visitors, the pair of Socrates and Hippocrates, and the sophists. This literary device further informs the view that distinctions between philosopher and sophist are complicated in the *Protagoras* (314c–e). The attendant's attitude toward the new arrivals is representative of the deflated status of the philosopher throughout the dialogue.

[49] At 316d, Protagoras gives a short history of sophism and how sophists conduct themselves.

[50] See Frede's introduction in Plato (1992) pp. xv–xvi. Frede describes the positive character traits exhibited by Protagoras in the text and refers to the desirable forms of argumentation used by sophists that influence Socrates's style of dialectic. Also, see passages 316d–317c: this section presents a positive account of the history of sophism and Protagoras indicates how earlier sophists had to mask their art and their identities. Aliases included poets, prophets and seers, physical trainers, musicians, and music instructors.

[51] Ebert (2003) p. 17.

theme of partnership determine the nature of the categories 'sophist' and 'philosopher'.[52] The contrast between Protagoras and Socrates is conditioned by this motif and the two are not depicted as representative of opposing perspectives, methods, and intentions.

### 4.7.3 The Attendees

The guests at Callias's house are a group of Athenian and non-Athenian privileged aristocrats, many of whom (Prodicus, Paralus, Charmides, Hippias, Critias, Callias, Alcibiades, Xanthippus, Philippides, Antimoerus, and Hippocrates) feature in other dialogues.[53] Socrates treats the guests as peers and the *Protagoras* does not depict him as opposing, challenging, or criticizing their rare and random input. This aspect regarding the secondary characters and the acceptance they receive from Socrates and Protagoras indicate that the social setting is traditional and conservative. Attendees are reluctant to upset the habits, structures, and standard customs.

## 4.8 Conclusion

Myth and philosophy interact in a mutual exchange in the *Protagoras*. The plot, symbols, and arguments partner to create a vision of citizenship with unequivocal connections with political practice and virtue. The dialogue interweaves the two genres to explain how citizens establish and maintain harmony within the state. Protagoras demonstrates how the pursuit of virtue pertains to living and thriving as a citizen and how achieving one's objectives involves learning to engage in committed and active political life. Mythic elements appear in the arguments to contextualize and help support Protagoras's position that virtue can be taught. The story prepares for examples introduced in the arguments and anticipates the

---

[52] Compare Protagoras's comments at 316c–317c with Socrates's situation in the *Apology*: cf. *Prot.* 317a–e about honesty regarding his profession, his disapproval of escape in the face of hostility, and taking precautions against harm targeted against sophists.
[53] For details on the characters, see Taylor's commentary in Plato (1996) pp. 68–69.

interaction between the pair of interlocutors by developing the theme of partnership and its role in successful inquiry. The arguments draw from the view of virtue projected by the myth; Protagoras's narrative describes how humans are naturally predisposed to justice, creating relationships, and forming societies.

The myth also provides a sociocultural and historical backdrop to Protagoras's discussion of virtue and defines the nature of the human capacities necessary for statecraft. Human ability for social organization is illustrated as an innate power granted by the gods; by connecting a myth about the origins of political skill with examples involving ingenuity and dexterity in civic life, Plato establishes a theory with authority and far-reaching influence. The dialogue links political skill and good citizenship with virtue by using narrative and when Protagoras subsequently constructs arguments using socially and culturally relevant examples, an integrity between the two forms of explanation is forged. Consequently, narrative and argument together justify and contextualize teaching virtue.

Mutual scaffolding reveals Plato's administration of literary and discursive elements in the *Protagoras* and how they function as a unity to argue that virtue can be taught. Myth does not simply illustrate or assist in conveying the point but plays an indispensable role in supporting and solidifying the arguments. By interweaving a narrative account of human nature into the discussion, Protagoras's account does more than address the issue of virtue: the account contributes to our understanding of language, sustainability, social organization, statesmanship, and conviviality.

Conducting an interdependent reading of myth and philosophy in the *Protagoras* also involves consideration of the medium: the different voices and forms of expression; social and cultural context; communicative devices; the characters' actions and personality traits; setting and backdrop; and tropes and themes. Meaning emerges out of the network of the particulars constituting the myth and arguments and the layers of meaning created through the interaction between them. In contrast to pursuing a realist allegorical interpretation of myth—looking for the essence of myth beyond or beneath the drama of the dialogue—one can explore richer and more intimate readings by considering the symbolic and dramatic language used to construct the myth and the philosophical project they feed into. Rather than interpreting Protagoras's myth in terms of realist allegory, my approach views the myth as antitype, or the continual perpetuation of mythic meanings. Ascribing an essential meaning demythologizes and strips myths of their heuristic possibilities; univocal interpretations distort and silence the dramatic language. The polymythic hermeneutics of myth and techniques such as radical typology, instead, create perpetual possibilities.

# 5
# Myth and Regulation: *Phaedo*

## 5.1 Binary Systems and Myth

At the forefront of recent myth studies is the influential social anthropologist and structuralist Claude Lévi-Strauss. Structural approaches to myth and ritual emerged in the early twentieth century and are characterized by numerous periods, internal debates, and variants.[1] The tradition has had a major impact on influential contemporary myth theorists such as Marcel Detienne, Jean-Pierre Vernant, and Pierre Vidal-Naquet in France and Edmund Leach and Mary Douglas in the Anglo tradition.[2] Since the publication of Lévi-Strauss's *Structural Anthropology* (1963), scholars from different disciplines have developed and modified many of the methods and ideas he introduced.[3] And the various branches and

---

[1] Lévi-Strauss's structuralism must be distinguished from another prominent form of structural analysis promoted by Vladimir Propp. Whereas Propp delineates the structure of myths by investigating narrative composition, Lévi-Strauss discloses the variety of binary oppositions underlying narrative structure. See Csapo (2005) pp. 189–199.
[2] For critical comparison between first- and second-generation structuralists, see Doty (1986) pp. 209–211.
[3] Lévi-Strauss is also influenced by Freud and Jung and shares their fascination for the inner workings of the mind. Like Freud, Lévi-Strauss situates myth in the unconscious. However, his analysis

© The Editor(s) (if applicable) and The Author(s) 2016
O. Tofighian, *Myth and Philosophy in Platonic Dialogues*,
DOI 10.1057/978-1-137-58044-3_5

movements within structuralism replicate and revive significant aspects of older myth theories.[4] Doty describes the importance of examining the nuances of structure in the study of myth:

> It is difficult indeed to speak of any myths or rituals *without* discussing something of their structure at some point: either structure as the elements that compose the myths or rituals, considered element by element, or as the structuration that differentiates one performance from another. It would be difficult to reach back to a point in mythographic history where these factors were not recognized and discussed.[5]

Structuralists do not focus exclusively on formal codes and classification of mythic elements. They disclose the deep structures underlying and ordering narratives—structures that correspond with formal aspects of the communities and cultures associated with producers of the myths. A structuralist approach emphasizes the inherent distinctions in myths that give rise to meaning—messages that resonate with the individuals living and creating myths within a culture. The methodology moves beyond the named oppositions expressed in myth to investigate the way elements are coded to reveal patterns that explain cultural values, concerns, and identities.

Lévi-Strauss argues that mythic units, or 'mythemes', acquire meaning in relation to other units. Mythemes, like the phonemes of language, are used to build more complex patterns of meaning that connect them to broader sociocultural frameworks. Lévi-Strauss also used the distinction between deep and surface structure: 'The deep structure is the underlying principle (at times approaching the Platonic ideal-forms, at other times the energizing dynamics of the Jungian archetypes) that generates surface (or peri-phrastic) structures—the actual linguistic forms one

---

of mythology and ritual looks to cognition rather than biology. In the tradition of Émile Durkheim's investigation of the collective conscience, Lévi-Strauss argues that a structural approach informs an understanding of the human mind. For a discussion of Durkheim's theory of myth, see Doty (1986) p. 43.

[4] See Csapo (2005) pp. 217–229. Lévi-Strauss was also heavily influenced by Marcel Mauss and Durkheim.

[5] Doty (1986) p. 193. Doty identifies Frazer, Van Gennep, and Eliade among scholars who reflect structuralist principles and methods although, in contrast to structuralists in the tradition of Lévi-Strauss, their interest in structure is concerned more with 'manifest structure' or 'surface manifestation'.

hears or reads when listening to or reading the language'.[6] Imitating this approach in linguistics, his theory abstracts from the stories by moving beyond the particular units of myth to uncover its hidden structure. Influenced by Saussure and Jakobson, Lévi-Strauss argues that the key to interpreting myth is language and understanding myth involves deciphering its grammar; instead of consisting of phonemes or words, sacred narratives consist of mythemes.[7] Structural anthropologists interpret social organization, interaction, and cultural expression in the same way structural linguists understand language.[8] Analyzing diverse languages requires examination of both form and content; the same formal principles and elements are found in the structure of every language. Similarly, content differs between the variety of myths but structure or form is consistent. According to Lévi-Strauss, the analyst must unearth the language-like foundations of culture and the generative logic of its grammar.[9] The aim is to develop an understanding of the unconscious and the underlying attitudes of the myth-producing cultures and communities.[10]

After the examination of various forms of 'oppositions' relevant to phonology, Lévi-Strauss uses the term 'binary oppositions' to inform his account of the thought process that creates social meaning. Binary oppositions are the universal logic of conflicting elements—a system of mental constructs paired against each other. Prominent examples include self-other, sacred-profane, good-bad, life-death, hero-villain, male-female, kinfolk-foreigner, culture-nature, and civilized-uncivilized.[11] Lévi-Strauss

---

[6] Doty (1986) p. 195.

[7] For Saussure's influential work, see Saussure (1983) and a summary of his core ideas by Csapo (2005) pp. 183–189. For a compilation of essays by Jakobson on comparative mythology, see Jakobson (1985), and Csapo (2005) pp. 212–217 offers brief commentary of his ideas. Also, compare with Heyne's notion of 'philosopheme'. See Feldman and Richardson (1972) pp. 216–217.

[8] Lévi-Strauss (1963) p. 211.

[9] Coupe addresses some of the criticisms aimed at Lévi-Strauss structuralist methodology: 'one cannot help but feel that, in pursuit of the grammar of the mind, one is leaving out almost everything that makes the interpretation of the particular text interesting. The richness of narrative is being reduced to the common denominator of universal "order"' ([2006] p. 90). Coupe refers to Geertz's critical analysis of Lévi-Strauss's abstract and essentialist mythography and Turner's critique of the closed and static system constructed by structuralists (Coupe [2006] pp. 90–91).

[10] Lévi-Strauss (1963) p. 87.

[11] Important criticism of Lévi-Strauss's theories deserve mention and need to be considered when interpreting some of the binaries he presents. For instance, his notion of the 'primitive' mind in

describes binary opposition as an integrated meaning-generating system. The binary code consists of categories connected by a logical structure where units mutually determine each other. The opposing categories define one another and, by virtue of this complementary relationship, give meaning to social activity and condition interpretation; it is the medium through which value and meaning are produced. For instance, binary systems operate to order diverse social phenomena such as family dynamics and agreements pertaining to human relationships such as marriage and social contracts involving property.[12] A structuralist approach to myth reveals the deeper structure underlying the complex, fluid, and disparate ethnographic or literary data. Myths are built up by cultural systems consisting of a limited set of types and reflecting human intellectual capacities; they also facilitate communication between social groups.[13] The structuralist aims to uncover the binary system of rules generating myths and maps it onto the wider cultural system constructed by the same complex rules.[14]

The myth of the afterlife journey in the *Phaedo* is structured by a systematic use of concepts and themes rooted in earlier religious and philosophical traditions conjoined with Plato's own intellectual and cultural vision. Binary oppositions pervade the *Phaedo* and impact the plot, literary themes, and arguments to convey a series of significant philosophical views and social commentary. Plato's interpretation and critique of pre-Socratic philosophy are framed within esoteric themes pertaining to the body and afterlife. And his personal and intellectual response to Socrates's execution is presented by using the same literary and cultural tropes. The plot structure of the dialogue and the dominant literary themes pervading the text are based on a set of strict dichotomies. Plato limits the philosophical discussions in the *Phaedo* by designing the plot, themes, and binary system for regulative purposes. These elements and their

---

contrast to modern ways of thinking reinforces derogatory stereotypes of Indigenous peoples and cultures, and his lack of attention to issues of power is exposed by Barthes.

[12] Lévi-Strauss (1969).

[13] Lévi-Strauss applies a theory of communication in interpreting society ([1963] p. 83).

[14] Lévi-Strauss looked for common features and contrasts in the Oedipus myth such as the distinction between patricide/marriage to mother. He examines forms of kinship binary structure in the myth as fundamental analytical tools. For Lévi-Strauss, these tools provide deeper insights than focusing primarily on plot structure. He demonstrates how myth functions as a compelling and provocative method for mediating social and cultural dilemmas ([1963] p. 230).

administrative roles in the text impact the dialogue's messages regarding metaphysics, epistemology, ethics, and religious expression. In addition, Socrates makes a cultural and intellectual statement directed toward advocates of selected pre-Socratic theories and figures.

Cultural productions such as myth are attempts to structure the world and classify the diverse experiences and elements into a meaningful order. Recognition and analysis of binary oppositions help decode culture; the concept is a device useful for inquiries into myth and gives access to deeper structures and patterns. Focusing on the structural features of the dialogue illuminates the language and symbols incorporated in the text and defines the primary audience it aims to address. The mythemes are carefully selected and appear according to a cultural logic that contrasts social phenomena; the same logic presents philosophical concepts in opposition to each other. Both sets of contrasting conjunctions generate meaning, and unpacking Plato's arrangement of binary opposites and the variety of themes, symbols, and arguments discloses important layers of meaning.

## 5.2 Theme Introduction, Setting, and Narrative Mode

The opening scene in the *Phaedo* is placed historically after the death of Socrates and features a narrator recounting Socrates's final moments and conversation (there are few dialogues with this post-execution retrospective quality). And it is one of few dialogues in which the narrator, Phaedo, is also a character in the story. The introductory prelude to the events of Socrates's last hours contains literary and symbolic details crucial for understanding the dialogue. The conversation is between Phaedo and Echecrates in the town of Phlius.[15] Both are devoted admirers of Socrates, and one of them, Echecrates, was also known to be a Pythagorean; at 88d, Plato informs us of his commitment to Pythagorean philosophy.[16]

---

[15] I detail the importance of the two characters in the Sect. 5.7.
[16] Hartle notes that the feeling of anger that is present in many other dialogues, particularly those related to Socrates's trial, is completely missing from the *Phaedo*. Instead, an amicable and cooperative tone is expressed in the interaction between Echecrates and Phaedo and later between Socrates and Cebes and Simmias ([1986] pp. 14–15).

Also, Echecrates is reported to have been the student of Philolaus.[17] In contrast, Phaedo had no connections with Pythagoreanism and had been Socrates's student and companion since Socrates freed him from the bonds of slavery.[18] Description of Phaedo's visit to Phlius and his discussion with Echecrates have an amicable tone, and Echecrates replaces his Pythagorean views quickly, easily, and without resistance. From the early passages, the reader is introduced to a Pythagorean character, who also has immense respect for Socrates,[19] and listens to an account from one who was intellectually enlightened by Socrates and literally freed by Socrates. This Pythagorean/Platonic dynamic pervades other parts of the dialogue; the motif is a regulating and structural device used by Plato for conveying the meanings behind critical passages and the placement of those passages in specific parts of the text. The Pythagorean/Platonic trope is also crucial for analyzing the myth at the end of the text.[20]

The lead-in conversation takes place in the Peloponnesian town of Phlius. Plato's choice of location for the introductory setting is a powerful literary and stylistic statement corresponding with the salient Pythagorean factor in the dialogue[21]; I return to this issue and discuss how it functions to characterize the myth and arguments. Pausanias tells us that Pythagoras's great-grandfather was Hippasus from Phlius, who fled to Samos after encountering political problems.[22] And it was well known that a number of Pythagoreans were once exiled to Phlius.[23] Phaedo is in conversation with a Pythagorean and describing Socrates's last conversation with two Pythagoreans in a town well known to have links with Pythagoreans. The pre-Socratic tradition, therefore, plays an important role in the structure of the dialogue and in the many levels of

---

[17] Huffman (1993) pp. 4 and 326. See 327 for comments on the problems with ascribing views to Philolaus based on the Pythagorean characters in the *Phaedo*.
[18] I also elaborate on the theme of incarceration and liberation and how they imbue the dialogue (the myth, the arguments, and specific symbols) and shape the character of Phaedo.
[19] He refers to Socrates as 'Master' (57a).
[20] A point emphasized by Ebert (2002).
[21] Dorter (1982) pp. 9–10.
[22] Pausanias. *Description of Greece, Book II: Corinth*, Chap. XIII, 2.
[23] Burnet (2003) p. 523. Also, see Hackforth in Plato (1955) p. 29.

## 5 Myth and Regulation: *Phaedo*

literary and philosophical meaning. In addition, Phliasian territory was the origin of the Phliasian Asopus, a river which flows through Sicyonian territory into the Corinthian Gulf. Supposedly, the river ran underground until it reached the Peloponnese. These geographic, cultural, and historical points are extremely important to consider for interpreting the place of the closing myth and its symbolic relationship with other features of the text.[24]

In relation to Phaedo's account, or the embedded dialogue, Plato's choice of setting and the circumstances surrounding the time period during which the scenes occur require further attention in order to understand the text's structure and semantics. The dialogue takes place in the prison where Socrates is going to 'leave the world',[25] and the story is narrated by a historical person who was released from the confines of slavery. These aspects are important on a number of levels. One of the most prominent themes in the text is 'deliverance' or 'release'—a major

---

[24] Pausanias: '[2.5.1] On the summit of the Acrocorinthus is a temple of Aphrodite. The images are Aphrodite armed, Helius, and Eros with a bow. The spring, which is behind the temple, they say was the gift of Asopus to Sisyphus. The latter knew, so runs the legend, that Zeus had ravished Aegina, the daughter of Asopus, but refused to give information to the seeker before he had a spring given him on the Acrocorinthus. When Asopus granted this request Sisyphus turned informer, and on this account he receives—if anyone believes the story-punishment in Hades. I have heard people say that this spring and Peirene are the same, the water in the city flowing hence under-ground [2.5.2]. This Asopus rises in the Phliasian territory, flows through the Sicyonian, and empties itself into the sea here. His daughters, say the Phliasians, were Corcyra, Aegina, and Thebe. Corcyra and Aegina gave new names to the islands called Scheria and Oenone, while from Thebe is named the city below the Cadmea. The Thebans do not agree, but say that There was the daughter of the Boeotian, and not of the Phliasian, Asopus [2.5.3]. The other stories about the river are current among both the Phliasians and the Sicyonians, for instance that its water is foreign and not native, in that the Maeander, descending from Celaenae through Phrygia and Caria, and emptying itself into the sea at Miletus, goes to the Peloponnesus and forms the Asopus. I remember hearing a similar story from the Delians, that the stream which they call Inopus comes to them from the Nile. Further, there is a story that the Nile itself is the Euphrates, which disappears into a marsh, rises again beyond Aethiopia and becomes the Nile [2.5.4]. Such is the account I heard of the Asopus. When you have turned from the Acrocorinthus into the mountain road you see the Teneatic gate and a sanctuary of Eilethyia. The town called Tenea is just about sixty stades distant. The inhabitants say that they are Trojans who were taken prisoners in Tenedos by the Greeks, and were permitted by Agamemnon to dwell in their present home. For this reason they honor Apollo more than any other god'.

[25] Edmonds (2004) pp. 176–178. Edmonds draws interesting connections between this feature of the setting and certain aspects of the arguments and the myth. When I analyze the arguments in the *Phaedo* and the plot structure in their respective sections, I refer to the use of the Orphic and Pythagorean idea of the body as prison—an idea that has a profound structural connection to narratives pertaining to the dialogue's prison location.

motif of the plot that operates in structural and literary ways and also impacts the arrangement and delivery of the arguments. There are a number of indications for the philosophical role of this theme: the arguments for the philosopher's attitude toward death, details and relevance of the afterlife, and the prescriptions Socrates gives for liberating reason from the senses. Plato also uses the deliverance trope to distinguish—or emancipate—his own philosophical positions from the major tenets and theories of pre-Socratic philosophy, particularly Pythagoreanism. The theme of deliverance or release, understood symbolically and represented structurally, is also manifested in the way Plato organizes the dialogue. The consecutive sequences represent a form of transition or development; they help explain how Plato's philosophy has a foundation in prior theories—both philosophical and religious. The function of this technique is to illustrate and enforce Plato's philosophy as a clear breakthrough in terms of method and theory. The first mention of Ideas through the use of unambiguous and detailed arguments (fundamentally anti-corporal in nature)—proofs for a particular version of the 'theory of Forms'—is well placed in this dialogue because of the overarching transitionary themes Plato implements (emancipation and deliverance). Particularly in Sect. 5.6, I explain further how the dialogue's plot consists of three major themes: deliverance, dualism, and a Pythagorean/Platonic dynamic.[26] In Sect. 5.7, I explore aspects of Phaedo's character, including the fact that he was liberated from slavery and how his identity corresponds with the three major themes in the text. Also, deliverance, dualism, and the Pythagorean/Platonic dynamic are informed by Plato's employment of the character Echecrates. Echecrates, as both a Pythagorean philosopher and devotee of Socrates, represents the point of departure from which Plato's own theory develops and facilitates the transition in dramatic form.

---

[26] Edmonds connects what he calls the 'traditional mythic pattern' in the myth to the 'Orphic' Gold tablets and Aristophanes's *Frogs*. However, he is careful to point out that these shared patterns may not be of primary importance when trying to discover the essence of the story or the author's message. Edmonds draws attention to the structural similarities between certain ancient myths. Using this framework allows one to recognize the traditional elements of a myth and from there reveal the manipulated features of each individual text ([2004] pp. 20–21). Similar to Edmonds, my analysis of the three major themes mentioned above acknowledges traditional influences on the plot, both religious and philosophical, and then moves toward exposing the modifications implemented by Plato.

## 5 Myth and Regulation: *Phaedo*

The second key factor in relation to the setting is that Socrates's execution is delayed because of a religious festival. I discussed the literary use of liminal figures in the *Meno* (trickster and slave), and in the next chapter I address liminal space (the setting for the *Phaedrus*). In the *Phaedo*, Plato presents us with the literary, emotive, and philosophical magnitude of liminal time. Scholars of myth and ritual have undertaken important studies on the sacred and existentially unique quality of the phase during which one performs a ritual or undergoes a rite of passage.[27] Plato stages the dialogue during the long delay between the announcement of Socrates's verdict and the actual execution. The time frame within which Socrates debates with his interlocutors is an instance of liminal time (i.e., a moment in limbo or liminal period where 'the characteristics of the ritual subject (the "passenger") are ambiguous; he passes through a cultural realm that has few or none of the attributes of the past or coming state').[28] In liminal time—for instance, during rites of passage or the moments leading up to and during the performance of a ceremony—traditional boundaries are broken down, conventional criteria are disrupted, accepted categories are problematized, and new hypotheses emerge. The liminal phase of a ritual or ceremony is also associated with purification, which is related to the plot and the important themes of deliverance and release. The ceremony delaying Socrates's execution is a purification rite.[29] This feature, employed as a literary device, renders the dialogue with important hermeneutic potential. In the following sections, I examine the possible reasons behind incorporating this particular festival in the dialogue.[30] Instead of simply stating that a random religious festival was taking place, Phaedo takes time to describe the origins of the tradition and its importance to Athenian identity.[31]

---

[27] The work of Victor Turner is particularly important in this respect. See my account in Chap. 2.
[28] Turner (1969) p. 94.
[29] Burger (1984) pp. 8–9. Burger also suggests a possible political message associated with Plato's mention of this particular ceremony—a critique of the Athenian judicial system's treatment of Socrates.
[30] The dialogue discusses the interval, the event giving rise to it, and the cultural importance of the event at 58a–c. Also significant is that Socrates decides to write poetry, rather than practice philosophy, during the interval (61a–b).
[31] Burger (1984) p. 23. For details concerning the myth associated with the ritual, the character of Socrates in the dialogue, and the company he shared on his last day, see Dorter (1982) p. 5.

## 5.3 Myth Analysis[32]

> There are many wonderful regions in the earth; and the earth itself is neither of the kind nor of the size that the experts suppose it to be; or so I'm led to believe (108c).

Socrates's statement appears prior to explaining the dimensions of our world and the real world. He prepares his listeners for what he is about to describe—an account that is in conflict with some of the basic tenets of pre-Socratic thought. Simmias seems disconcerted and curious in his response to Socrates's assertion which indicates, at least in the context of the dialogue, that the account that follows is novel. Socrates begins by postulating that the earth is spherical and situated in the middle of the heavens for logical reasons of uniformity and equilibrium. He indirectly criticizes pre-Socratic theories that hold that some physical force is the reason the earth is suspended and does not fall (109a). Socrates then focuses on the surface of the true earth after he determines that we live in only one of the earth's hollows, which we think is the true surface (109b–110a). The true earth's surface is a dodecahedron and is the origin of all the things in our world and the standard by which things are gauged. For instance, Socrates tells us that the colors of the true surface, flora and fauna, geology, and the appearance of gods are imitated on our earth. Our earth, since it is only one of the hollows, contains air, mist, and water whereas the true earth is positioned among 'ether'. The ether is the source of the air, mist, and water (called dregs) occupying the hollows (109b–c). The details concerning the true earth and its contrast with our world reflect fundamental binaries that also define and delineate many other elements in the dialogue; these basic opposing sets are the distinctions between superior and inferior/original and copy/uncontaminated and diluted. Literally, Plato distinguishes between a sublime, pure, and original surface and an inferior and degraded underground cavern. Dualism is one of the most prominent tropes in the myth together with the theme of deliverance, and all of the motifs and ideas constituting the tale are regulated by the combination of the two.

---

[32] Hackforth states that the myth supports Plato's bare doctrine of immortality. His view is one interpretation of the myth that I challenge in my approach (Plato [1955] p. 171).

## 5 Myth and Regulation: *Phaedo*

The notion of a true dodecahedron-shaped earth is an important symbolic element in the myth. For Pythagoras, the solid sphere represents harmony and therefore it made sense to postulate the shape of the earth as round. This concept influenced Greek thought to such an extent that from the fifth century onward practically all important Greek thinkers shared the view. The sphere represents perfection, harmony, and equilibrium. But there is an important distinction between the Pythagorean view and Plato's use of it in the myth. For adherents of the Pythagorean view, our world is the true earth because it is spherical. For Plato, our world is merely a cavity within the true earth, the surface of which lies well beyond our sphere of existence. The true earth is privileged with the dimensions of a dodecahedron (not a sphere)—a shape that came to be known as a 'Platonic solid'.[33] (Philolaus links the dodecahedron to ether but considers the shape merely a representation of an element like the others.) The Pythagorean/Platonic contrast is significant and pervasive and, I argue, is in harmony with other themes and arguments.[34]

After Socrates describes some brief details pertaining to the appearance and inhabitants of the true earth, he gives an account of the places within the earth—the 'hollow regions' (111c). These regions consist of hollows of different depths but are connected by underground rivers. The rivers consist of different elements and substances: hot and cold water, fire, and mud and lava. These rivers oscillate as a result of flowing into a pumping central chasm called Tartarus—the earth's deepest chasm. Socrates mentions the four main streams, which are Oceanus, Acheron, Pyriphlegethon, and Cocytus. He also refers to two lakes and the region that contains one

---

[33] Some ancient sources credit Pythagoras with the discovery of the 'Platonic solids', whereas others say Theaetetus was the first to describe all five. Pythagoras mentions only the tetrahedron, cube, and dodecahedron (Ferguson [2008] pp. 155–157).

[34] The details in the myth such as the geometrical contours of the true earth—a dodecahedron as opposed to a sphere—represent a contrast with Pythagorean thought without completely breaking ties with the tradition. In terms of the world we inhabit, Pythagoreans believe it to be the only earth, displaying the perfection of numbers, and therefore spherical. However, for Plato, our world is an inferior hollow within the true dodecahedron-shaped earth. 'The Pythagoreans, Aristotle argues, differ from Plato only in denying any separation between the first principles—which they identify with numbers rather than "ideas"—and the things said to be their imitations; the Pythagorean teaching on reincarnation, on the other hand, presupposes the separability of the psyche from the body. The attempt to reinterpret the meaning of "separation", and in so doing to reverse the Pythagorean position, is, one might say, the fundamental intention of the *Phaedo*' (Burger [1984] p. 7).

of the lakes. Socrates tells of the fate of souls that have committed certain kinds of sin (113d–114b). Their conduct determines the journey they undertake through the four-river system, past the Acherusian Lake and, if necessary, into Tartarus. The crimes that determine one's afterlife fate are described by Plato in very general categories; he does not articulate, or differentiate between, the nuances associated with the variety of immoral acts or consider the contextual elements which may have influenced the perpetrator. For this reason, it is fair to assume that he infers the basic idea that injustice deserves punishment and that different crimes require different forms and degrees of punishment.[35] Owing to the brevity of his illustration, I argue that Plato endeavors to make a simple point about the punishment of sins and that the more significant issues conveyed in these passages—or embodied in the myth—must be derived from Socrates's narrative; meaning is mediated through Plato's intricate design of the peculiar underground river system. The motifs interwoven through the story help connect the myth and the corresponding arguments and are regulated by the plot and characterized by the themes associated with the binaries separating pre-Socratic and Platonic thought. The underworld typology in the myth is a deliberate attempt by Plato to symbolically represent Phlius, the location of the opening scene of the dialogue. And as for my argument, the significance of Phlius for the text is to emphasize the pivotal place Pythagoreanism occupies in the overall plot and meaning of the *Phaedo*.

In the passage following the myth, Plato makes reference to the deliverance motif prevalent throughout the dialogue. The righteous individual is liberated from the lower regions of the earth, and if one is committed to philosophy then one remains on the true earth for eternity without a body. These comments reaffirm the dualism theme. The dualism trope is replicated and reinforced after Socrates concludes the myth (114e). The pleasures associated with the body are represented as a hindrance to one's acquisition of knowledge; he confirms that detachment from the body and acquiring knowledge are prerequisites for salvation—a desirable afterlife on the true earth. And, in accordance with the theme of release, Socrates states: 'But those who are judged to have lived a life of

---

[35] Edmonds (2004) pp. 197–198.

surpassing holiness—these are they who are released and set free from imprisonment in these regions of the earth, and passing upward to their pure abode, make their dwelling upon the earth's surface' (114b–c).

## 5.4 The Philosophical Arguments

In my analysis of Plato's arguments in the *Phaedo*, I address the three major themes in the text: deliverance, dualism, and a Pythagorean/Platonic connection. Before engaging in a study of the arguments, I provide some explanation of the significance of the three main themes in order to illuminate their literary and philosophical roles. In the *Phaedo*, Plato distinguishes his philosophy from pre-Socratic philosophy, in general, and Pythagorean thought, in particular (possibly Pythagorianism as interpreted by Philolaus). To mark this distinction and clarify the differences, he provides an account of the existence and nature of Forms in a comprehensive manner and explains how the notion pertains to the idea that learning is recollection.

At 62b–c, Socrates offers an explanation to Cebes for the notion that suicide is immoral. What he presents is an argument based on a belief.[36] Before Socrates discusses his view, Cebes anticipates that he has heard explanations for the same conclusion from Philolaus and others (a point that Socrates acknowledges). What Plato conveys in these passages is important for two reasons: (1) for understanding the subsequent arguments and (2) for characterizing the stage of the narrative or plot. First, Plato has Socrates elaborate the Orphic concept of the physically imprisoned soul.[37] Socrates explains the idea that incarceration was divinely ordained and concludes that it is unethical for the soul to escape from the body before the gods decide to liberate it.[38] Socrates asks Cebes to put himself in the place of the gods: 'Then take your own case; if one of your possessions were to destroy itself without intimation from you

---

[36] For a discussion of the religious discourse in the *Phaedo*, see Morgan (2010).
[37] Hackforth in Plato (1955) p. 4.
[38] Socrates refers to the hidden messages of the mystics at 62b and 67d. Also, see 81e–84b for discussion of the body as prison.

that you wanted it to die, wouldn't you be angry with it and punish it, if you had any means of doing so?' (62c). Socrates's commitment to the anti-suicide position functions in the subsequent passages as support for the arguments that follow.[39] The arguments can be interpreted as prescriptions to live a moral life with the intention of completing one's life. And life under these conditions must involve the aim of philosophical perfection and, as a consequence, remaining confident and steadfast in the face of death. The hypothesis employed here is the view that pursuit of a philosophical life is necessary if one wants to achieve true freedom; that is, philosophy (in the form described by Socrates) and liberation are interdependent. The subsequent arguments, or the combination of arguments and dramatic effect, build on this hypothesis. The argument for opposites that follows is associated with Philolaus.[40] Plato introduces the hypothesis by employing the Orphic theme of the imprisoned body characteristic of Pythagoreanism, which impacts the initial part of the discursive section.[41]

The passages in the dialogue dealing with the prohibition of suicide illuminate many salient characteristics of the Pythagorean/Platonic dynamic.[42] At 62b, Socrates presents his argument against suicide. He makes reference to the Orphic belief that interprets physical existence as imprisonment of the soul, indicating that he shares this view.[43] This belief is adopted by Pythagoreans, who also hold that taking one's own life is immoral. However, Socrates and the two Pythagorean interlocutors disagree when it comes to how one should feel about dying. Socrates renders a defense of his conviction that his death will be advantageous and therefore desirable. In the arguments that follow, the reader is exposed to a worldview consisting of the strictest form of dualism.[44] At 65d, Plato

---

[39] At 63c, in support of his position, Socrates adds to his belief that he will 'find there divine masters who are supremely good'.
[40] Huffman (1993) pp. 133, 140, and 325.
[41] Hackforth in Plato (1955) p. 38.
[42] Hartle argues that arguments are not objects and infers that juxtaposition and separation of arguments 'generate' truth and falsehood. Her observations are important for interpreting the Pythagorean/Platonic dynamic in the text ([1986] p. 64).
[43] Edmonds (2004).
[44] For the soul/body dichotomy throughout the text, see 64c–65d, 66b–67d, 71e, 72a, 73a, 76c, 76e, 79c–80e, 81c–d, 84b, 105d, 106e, and 107c–d. For the sense/intellect dichotomy throughout the dialogue, see 64d, 65b–d, 66a, 66d, 67b, 79c–80b, 81b–c, 81e–84b, and 114e.

## 5 Myth and Regulation: *Phaedo*

presents an argument involving a premise interpreted as the first subtle indication of the theory of Forms; the stronger account is yet to come.[45] The following argument is framed by the dualism trope and Socrates emphasizes that philosophers find salvation in death—the ultimate release from physical embodiment. At this point (69e), there is no serious diversion from Pythagorean philosophy.

The passages in the dialogue prior to the myth consist of four main lines of argument: the logic of opposites in the recycling of life, recollection, argument for affinity, and the immortality of the soul.[46] In presenting these arguments, Plato uses an accepted Pythagorean idea as his gambit and then reinterprets it to introduce his own philosophical theory and surpass the limits of his predecessors; he manipulates the logic of opposites. He begins with an argument in support of the theory that life comes from death and death comes from life. Plato provides 'background information' to assist in understanding the origin of his arguments. At 70c–d, Socrates refers to the religious belief that souls exist in another realm before re-entering the physical world. In the *Meno*, Plato makes the same reference and uses the theory of recollection and the slave experiment to support the belief. In the *Phaedo*, one finds a multidimensional use of the belief, which includes the attitude toward death as pretext for introducing a theory involving Forms. After announcing his belief, Socrates indicates that more arguments are required if it is to be accepted and then the myth is presented. A form of prenatal experience/afterlife narrative is illustrated in order to frame the belief.

The logic of opposites features variously in almost all pre-Socratic philosophy and particularly characterizes Pythagorean philosophy. Philolaus, who was connected with the Pythagorean exiles at Phlius, taught Simmias and Cebes and was well known for his concern regarding the philosophical significance of opposites. Plato begins the discursive part of the dialogue by addressing similar philosophical issues pertaining to opposites. Although the argument from opposites is not a central concern of the dialogue (the three more important arguments do not depend on it), it does function as a foundation for the arguments that follow: recollection, affinity, and immortality of the soul. The recollection argument, for

---

[45] Hackforth in Plato (1955) pp. 50–51.
[46] See comments by Patterson (1965) on immortality.

instance, makes use of it but its validity is not contingent on the principle of opposites. During the frame dialogue, Phaedo expresses his own mixed feelings regarding the opposites of pleasure and pain to Echecrates; this occurs as he begins giving his account and setting the theme and mood for the scene (59a). Plato's theory of opposites in the *Phaedo* differs from the description of pleasure and pain in the *Gorgias* (consider the different views of punishment in each dialogue). The theory of opposites in the *Phaedo* is closer to the Pythagorean view (it is closer to Philolaus's view, to be precise), which corresponds with the Pythagorean/Platonic comparison and contrast pervading the dialogue.

In subsequent passages, Socrates introduces recollection. The passages containing the argument for recollection begin at 73a and function in two ways. First, the theory accepts the conclusion from the opposites argument—a factor that agrees with tenets of Pythagorean or pre-Socratic philosophy. But the theory of recollection, as mentioned, is not contingent upon any kind of argument that uses opposites and it is from this scene in the dialogue that Plato begins to make a clear distinction between his philosophy and the theories of his predecessors. The theory of recollection was introduced in the *Meno*, and in the *Phaedo* Plato does not challenge the view in any significant manner but reiterates and reinforces the idea by using different arguments—arguments using the concept of Form (the Form of Equality). The function of the recollection argument is to prepare the description of the concept of Form and examination of its place in Platonic philosophy rather than another attempt to justify *anamnesis*.

After Plato addresses the argument for recollection, the dialogue focuses on explaining the significance of Forms.[47] He provides an argument that (1) supports his use of the concept of Form in the earlier line of argument and (2) elaborates how Forms are interpreted in relation to the soul. To make this connection, Plato offers the affinity argument. This argument clarifies the indivisible and eternal nature of the Forms and, as a result, the epistemological attraction of the soul to the Forms. Because of this shared essence, the nature of the soul and the nature of Forms are

---

[47] Dorter identifies the relevance of the purification theme in Plato's recollection argument in the *Phaedo* ([1982] pp. 65–69).

interpreted as correlative. The next series of arguments are a response to the objections of Simmias and Cebes to Socrates's arguments for the immortality of the soul. Cebes, in particular, presents the Pythagorean attunement theory.

The attunement theory was a popular Pythagorean view of the soul elaborated by Philolaus and also held by Parmenides. Cebes presents the argument and seems to have convinced those listening in the scene. After Cebes completes his critique, Plato employs a literary technique that redirects and complicates the narrative and the rhythm of the arguments and influences interpretation of literary and philosophical dynamics. At 89b, the frame dialogue and the main dialogue interweave: the narrator, Phaedo, refers to himself in the embedded dialogue and the main character in the narrative, Socrates, interacts with Phaedo as they sit in the prison. Once Phaedo's presence is highlighted in the dialogue's main narrative, a shift occurs in the topic and theme of the arguments; what follows is an elaborate account of what we know as the theory of Forms.[48] The shift I refer to is first represented when Socrates focuses on meta-philosophical concerns such as misology, elaboration on the place of hypothesis, the problems with basing knowledge on likelihood, and the importance of considering theoretical consequences. Socrates raises these topics in response to a theoretical challenge to his philosophical position and the literary dynamics conditioning these passages deserve special attention.[49]

> While Socrates' conduct may provide the most effective weapon against the fear of death, the only defense against misology that is capable of protecting the psychē from blinding itself is an art of argumentation. This *technē* of logos Socrates identifies as a "second sailing": it abandons the attempt to investigate the beings themselves in order to investigate their truth through logoi and is illustrated by the turn from the first to the second half of the dialogue.[50]

---

[48] Dorter links the theme of liberation with the scene in which Phaedo enters and the new subjects that Plato introduces into the dialogue ([1982] pp. 89–97).
[49] Hartle also highlights, among other transformations that occur during the course of the dialogue, the changes that Echecrates goes through as a result of Phaedo's interlude and the shifts in the arguments that it triggers ([1986] pp. 79–80).
[50] Burger (1984) p. 10.

Why does Plato decide to change the direction of the discussion and introduce new issues at this point in the dialogue? First, he warns against mistrusting argument and criticizes those who fail to provide convincing support for a proposition and instead blame the arguments themselves or the value of argumentation (90d).[51] Then Simmias states an important feature of the hypothesis used for the theory of recollection. 'But I realize that theories which rest their proof upon likelihood are imposters …. On the other hand, the theory of recollection and learning derives from a hypothesis which is worthy of acceptance' (92d). Simmias reiterates that the soul has the same status as Forms and rejects the alternative attunement theory. Following Simmias's agreement, Socrates renders further arguments against the view that the soul is attunement. It becomes clear at 93c that recollection accounts for the place of goodness and badness and, in contrast, the attunement view is inconsistent with a cogent moral theory. In addition, the explanatory value of the attunement theory in terms of the soul's governing power is limited. Socrates exposes this at 94b–e. Therefore, on the basis of desirable consequences, the hypothesis stating that the soul is immortal and has affinities with the Forms is superior.[52]

Socrates's response to Cebes (96a), like his response to Simmias, has a number of important dimensions worth unpacking for its dramatic and philosophical import. Plato chooses to extrapolate his metaphysical theory through an analysis of generation and destruction. Socrates describes his early interest in natural science, which led him to focus on philosophy. He expresses his dissatisfaction with pre-Socratic causation but finds potential in Anaxagoras's view that intelligence rules everything. Ultimately, Socrates distinguishes between the cause and the conditions surrounding the cause. He recognizes that the physical conditions for generation and what is generated could be otherwise, whereas he was looking for an explanation which is necessary and which gives rise to an outcome that could not be otherwise. Socrates also draws a connection between the cause and the highest good: things come to be because it is best for them to be that way according to a certain order. Next, Socrates

---

[51] For further details, see Hackforth in Plato (1955) pp. 109–111.
[52] Socrates's arguments for the immortality of the soul and his conception of soul in the *Phaedo* are determined by the unique structural network and context of the dialogue. For accounts of the soul in other dialogues in contrast to the *Phaedo*, see Hackforth in Plato (1955) pp. 19–24.

## 5 Myth and Regulation: *Phaedo*

acknowledges the use of hypotheses in investigation and refers to the procedure as 'employing images' (100a). He conducts his inquiry into reality by using the hypothesis referred to earlier in this section: that individuals must live a life devoted to philosophy without compromise, even if faced with death; happiness at the thought of death has special meaning in this discourse. Plato's metaphysical theory is constructed as a necessary argument in this context and relates directly to the hypothesis. I engage with the relationship between the myth and the arguments in the next section by drawing attention to this last argument and noting the correlation between the hypothesis and the moral of the myth.

In the remainder of the argumentative part of the text, Plato submits some of the most important details concerning his metaphysical theory. Socrates points out that what he describes is nothing new and has been directly referred to, or indirectly implied, from the beginning. 'I do not go so far as to insist upon the precise detail; only upon the fact that it is by Beauty that beautiful things are beautiful. This, I feel, is the safest answer for me or for anyone else to give, and I believe that while I hold fast to this I cannot fall' (100d–e). Socrates states the reason he holds on to his philosophical position: it achieves impenetrability and infallibility because the conclusions coincide with the highest good. For Socrates, this theory, more than any other, has the potential to lead to consequences that correspond with the highest good and deserve full commitment.

At 103, Plato distinguishes Platonic metaphysics from pre-Socratic thought with the purpose of distinguishing his philosophy from theories based on the logic of opposites. This section of the dialogue refers to the earlier line of argument prior to Plato's examination of the Forms.[53] Plato acknowledges that the logic of opposites is relevant, but only on the level of particulars. His theory of reality limits the efficacy of empirical analysis; in the *Phaedo*, Plato transcends particulars to provide an account based on the Forms. The dialogue marks one of the most distinctive ideological differences between Plato's views and those of his pre-Socratic predecessors—particularly, Pythagorean philosophy.[54]

---

[53] Dorter (1982) pp. 74–75.

[54] Pythagorean/Platonic dynamics running through the dialogue include Echecrates/Phaedo, events taking place in Phlius (frame dialogue)/events taking place in Athens (emphasized dialogue), Simmias and Cebes/Socrates, the hollows/real earth, and spherical earth/dodecahedron.

## 5.5 Mutual Scaffolding

The myth at the end of the *Phaedo* has a structural role in the dialogue and functions as a regulating device. The myth's structural influence manifests in the plot, character selection, symbolism, and the arrangement and style of different arguments. The various ways myth and argument operate are connected through synecdoche. The afterlife myth invests in the plot and dominant narrative themes: dualism, deliverance, and the symbolic and theoretical Pythagorean/Platonic distinction. The myth functions in ways other than those I propose; the dialogue also aims to give hope and encouragement to the others in their pursuit of philosophy and for living a moral life. Emotive, illustrative, or allegorical interpretations are important and exemplify the richness of the myth; the scenes and situations are designed and ordered for multilayered meaning and affect. However, the plot, characters, and symbolism Plato employs to mold his literary creation are orchestrated to make a definitive point to and about Pythagorean thinkers. The dramatic features flow into the arguments and contribute to this particular philosophical message of the text.[55]

Plato's afterlife myth addresses pre-Socratic and Pythagorean ideas directly by using identifiable cosmological symbols.[56] The status, arrangement, and relationship between these symbols in the narrative correspond with the arguments. A major theme in the dialogue is dualism (metaphysical, epistemological, and ethical) and the myth reflects this trope through the distinction between the true earth and our inferior world deep within it. The account provides the pattern for interpreting the difference between the world of intellect and the world of sense experience and how the latter receives its characteristics from the pure reality of the former. The arguments in the dialogue are structured by a strict dualism trope and worldview, and the myth assists in making this framework and related features transparent. The distinction between the two realms is told through a story about a cosmic dichotomy, and the structure of the narrative also regulates how the differences between Pythagorean and Platonic

---

[55] Rowe argues for an integrated view of the philosophical and non-philosophical parts of the text. Integration, for Rowe, means the extent to which arguments can convince us to live a Good life and reduce the fear of death connected to the vision of the soul's afterlife fate (Plato [1993b] pp. 2–3).
[56] Ebert (2002).

## 5 Myth and Regulation: *Phaedo*

theories are communicated and how they function in the dialogue's interpretation of the world. The ideological, theoretical, and practical contrasts in the myth also feature significantly in the arguments. Plato's true earth is the shape of a Platonic solid, the dodecahedron, and not a sphere.[57] The notion of a spherical earth was a commonly accepted idea among pre-Socratic thinkers and particularly important to Pythagoreans.[58] Plato marks off a Platonic theory of reality from a Pythagorean one by introducing the distinction between the two worlds.

The myth uses imagery of an underground river system and a central fire to describe the fate of souls. This geography exists underneath our cavernlike world and has no influence on the true surface. The significance of this symbolism is associated with the town of Phlius, where Phaedo the narrator transmits the story to Echecrates. The town has numerous links to Pythagorean figures and was known for its unique underground river system. Also, the idea of a central fire is common in pre-Socratic philosophy and features prominently in Philolaus's thought. The illustration of the two worlds correlates with the arguments both structurally and symbolically. The description of the physical world uses geographic and natural icons familiar to Pythagoreans. And the arguments and ideas presented by Socrates's interlocutors are recognizably Pythagorean. The account of the true earth uses geometry and concepts embedded in other dialogues and indicative of Platonic theories. The arguments conveyed by Socrates reflect the Theory of Forms and Recollection.

The Pythagorean/Platonic contrast is represented clearly in other aspects of the text. The character of Echecrates introduced in the opening scene and the pair of Simmias and Cebes as interlocutors in the embedded dialogue are Pythagoreans who undergo change or transformation (release or deliverance) through the discussions that take place. 'What we are presented with at this level of the dialogue is a change that takes place in Echecrates, a change brought about by Phaedo's narration and which mirrors the change in Simmias and Cebes brought about by Socrates'.[59]

---

[57] Philolaus also discussed the importance of geometrical shapes such as those now termed Platonic solids; however, Plato attributes a noetic quality to them. Philolaus identified geometrical shapes with elements, and the dodecahedron was associated with the universe.
[58] Compare 108c and 108e–113c for distinctions pertaining to shapes.
[59] Hartle (1986) p. 79.

For the myth, Plato uses the themes of release or deliverance to explain the judgment of the soul. Different degrees of unjust souls must journey through the river system and Tartarus and suffer different forms of punishment. Virtuous souls are released from reincarnation into the physical world and dwell in the intellectual world of perfect entities. Dualism plays a strong role in accommodating the theme of deliverance and communicating its literary and philosophical impact. The eschatological myth consists of a dichotomy between the lower world and the upper world and provides the appropriate framework for administering the deliverance trope. The quintessential Orphic or Pythagorean qualities of the tale merge with Plato's understanding of the essential connections between reason and freedom. The myth prioritizes rational endeavor over empirical investigation and is in harmony with Plato's philosophy presented in the *Phaedo*. Earlier philosophical and religious traditions are represented, appropriated, and then superseded.[60] The lower world is characterized to link with other motifs in the myth such as dualism and deliverance from physical imprisonment. The language and imagery are familiar to Pythagoreans and Plato uses numerous Pythagorean characters to instantiate stages in the arguments, the binaries underlying the arguments, and the moral and religious dimensions of the arguments. The dialogue maneuvers through theories, acquainting us with Pythagoreans and then reworking core issues and concepts to accommodate a new metaphysics, epistemology, and ethics.

A mutual scaffolding interpretation illuminates the interdependent and multidimensional relationship between *mythos* and *logos* in the *Phaedo*. Interpretations that rationalize narrative elements by reducing them to moral allegory or illustration are based on the *mythos/logos* dichotomy. Mutual scaffolding, however, explores the regulating function of the myth, explaining how it directs arguments and conditions the literary rhythm.[61] The myth's plot is an indispensable part of the dialogue

---

[60] Pythagoreans saw the physical world as manifesting number and therefore worthy of serious contemplation. The fact that Plato's philosophy infiltrates and shapes an otherwise Pythagorean-themed story re-enforces the Pythagorean/Platonic motif.

[61] Edmonds attempts to interweave *mythos* and *logos* when analyzing the *Phaedo*. He uses metaphor or metonymy to connect them, influencing his description of myth as an addition to argumentation or simply illustrative: '… Plato carefully crafts the myth Socrates tells of the soul's journey after

that elucidates the integrated nature of different scenes and features. The regulating influence of the myth is also reflected in Plato's arguments; narrative plot and symbolism inform both the literary and intellectual peculiarities pervading the *Phaedo*. Sensitivity toward the structural intricacies in *mythos* highlights the themes of deliverance, dualism, and the Pythagorean/Platonic dynamic. These important aspects of the plot help guide interpretation of the argumentative structure. Both arguments and myth are regulated by an overarching narrative framework—a format that governs and sets the tempo for the movements and signals in the dialogue.

The myth describes the possible afterlife existence of souls depending on the degree of virtue practiced during earthly existence. It promotes a life dedicated to philosophy aimed at achieving complete release from the cycle of reincarnation into the physical world or avoiding descent into eternal punishment.[62] The myth perpetuates a dichotomy involving two distinct realms; the inferior world acquires its qualities from the superior. The lower world must be transcended in a form of escape. Eternal salvation is depicted as a flight from bondage; one must first tolerate existence in a body and struggle intellectually and morally through life in order to release the soul. The 'two-worlds' theory used in the literary framework determines the rhetorical style of the discursive sections.[63] Therefore, the order of various arguments by the different interlocutors and their inferential logic is driven by structural and thematic elements from the myth.

The arguments in the dialogue begin with Socrates and the Pythagoreans agreeing to some basic principles (release from the body and opposites) but disagreeing about some metaphysical consequences each party infers. The Pythagoreans use the theory of opposites but attempt to connect it to neither their beliefs regarding the afterlife nor their views on living a moral life. For Pythagoreans, the principle regarding opposites is restricted to cosmology. Socrates introduces the general hypothesis that a philosopher should welcome death and manipulates the principle of

---

death to highlight important ideas raised in the earlier arguments, shaping the traditional tale to expand and reinforce these arguments' ([2004] p. 160. Also, see pp. 166–167 and 170).

[62] For the hypothesis that the philosophical life is a preparation for death, see 64a–e; 81a; 95b–c.

[63] Benetiz (2007) suggests that myth informs Plato's distinction between appearance and reality and characterizes the descriptive language used to represent the two worlds.

opposites to support it. He also employs the argument from opposites for his ethical theory. The *Phaedo* exemplifies a move away from some of the standard tenets of pre-Socratic thought; Plato explicates and replaces them with Platonic theories and ideas; he officially liberates his thought from his predecessors. Plato's choice of plot accommodates salient motifs in the text, particularly imprisonment—a motif that was recognizable to the philosophical and religious community present in the embedded dialogue. The dialectical unity in which the arguments and the myth engage is defined by these literary and ideological characteristics.

> Why, really, Simmias, I don't think that it calls for the skill of a Glaucus to explain what my belief is; but to prove that it is true seems to me to be too difficult even for a Glaucus. In the first place I should probably be unable to do it; and in the second, even if I knew how, it seems to me, Simmias, that my life is too short for an explanation of the required length. However, there is no reason why I should not tell you what I believe about the appearance of the earth and the regions in it (108d–e).

Truth regarding the earth is too difficult to prove discursively but the interlocutors agree that it is sufficient to tell a story about the 'appearance of the earth and the regions in it'. Socrates deems it more appropriate to describe the earth in a way coherent with an organized and operational literary system. Correspondence with physical reality is clearly not the aim of the myth. Dorter explains that the account at the end of the *Phaedo* has the potential to be 'true' under different conditions: 'the "truth" of entities would seem most naturally to refer to their teleological reason for being, for this is the truth that Socrates is pursuing. In this case, the "things", or entities in their true being (99e3), would indeed refer to physical things conceived, however, not in terms of their physical operations (efficient and material causality) but in so far as they are manifestations of the teleological principle, the good'.[64] The narrative plot structure infuses the dialogue with examples, themes, and references and creates necessary conditions for commentary of Plato's ethics; metaphysics and epistemology are inseparable from moral theory. The task of

---

[64] Dorter (1982) p. 122.

creating and inserting the myth as an essential regulating element is justified and the hermeneutically instructive passages bolster this perspective.

Of course, no reasonable man ought to insist that the facts are exactly as I have described them. But that either this or something very like it is a true account of our souls and their future inhabitations—since there is certainly evidence that the soul is deathless—this, I think, is both a fitting contention and a belief worth risking; for the risk is a noble one (114d).

## 5.6 Plot Structure

Not only can an extrapolation of the various ways in which authors use a common set of elements uncover the different agendas of these authors and provide a deeper understanding of the individual texts, but it can also shed light on the ways in which myth was used by the Greeks in the late fifth and fourth centuries BCE—not as sacred scripture, not purely as entertainment, but as a device for communication, a mode of speaking in which they could convey meaning densely through the manipulation of mythic motifs and patterns that each had its resonance for the audience.[65]

Plato's dialogues and the different kinds of stories embedded in them incorporate plots that determine order, style, and meaning and facilitate communication with other elements in the text. The plot structure of the *Phaedo* myth consists of a number of pivotal themes that embolden its tapestry of sociocultural and philosophical concerns and messages. Plato specifically devised the plot with an agenda; he directed his philosophical work toward those with Pythagorean affiliations or sympathies and constructed the dialogue by using an almost proselytizing communicative approach. Socrates's responses to his Pythagorean counterparts convey an evangelical tone that is also reproduced in the myth; the afterlife journey inspires conversion. The mutual cooperation between myth and arguments amplifies the dialogue's persuasiveness, and the combination of care and zeal exhibited by the plot contributes to the success of the text. The plot structure driving the myth, the arguments, and the narrative

---

[65] Edmonds (2004) p. 4.

direction of the *Phaedo* is designed by Plato by using mythic motifs that express religious fervor, moral well-being, and genuine concern for protection, guidance, and emancipation.

> [Phaedo's] life was characterized by liberation from bondage both in the literal sense and in the figurative sense of conversion to philosophy (82e ff) and the dialogue is pre-eminently about the theme of bondage and liberation: Socrates' literal imprisonment, the imprisonment of the soul within the body and its liberation by death, the imprisonment of reason by corporeal pleasure and pain and its liberation by philosophy, the subterranean rivers, as well as Socrates' account of his ascent to philosophy, which parallels the *Republic*'s account of the liberation from the cave. Our constant awareness of Phaedo, like the references to Theseus' liberation of the fourteen, helps make us sensitive to the theme of liberation that runs as an undercurrent throughout the work.[66]

Plato uses the motifs of deliverance and dualism to express religious and philosophical ideas. The myth, the dramatic scenes, and the arguments imply a religious practice or process of ascension; Socrates, the interlocutors, the characters from the frame narrative, and the intended audience (Plato's contemporaries and later readers) are encouraged to engage in a 'ritual' of release.[67] Deliverance is represented in numerous ways, and the plot is reflected continuously and reinforced until it culminates in the final eschatological story—a narrative involving the soul's afterlife liberty and Socrates's departure from his body.[68]

The plot imports a strict version of Orphic and Pythagorean cosmic dualism. This involves the idea of the soul as imprisoned and Plato modifies the traditional system by interweaving his views on knowledge acquisition and morality.[69] The theory of Forms is introduced in the dialogue and is explored and represented in arguments and in the myth ending the *Phaedo*. And the dialogue's plot creates the philosophical, literary,

---

[66] Dorter (1982) p. 10.

[67] Inspirational liberation tropes pervade the text: the release of the soul from the body, prisoner from the prison, Platonic philosophy from Pythagorean philosophy, real world from physical world, and so on.

[68] For examples representing the influence of the deliverance trope in the myth, see 113e–114c.

[69] For instance, see 82c–84b.

and religious conditions for convincing the interlocutors and the reader of the validity, moral import, and emotional appeal of the theory. My interpretation does not suggest that the epistemology and metaphysics of different dialogues are contingent on the plot specific to *that* dialogue. Intertextual patterns exist and Plato's philosophy is systematic; he is not only engaging in dramatic experiments. But one must be aware of the nuances associated with the plot and its regulative function in relation to the stories and scenes contained in the text. And understanding the way plot affects the delivery of the discursive sections is crucial for reading both the Pythagorean and Platonic perspectives portrayed in them. A mutual scaffolding approach isolates these factors for deliberation, highlights the need for analysis of their relation to the structures and symbolism of the myth, and encourages re-entry into the dialectical unity.

## 5.7 Character Selection

Character selection in the *Phaedo* is complex since the dialogue has an opening scene framing the embedded dialogue and the Phaedo character appears in both parts. The characters in the opening and the main dialogue reflect each other, and the myth impacts the structural and thematic conditions influencing the context for each set of individuals or discussants. The plot exemplified in the myth helps clarify the relationships between the individual characters and the connection between the two sets of characters (from both the frame and emphasized dialogues).[70]

### 5.7.1 Phaedo

Phaedo narrates the events surrounding the final moments of Socrates, and Plato introduces him in the frame story opening the dialogue. He is a slave freed by Socrates and becomes a keen student of the philosopher. His character was once a liminal figure now freed from the ambiguous, transitional, in-between status associated with anti-structure and has re-entered

---

[70] See Colloud-Streit (2005) pp. 121–124.

a socially sanctioned and structured existence. Phaedo exited the stage of limbo defining an enslaved person and retains insights from dwelling in liminality. Phaedo's personality in the dialogue is characterized by his post-liminal life and corresponds intimately with themes connected to the plot. The Phaedo character is a living example of the liberated soul venerated in the myth. And the fact that the events of the dialogue occur during liminal time ties the narrator's recollection with the afterlife story in substantive terms; that is, both Phaedo's liminal past and the liminal moment of Socrates last hours indicate disorientation, deconstruction, recreation, and transformation. Every time Phaedo appears in the dialogue, whether as narrator or in the one instance as character, a significant shift occurs theoretically or methodologically.[71]

### 5.7.2 Echecrates

Echecrates is a Pythagorean from the Peloponnesian town of Phlius, where the opening scene of the text is set. His role in the text is symbolically significant not only because he was a Pythagorean but also because he was a supporter of Socrates and a student of Philolaus and was linked with the exiles in Phlius.[72] Echecrates is equivalent to the figures of Simmias and Cebes, thus supporting the Pythagorean trope or dimension pervading the dialogue.

### 5.7.3 Socrates

As a consequence of the deliverance theme, Socrates's role is presented as heroic; he gave up his life because he refused to compromise his philosophical ideals.[73] The deliverance trope, as it is employed in the *Phaedo*,

---

[71] Socrates presents his final and most convincing arguments after Phaedo as narrator breaks the flow of the embedded dialogue with additional remarks and simultaneously appears as a character at 88–89 and 102.
[72] Echecrates's association with Philolaus may clarify doubts that he was a Pythagorean because of his unorthodox ideas (Plato [1993] pp. 6–7).
[73] Edmonds (2004) pp. 159 and 202–205.

has similarities with myths portraying the death and resurrection of a god or hero.[74] The dialogue's literary style is heavily influenced by the themes of dualism and deliverance, and Socrates is the hero who is ultimately resurrected as divine. Parallels between the tales of Dionysius, Heracles, the Egyptian god Horus or Osiris, and possibly even Christ are appropriate.[75] One of the major factors distinguishing Plato's *Phaedo* from other narratives based on a deliverance plot is the specific context in which the text was written and the audience for which it was written. The ideological pre-Socratic-Pythagorean factor influencing the dialogue reduces the moral of the *Phaedo* from a universal message to a very idiosyncratic and temporally and culturally specific 'community announcement'.

Plato's dialogues challenge preconceived notions, question hypotheses, and reinterpret traditional views. These activities are performed in the *Phaedo* with ritual connotations and a dominant and urgent mood of spiritual aspiration. The discursive steps and moves in the text are also imbued with religious enthusiasm encouraged by the sacrificial hero figure of Socrates, whose deliverance from the physical world is imminent. These qualities saturate the *Phaedo* with a particular liminal quality not found in other dialogues; Plato's account communicates a unique balance of solemnity and euphoria.

### 5.7.4 Simmias and Cebes

Socrates's two interlocutors in the embedded dialogue occupy a function similar to that of Echecrates; Simmias and Cebes are the Pythagorean contrast to Platonic philosophy—a contrast dictated by the plot. They also resemble Echecrates in that they are both students of Philoaus and devotees of Socrates. Their function corresponds with the Pythagorean symbolism of the myth and operates within the dualism and deliverance tropes as the inferior state from which one must find release.

---

[74] For a different interpretation of Socrates fulfilling the role of hero in the *Phaedo*, see Hartle (1986) p. 24. Also, see Chap. 15 'Socrates: The New Aesop' in Compton (2006) pp. 154–165.
[75] Compton (2006).

## 5.8 Conclusion

The *Phaedo* is characterized by the religious theme of deliverance, a strict form of dualism and a Pythagorean/Platonic dialectic. The plot, literary themes, and arguments are synchronized according to these themes; the three tropes also impact the settings, characters, arrangement of arguments, and dramatic scenes constituting the narrative. The narrative style resembles religious scripture or epic and evokes both solemnity and inspiration. The mood created by the plot and prominent themes adds an emotive quality to the presentation of Plato's philosophical arguments and commentary of other philosophical positions. Using mutual scaffolding to approach the relationship between myth and philosophy, I highlight the structural similarities between the two parts of the dialogue. Also, an approach to the *Phaedo* that focuses on structure illuminates the regulating role of the myth's unique literary themes and symbolism and how they are reinforced in the argumentative sections; myth and philosophy are part of a dialectical unity combined through structural similarities.

The dialogue is structured by sets of dichotomies that regulate philosophical discussions and dramatic presentation in the *Phaedo*. In addition to the plot and literary themes, a binary system underlies the text and regulates the meaning and direction of the dialogue. These opposing conjunctions determine each other and create meaning by providing appropriate elements for describing and justifying Plato's metaphysics, epistemology, and ethics in the context of Socrates's final hours. Rather than a rhetorical strategy influencing the dialogue's plot and themes, the binaries in the text both foreground the energy of Socrates's last moments and contribute to distinguishing Platonic thought from prominent ideas and traditions characterizing intellectual society at the time. Religious sentiment in the dialogue is coupled with philosophy, and a sense of ritual and liminal experience pervades the narrative; the combination of these factors also creates anticipation for the myth at the end of the *Phaedo*.

The key to understanding Plato's sets of mythic elements and philosophical concepts in the *Phaedo* is the notion of opposition. This structural principle elucidates the dialogue's special emphasis on cosmological dualism, life and death, soul and body, reason and the senses, and a range

## 5 Myth and Regulation: *Phaedo*

of other nuanced oppositions that reciprocally determine each other for the purposes of the text. The myth articulates the binaries and directs the scenes, the discussions, and the purpose of the arguments. Plato's fusion of narrative and discursive argument in the *Phaedo* reflects his interest in abstraction and systematic thinking. It also reflects his interest in the power of culture and imagination expressed through creating myths. A structuralist reading of the dialogue does not imply allegorical interpretation. Instead, by focusing on the logic of binaries used by Plato—the rules imposed for creating meaning from contrasting categories—I present a reading that reveals important symbolic and conceptual patterns. These patterns develop the structural foundations organizing myth and philosophy into a reciprocal unity. Disclosing these elements and their interdependent formal relations helps examine the various ways religious and philosophical meaning are constructed in the *Phaedo* without reducing the literary messages to allegory.

# 6
# Myth and Transition: *Phaedrus*

## 6.1 Cultural Standpoint and Myth

The majority of dominant modern approaches to myth overemphasize the 'fabulous' nature of mythology as opposed to its scientific, historical, or philosophical potential, connections, and qualities. Beginning from the late seventeenth century, there emerged a set of reductive theories that continue to stigmatize myth and identify it in contrast to modern ideals, norms, and aspirations. However, attempts to rationalize myth date back as early as Thales in the sixth century and later were enforced by Euhemeros (330–260).[1] The linguistic and cultural shift from the Greek *mythos* to the Latin *fabula* directed emphasis to the poetic aspect of myth, relegating it to the imagination and establishing interpretative methods that continue to the present.[2] Myth is fictional, but fiction does not necessarily equate to unempirical or unreal; and the mysterious does not imply incomprehensible. Contemporary myth studies carry heavy

---

[1] Doty (1986) p. 4. Also, see Hawes (2014).
[2] Doty (1986) pp. 3–4. This technical interpretation and application of the term myth as non-scientific entered modern usage in various phases: 1830 (English), 1815 (German), and 1818 (French) (Doty [1986] p. 4).

historical baggage generally encouraging one to rationalize the images and narratives of myth and replace them with one's own scientific or philosophical theories.[3]

The legacy of Euhemerism lived through early Roman writers followed by later Christian apologists who attempted to denounce the Greek pantheon to help justify the reality and message of Jesus Christ. Müller's philological and etiological approach and Frazer's 'myth and ritual' school are described as nineteenth-century manifestations of Euhemerism—interpretations that see myth as a problem for modern rationality and attempt to substitute it for something else.[4] Contemporary myth theorist William Doty, however, presents a multifaceted and inclusive definition of myth that creates interpretive space for the rich variety of myths with different functions and from diverse sociocultural settings. The matrix he proposes is not designed to constrain meaning by reducing myth to a set of universal indicators but to establish a framework for a polymythic hermeneutics that engages the multifarious and fluid examples of myth and the unique functions they represent within their own contexts.[5] Doty stipulates his vision in what he terms 'a comprehensive working definition':

> A mythological corpus consists of (1) a usually complex network of myths that are (2) culturally important (3) imaginal (4) stories, conveying by means of (5) metaphoric and symbolic diction, (6) graphic imagery, and (7) emotional conviction and participation, (8) the primal, foundational accounts (9) of aspects of the real, experienced world and (10) humankind's roles and relative statuses within it.
>
> Mythologies may (11) convey the political and moral values of a culture and (12) provide systems of interpreting (13) individual experience within a universal perspective, which may include (14) the intervention of superhuman entities as well as (15) aspects of the natural and cultural orders. Myths may be enacted or reflected in (16) rituals, secondary elaboration, the constituent mythemes having become merely images or reference

---

[3] For recent studies of myth theory, see Csapo (2005), Lincoln (1999), and Segal (1999, 2004).
[4] Doty (1986) p. 5.
[5] Doty avoids past monomythic definitions and encourages the view that appreciates the polyfunctionality of myths (Doty [1986] p. 13). Also, see Wiles (1976). Wiles identifies the dilemma associated with definitions of myth: that they must simultaneously account for myth's particular local, historical, and ethnic features and its transcultural reach.

points for a subsequent story, such as a folktale, historical legend, novella, or prophecy.[6]

Doty's theory pertains to my reading of the *Phaedrus* and I explore the relevance of his definition with attention to points 1, 2, 3, 5, 8, 9, and 11. According to Doty, every example from the vast array of myths is part of a particular network interlocking different narratives through common elements and thematic connections. And certain versions of myth actualize elements of the worldview characterizing the particular mythological network.[7] The many interconnected stories should not be interpreted individually but as part of a canon that enriches a multidimensional worldview. When myths are transmitted from one context or situation to another, an organic process of adaptation and change occurs with additions, expansions, deletions, and substitutions of mythemes (using the term popularized by Lévi-Strauss). In this respect, the quest for original versions of myths is misguided and often inconsequential for understanding the development and contemporary relevance of myth; inquirers run the risk of ascribing to myth their own biases, desires, and agendas, distorting meaning and limiting interpretative potential. Study of the network integrating divergent examples has proven to be more fruitful than extracting and isolating a mythic narrative from its complex web of interrelated myths and cultural contexts.

Doty applies the term 'culturally important' to mean that myths have a unique ability to represent their respective societies and must not be addressed simply as private fictions.[8] Although myths are a mix of different stories expressing different intentions and constructed for various purposes they are socialized to be aesthetically engaging, socially acceptable, and communicable in the public arena. A myth's importance and its implications for the community are determined by social consensus; for this reason, myths exist in their current forms or were documented in the past. But the specific community impact of sacred stories and the inner meaning of ceremonies or representations of divine beings are often

---

[6] Doty (1986) p. 11.
[7] Doty (1986) p. 12.
[8] Doty (1986) p. 13.

restricted to initiates who are protective in relation to interpretation and interaction.[9]

> Imaginal expressions and stories are the embodiments in which interpretations are applied schematically to experienced reality; meanings are 'invented' and 'fictionalized' onto the world.
>
> In this sense the "fictional" range of a culture includes sacred myth and philosophical reflection as well as fable or anecdote, poem, or novel. Hence myths share a large imaginal spectrum, and it is the "culturally important" criterion in the definition used here that distinguishes their communal and lasting significance from the more idiosyncratic imaginings of the individual entertainer or artist.[10]

Artists are pivotal actors in the nexus that establishes a myth as culturally important. Although creators of myth may be rejected at first and conflict with the traditions and norms of the network in which they operate, they initiate new and innovative languages and images with the potential to shape or change cultural viewpoints. Myths also develop corresponding forms of performance and create opportunities for profoundly meaningful enactment through recitation, ritual, or contemplation. The myth of the charioteer in *Phaedrus* represents the power of sacred narrative to depict visceral and kinesthetic experiences. Both rhythmic ritual movement and interactive social experiences are portrayed, and models for communicative performance are reflected in Plato's vision of the world. The approach of modern myth theorist Theodor H. Gaster is appropriate for understanding the ritual aspect of the *Phaedrus* myth. He departs from the 'myth and ritual' schools associated with Frazer by shifting analysis from questions of cause and effect to interpreting myth and ritual as mutually interdependent; ritual is depicted in Plato's myth as an embedded form of mythic expressions, manifesting differently but responding to the philosophical and literary context.[11]

Mythic language combines 'poetic, emotive, and attitude-conveying diction', rational discourse, and sense experience to help situate thinking

---

[9] Doty (1986) p. 14.
[10] Doty (1986) p. 15.
[11] The 'parallel expression' perspective is explored in Gaster (1954) republished in Dundes (1984) pp. 110–136. Also, consider the interpretation of myth and ritual by Clyde Kluckhohn (1942).

within embodied encounters.[12] The literary language of the *Phaedrus*, in particular, promotes the importance of sense experience by describing nuanced social situations. It pushes the boundaries to reveal unconventional and unprecedented meanings that inform unique physical, emotional, and intellectual encounters; 'mythical metaphors, symbols, and allegories provide concrete conveyances for (abstract) thought'.[13] Myth is also a set of stories from a culture or society and expresses 'roots' or origins; mythic tales form and project significant framing images and self-conceptions.[14] Historical sequence or logical order is not factored into mythic accounts; rather, priority is given to a particular form of social and cultural appeal. Essential mythemes are foregrounded for people who find them worth defending and honoring because they resonate with communities and tie multiple levels of individual lived experiences. Therefore, myths are exclusory; they are not designed to accommodate outsiders or the uninitiated. They must be interpreted or translated to speak to people belonging to a different mind-set or cultural identity. Myths justify actions, behaviors, goals, objectives, performances, celebration, and mourning; they convey a sense of wholeness and purpose and link the past to the present and future in a socially and culturally identifiable way. Doty identifies the distinction between meaningful history (he refers to the German *Geschichte*) and history as chronicle (*Historie*) and explains how 'mythic chronology' represents a perception of time as 'time experienced as bearing meaning'.[15] Mythology expresses something other than actual historical facts or events; what is conveyed is grander and its meaning is not necessarily constrained by the time period and social context that cultivate it.

The purpose of myths is to encourage a perpetual and sympathetic response through ritual and recital. The myth of the charioteer is a powerful example of how myth evokes emotional participation—an outcome of mythic performance. In this mode, myth communicates absolute truth with far-reaching significance for those operating within the relevant

---

[12] Doty (1986) p. 19.
[13] Doty (1986) p. 20.
[14] Doty (1986) p. 25.
[15] Doty also reiterates an earlier distinction he makes between the historic (*geschichtliche*) and historical (*historische*) (Doty [1986] p. 27).

cultural and philosophical framework. Doty clarifies this point by quoting Herbert Mason:

> we might perceive myth to be, not a mere untruth, but a story rooted in a place where one has been in the past and that one has to reach urgently in the present and that someone at a crucial point on the way says does not exist. It is a story, like most, of facts familiar to oneself but to which, until something happens to make returning to them impossible in the familiar way, one gives no thought.[16]

Myth theorists in the functionalist tradition such as Malinowski interpret myths as 'charters' for social orders.[17] For functionalists, political and moral values reflect the structures inherent in myths and rituals.[18] Myths provide frameworks that correspond with social order and convey principles and rules for action and behavior. The values communicated by myths operate in a wider network and pertain to various forms of phenomena and interaction, particularly those characterizing the religious and social spheres.

The myth in the *Phaedrus* is a fusion of different units and features and is a product of Plato's sophisticated appropriation of traditional materials and religious traditions. He incorporates and develops themes and ideas from earlier accounts, combining them with his own philosophical project. Plato constructs the dialogue to address his audience, close circle, and critics directly. He arranges a unified and culturally relevant argument infused with diverse mythic elements in harmony with a vivid and philosophically potent mythic narrative. Myths function in different ways by virtue of incorporating different units once part of other networks. One function of the *Phaedrus* myth is to represent ritual performance and evoke the emotive response associated with sacred rites. A monomythic definition constrains a reading of the myth and does not accommodate its dynamic and multilayered nature and function. Features and functions pertaining to ritual performance and philosophical transition are

---

[16] Mason (1980) p. 15, quoted in Doty (1986) p. 27.
[17] See Doty (1986), Chap. 2. Also, see introductory comments and references related to Malinowski in Dundes (1984) pp. 193–195.
[18] Doty (1986) p. 29.

actualized in the *Phaedrus*. The ritual nature of the narrative addresses philosophical debates and questions specific to the dialogue and Plato's religious interests.

## 6.2 Theme Introduction, Setting, and Narrative Mode

Determining meaning in Plato's dialogues requires an understanding of the status of interlocutors introduced in the text, their relationships with each other, and their representation by narrators or others.[19] Plato's representation of Socrates, for instance, is variable and contingent on the structure and multilayered messages of each text. And in the *Protagoras*, the depiction of sophists diverts from that of other dialogues. Narrative voice, setting, and sociocultural context play fundamental roles in characterizing key figures in addition to philosophical content and perspective. One particular philosophical perspective does not feature across dialogues. Plato chooses different narrators (or none at all) and characters to represent degrees of status and personality types to correspond with and convey nuanced and multidimensional scenarios, questions, and debates. In the *Protagoras*, for instance, the plot and important themes are expressed through the myth, which in turn influences the ideas, theories, and arguments. In the dialogue, (1) a sophist, and not Socrates, tells the myth that governs the direction and meaning of the dialogue and (2) the outcome of the debate is in favor of Protagoras. These factors are inextricably connected to the representation of Socrates in the frame narrative where he appears as explicit narrator.[20] Therefore, character depiction and interaction in Plato's dialogues suggest the methodological strategies employed in the work, offer interpretative possibilities, and reveal crucial structural features. The way Plato portrays characters evokes a variety of questions about communicating perspective and the intentions behind hierarchies and status. He foregrounds perspective and

---

[19] See Werner (2014), Chap. 2.
[20] In the chapter on the *Protagoras*, I explain how the character of Socrates is constructed, presented, and used in a radically different way in contrast to the other dialogues.

intension by introducing and developing character attributes, habits, attitudes, and personal idiosyncrasies. Dialogue settings accommodate the range of character dynamics and both aspects require further literary, cultural, and philosophical analysis.

The *Phaedrus* does not employ a framing dialogue; the opening scene is the beginning of the exchange between interlocutors without prelude by an explicit narrator.[21] In conversation with Socrates, Phaedrus recalls an earlier encounter with Athens's best orator, Lysias. In the initial exchange with Socrates, Phaedrus tells of his prior engagement that day when Lysias presented a speech on love. Phaedrus agrees to read to Socrates from a copy of the speech; this scene introduces many of the upcoming topics for discussion and evaluation. As Socrates and Phaedrus venture outside the city, they divert from the country path to walk along the Ilisus in search of a tranquil spot. Under the shade of a large tree and beside the spring, Phaedrus reads Lysias's speech.

In the absence of an explicit narrator and frame dialogue, the opening scene conveys interpretative suggestions necessary for contextualizing the myth and arguments.[22] Phaedrus's description of his prior engagement, the arrangement made between the two characters to depart from the city, the environment in which the discussion occurs, and the cultural allusions made in the process are symbolic and suggestive precursory events. The mise-en-scène and development of the discussion on the way to the country are rich with literary meaning and help position the philosophical purpose of the text. No other figure is present during the conversation between Socrates and Phaedrus. The interlocutors contrast their position outside the city with that of Lysias left back in the city. And Phaedrus states that he wishes to walk along country roads following the advice of

---

[21] For an interpretation that recognizes the importance of considering narrative mode, see Ferrari (1987) pp. 2–4. Ferrari recognizes the fact that in the *Phaedrus*, *Protagoras*, *Phaedo*, and *Symposium* Plato makes a special effort to elaborate on the setting and background. But in contrast to the other three, Ferrari explains, the *Phaedrus* does not contain an explicit narrator. He argues that using an explicit narrator in the *Protagoras*, *Phaedo*, and *Symposium* helps Plato illustrate the distinction between a premeditated manipulation of the environment, expressed by the narrator, and a spontaneous reaction to the immediate surroundings and events. However, Ferrari does not return to the significance of narrative mode, or lack of it, to test the possible influences it may have on other aspects of the *Phaedrus*.

[22] For a comprehensive study of the different kinds of authors, narrators, and readers one can consider in the study of literature, see Booth (1987).

the Athenian physician, Acumenus, only for Socrates to suggest later that they leave the path and walk along the river. These scenes and literary techniques depart from structure to cross thresholds and are instructive in reading the discursive and non-discursive parts of the dialogue.[23]

The beginning of the *Phaedrus* is possibly the most detailed and vivid of all the dialogues.[24] The setting is the country or the outskirts of the city and this is unique in relation to other dialogues, most of which are situated within the city walls.[25] The pair decide to traverse beyond the threshold of the city, where all the mundane activities are performed, to converse before returning to the *polis*. This sequence of events, or process, represents an important sociocultural theme and assists in identifying plot structure. The theme is ritual performance—a sacred activity that takes one from a mundane state to a liminal phase, and back again. The threshold of the city, the countryside, or outer ring represents liminal and outsider space (i.e., symbolically, the spatial fringe of 'reality'), which shares qualitative affinities with liminal/marginal characters (tricksters, shamans, outcasts, and minoritized or stigmatized individuals or groups) and liminal moments (periods in limbo, initiation rites, or phases in transition). This feature of liminality is important for analyzing the plot of the dialogue which relates to ritual initiation or 'rite of passage' (in terms of both Phaedrus's enlightenment and Plato's philosophical project). The theme of ritual practice facilitates transformation or transition; the literary setting of the text exemplifies the move away from 'normal social space' and acts as a frame for the unique philosophical dimension of the text. The ritual transformation theme is a device that prepares for a 'rite of passage' in terms of Plato's theories.

---

[23] The *Phaedrus* represents liminality and outsiderhood in multiple ways. The discussion takes place outside the city walls and in the countryside. There are no inhabitants, and references are made to supernatural beings and sacred symbols (cicadas are a symbol for transformation). The description of the location is important because of the contrast to the location where Lysias gave his speech and the company he entertained. The palinode replicates the 'outer rim' trope to depict the domain of the gods and Forms.

[24] Nicholson (1999) pp. 15–17. Also, see Griswold (1986). The first chapter, 'The Dramatic Scene and the Prologue', acknowledges the importance of literary and aesthetic devices for understanding the meaning and message of the dialogue. Griswold limits his analysis to the importance of one theme (i.e., the necessity of self-knowledge).

[25] For an interpretation that links Socrates's trip out to the country with his loss of composure and enthusiasm for listening to Lysias's speech, see the introduction by Nehamas and Woodruff to Plato (1995) pp. x–xi.

Transition manifests in various parts of the text and helps integrate different sections and elements. Phaedrus claims in the dialogue, for instance, that he had come from Epicrates's house, which once belonged to Morychus, where Lysias was entertaining a group of people. Epicrates and Morychus, as well as Lysias, were not known for living virtuous lives. The scene depicts a clear contrast between the place and company Phaedrus experienced when in the city and the place and company he enjoys in the country. I examine the relevance of the transition trope in detail later in the chapter and demonstrate the important thematic implications of the introduction and setting.

The dialogue makes explicit from the beginning that Socrates and Phaedrus are close friends. The pair shares significant interests: a love of speeches and a passion for the topic of love. But there is an imbalance of power distinguishing the two. Throughout the dialogue, Phaedrus seeks Socrates's approval of Lysias's speech, admires Socrates's myth of the charioteer, and accepts Socrates's theory of rhetoric. There are many factors indicating that Phaedrus occupies the inferior role in a master/student relationship. The interdependent relationship between a sage-guide and initiate is essential for ritual initiation or ritualized transformation and is enacted in the interaction between Socrates and Phaedrus.[26]

The motif of transition and transformation through performance is replicated throughout the dialogue and indispensably linked with the plot structure. The notion of transformation directs the discursive sections and the narrative design of the text; in the *Phaedrus*, meaning is conveyed in the context of ritual practice or the ceremonial process of change. Performance is described in the literary scenarios of the *Phaedrus* to evoke experiences of change; in particular, Phaedrus's transformation is aided by the vivid and active nature of the myth of the charioteer. The exchanges between the two interlocutors develops within the framework of a master/student relationship indicative of mystery cults and other esoteric religious traditions. Communication between the two culminates in the philosophical initiation of the student/Phaedrus. Performance is integral to initiation, and the stages of the plot illustrate forms of physical

---

[26] The opening line indicates transition: 'Where have you come from, my dear Phaedrus, and where are you going?' (227a).

movement involving Socrates and Phaedrus as sage-guide and initiate, respectively. Ritual movement is explicit and amplified in the journey of the charioteer, which becomes the model for epistemic maturation.

The ritual initiation plot resonates through and administers the structure of the philosophical discussion and the contemplative aspect of the narrative. Performance is an integral part of ritual, and the choreographed physical activity depicted in the scenes is concomitant of the plot. There are several important elements in relation to the ritualized narrative: the preparation and events leading up to it; gestures and movements at the beginning, middle, and end of the process; and the sensations encountered by master and student during the course of the initiation. All are important contextual elements for analyzing the dialogue and the performative; philosophical and literary components function together to create meaning. The myth of the charioteer manifests the structure of the ritual initiation process—a process also exhibited in the interaction between Socrates and Phaedrus. An elaborate form of kinesthetic learning takes place in the dialogue conditioned by the elements, principles, and narrative sequence constituting the myth. The dialogue demonstrates the performative nature of learning and illustrates stages of knowledge acquisition in the context of initiation. Unpacking the ritualistic theme pervading the structure of the dialogue clarifies the important role myth plays in the sections that present arguments. Myth introduces performance as a key factor in philosophic education and intellectual transformation. The *Phaedrus* also represents Plato's attempt to transform earlier methods and views on metaphysics and epistemology. Plato employs the ritual initiation narrative in the dialogue to epitomize philosophical change and constructs a literary account that interweaves learning, transformation, and embodiment. Ritual performance is the trope that facilitates the introduction of Plato's methodology and outlook in the *Phaedrus*.

## 6.3 Myth Analysis

In the passages leading up to the myth of the charioteer, the dialogue describes the four different types of divine madness: the gift of prophecy from Apollo, madness arrived at through the mystic rites associated with

Dionysus, poetic madness evoked by the Muses, and the bestowal of *eros* by Aphrodite. Socrates then gives a brief account of the immortality of the soul followed by the myth. He clarifies that the explanation of the soul only resembles the truth, acknowledging the limited capabilities of human beings; the ability to provide true exposition resides with gods (246a). A likely story, an appropriate myth, is the most that is humanly possible.[27]

> There is not a single sound reason for positing the existence of such a being who is immortal, but because we have never seen or formed an adequate idea of a god, we picture him to ourselves as a being of the same kind as ourselves but immortal, a combination of soul and body indissolubly joined together (246c–d).

Plato explains that certainty about the existence of gods is a matter beyond human understanding. The interaction between gods and pre-embodied souls as presented in the myth can be judged similarly; the validity of the narrative cannot be demonstrated by using logic or verified by experience. Socrates illustrates how virtuous qualities nourish wings of the soul to support growth whereas opposite qualities lead to deterioration of wings. Elevating toward the gods by using wings and transcending the senses through knowledge of Forms are both explored as 'divine' quests in the *Phaedrus*.

> The function of a wing is to take what is heavy and raise it up into the region above, where the gods dwell; of all things connected with the body, it has the greatest affinity with the divine, which is endowed with beauty, wisdom, goodness and every other excellence (246d–e).

The plot structure links both the ascent to knowledge and flight to the gods by creating a framework that stipulates the process of initiation.[28] A soul's previous existence is evaluated as having been virtuous or unjust depending on an individual's current social status and the right and wrong behavior he or she practices as an embodied soul. Reasons for why

---

[27] Werner (2014), Chap. 3.
[28] I return to this point later in the chapter.

perfect souls are punished and stripped of their wings—fallen from their metaphysically perfect state—are interpreted retrospectively.

After the preamble to the myth, Plato delivers his mythical narrative about the prenatal journey of the soul. The dialogue accords three capacities to the soul: Socrates describes humans as rational (having the ability to know and control), as influenced by emotions or spirit (easy to restrain), and with desires (difficult to restrain) which he symbolizes in the form of horses. The horses are controlled by a charioteer (the rational part of the soul) who must steer the two opposing horses (the other two parts of the soul: emotions and urges)—a task Socrates describes as both difficult and troublesome (246b). Only gods are unrestrained by emotions and desires and exercise reason free of the constraints of the body. Humans must overcome the pressures of embodiment that hinder advancement of the soul and endeavor to break the cycle of reincarnation.

Immediately after explaining the connection between the wings of the soul and virtue, Plato shifts to describing the divine chariot procession. The myth describes the different divine characters and their roles in the story. Zeus is the 'mighty leader' of the gods who governs everything that takes place. Following him is 'a host of gods and spirits marshaled in eleven bands' (247a). Twelve gods each lead their own group of souls while another god, Hestia, stays behind in the house of the gods. The gods witness amazing spectacles on their journey, and souls who are able and interested in following the gods view the same things. When the followers approach the 'summit of the arch' of the outer heaven, they must struggle against a steep stretch. The bad horse driven by physical desire can disrupt this critically important course of the journey by redirecting itself back to the material world—the place where its interests lie.

Souls who control their 'dark horse' reach the summit and perceive the other side of the heavens while standing on the outer surface of the universe as it rotates. After souls arrive on the outer rim, the glorious sights along the path upwards are replaced by the realm of absolute reality—the reality that is the object of true knowledge and realized only by intellect. Plato explains that the gods enjoy the full revolution of the universe and behold absolute justice, discipline, and knowledge; they satisfy themselves with the advantages of experiencing absolute reality, before returning from the heavens. Then they set up their horses at their mangers, feed them with ambrosia, and quench their thirst with nectar. In contrast, human souls have a limited encounter with absolute reality and some even miss the experience altogether. The myth mentions three kinds of experience: (1) the best a soul can hope to achieve after following a god is an impaired vision of reality because the height reached only allows the charioteer to peer above into the outer heavens, (2) the chariots of some souls oscillate up and down and do not enable the soul to acquire a complete view of the higher heavens, and (3) the third group remains below the surface at all times and spends the journey competing with others for a better position; therefore, the souls in this group damage their wings and, as a result, hold opinions in life rather than seeking knowledge (248b).

After establishing and elaborating the three possible journeys on which souls embark, Plato divides the three categories further by detailing the different kinds of people each experience produces and the hierarchy of incarnations they undergo:

1) souls that witness the outer heavens in a substantial way become (a) seekers of wisdom, (b) seekers of beauty, or (c) followers of the Muses (i.e., a lover) (see the four kinds of divine madness I describe at the beginning);
2) souls that experience reality to a slightly lesser extent through fragments become (a) law-abiding monarchs or (b) warriors and commanders;
3) souls one rank lower become (a) men of affairs, (b) managers of households, or (c) financiers;
    The following social categories constitute a regressing list of social groups:
4) (a) lovers of physical activity, (b) a trainer, and (c) a physician;
5) (a) soothsayers and (b) officials of the mysteries;
6) (a) poets and (b) practitioners of other imitative arts;
7) (a) artisans and (b) farmers;
8) (a) popular teachers[29] and (b) demagogues;
9) the last are destined to be tyrants (248d–e).

---

[29] Consider the depiction of Lysias in the dialogue as a popular teacher and rhetorician.

## 6  Myth and Transition: *Phaedrus*

Plato explains how fate is determined by actions and choices from a previous life. One only returns to a disembodied state after ten thousand years unless one lives the life of a philosopher three times in a row, after which a process begins to achieve salvation in shorter time and fewer incarnations (249a). Those who do not choose the philosophical life are judged according to actions from previous lives and either reap reward in one of the levels of heaven or undergo punishment in one of the levels beneath the earth. After one thousand years, they draw lots and choose the kind of life they wish to be reincarnated into, which may include non-human species.

Socrates begins describing the realm beyond the heavens and states that he will speak the truth. This contrasts with his earlier disclaimer about the likelihood of his account. Plato indicates that a different sense of truth applies in this context:

> Nevertheless the fact is this; for we must have the courage to speak the truth, especially when truth itself is our theme (247c).

Plato's account involves a description of the ontological status of Forms. He refers to the intangible subjects of true knowledge that constitute ultimate reality beyond the heavens. Only the gods have complete and unlimited access to this reality, whereas human souls experience it in the ways described in the myth of the charioteer. The passage gives one version of the theory of Forms, and the complete myth confirms the function of the theory in the dialogue and its link with Plato's notion of truth.

At 249c, Plato introduces the theory of recollection and explains its significance in relation to the myth. The soul's prenatal journey establishes the basis for knowledge acquisition. When one transcends worldly concerns and thinks philosophically, one is in fact remembering the Forms one encountered while traveling with a god; Plato identifies philosophy as a divine pursuit. Socrates refers to the fourth type of madness and how encounters with beauty in the world are actually reminders of the true beauty witnessed prior to embodiment. Alternatively, some individuals do not make connections between beautiful things and the beautiful sights perceived during prenatal experience; they divert from virtuous lives and do not gain knowledge (250a). 'But beauty, as we were saying, shone bright in the world above, and here too it still gleams clearest, even as the sense by which we apprehend it is our clearest' (250d). Socrates acknowledges that even though sight does not lead to knowledge, it is the keenest of the senses and sparks our memories of true reality in the strongest way possible.

## 6.4 The Philosophical Arguments

The myth of the charioteer has an intertextual relationship with arguments in earlier dialogues and indicates movement toward arguments in later dialogues.[30] By making connections in the myth between passionate love, the soul, and knowledge, Plato establishes a framework or point of reference for future metaphysical and epistemological arguments. However, the distinction between myth and exegesis remains unclear in many passages of the *Phaedrus*; a blend of narration and explanation complicates demarcation of genre. The myth alludes to philosophical concepts and theories but these passages do not constitute arguments. Rigorous arguments are contained in the second half of the dialogue when Plato revisits the subject of rhetoric; the next section on mutual scaffolding discusses the influence of the myth on Plato's analysis of rhetoric. The second half of the dialogue after the myth demonstrates the philosophical significance of the story, and the dialogues after the *Phaedrus* employ a complex metaphysics and epistemology that, for the first time, involve the method of collection and division.

The order and delivery of details in Socrates's second response to Lysias's speech share features with Plato's more complex philosophical methodology characteristic of later dialogues. Socrates's first speech reflects the philosophical views of dialogues such as the *Phaedo*; the speech incorporates notions such as outright rejection of passions, dismisses knowledge acquired through the senses, and disavows the body completely. In contrast to the first speech, the second speech recognizes the importance of

---

[30] Santas lists the theories referred to in the second speech as '1. The immortality of souls, not the personal immortality by offspring in the *Symposium*, but the everlasting existence of all souls as in the *Phaedo*. 2. The tri-partite division of the soul, as in the *Republic*. 3. The theory of Forms, realities, "colorless, shapeless, and intangible" (247c). 4. The recollection of Forms' ([1992] p. 305).

*eros* and the myth introduces a more sophisticated and multidimensional interpretation of love in which physical love and mental love are united and complementary.[31] The integration of soul, the body, and intellect demonstrated in the mythic account becomes the basis of investigation in the *Phaedrus*. The myth in the second speech facilitates the transition from a dualist perspective to a more complex theory that acknowledges and explores love, passion, and embodiment—integral features necessary to explain the richness of human experience. The myth's interpretation of the soul/body relationship anticipates the metaphysics and epistemology of later dialogues and the methodology required to address new questions and concerns.[32]

> The *Phaedrus* does not suggest that logos is bent on deceiving us, or that the truth it images only approximates what is. Nor does it suggest that all articulations of, say, the nature of justice are equally good. On the contrary, the *Phaedrus* itself shows how progress can be made from partially true logoi about something (such as eros) to more adequate logoi that call upon a larger context closer to the whole truth of the matter.[33]

## 6.5 Mutual Scaffolding

The brief details concerning the four kinds of madness and the immortality of the soul, together, act as a preamble for the myth, indicating that the narrative is a serious philosophical component of the dialogue. The description of the four kinds of madness and immortality of the soul is intended to facilitate the myth. Plato establishes a dynamic relationship between a particular kind of madness and the soul—the indispensable connection between passion and knowledge.[34] The association between the preface and the account of the soul's journey is clarified in certain

---

[31] Also, there is a contrast with the view of love in the *Symposium*, which asserts that love is an intermediary between humans and the divine, whereas in the *Phaedrus* love is something divine (White [1993] pp. 55–56).
[32] White (1993) pp. 1–2. White indicates that the metaphysical, epistemological, and methodological platform for later dialogues is established as a transformation or extension of earlier theories.
[33] Griswold (1986) p. 120.
[34] Nehamas and Woodruff, introduction to Plato (1995) p. xx.

parts of the myth. Pre-embodied situations and events, such as following a certain god (252c–253c) and the degree to which one witnesses the realm above the heavens (248a–d), influence predispositions and inclinations in this world such as attraction to particular virtues and the talent for recognizing, or ability to comprehend, truth when one is confronted by particulars (252d–253c). Being taken over by the fourth kind of madness, which leads to the acquisition of knowledge, depends on the way one becomes aware of one's own natural capacities.[35]

Based on the myth, the dialogue argues that we are enticed by certain objects of love more than others—objects that lead one to knowledge of the truth while in an embodied state. The attraction to these objects is determined by our soul's prenatal adventure—a theory made possible because Plato has already set up the framework or context in order to make the view meaningful. This was done by proposing, as a hypothesis, the essential relationship between beauty, love, and the soul and the different dimensions and degrees to the relationship. Basically, the introduction to the myth defined the terms and conditions with which Plato could construct his myth. He attributes these initial beliefs to the poet Stesichorus, whose name means, very appropriately, 'he who sets up the chorus'. 'Socrates conceals himself under the name Stesichorus in order to speak on behalf of the lover, and he addresses a boy (243e4) who is played by Phaedrus. Socrates is concealed as a poet and as an advocate of noble love, and Phaedrus as a potential philosopher. A new rhetorical framework is thereby created for this speech'.[36]

There are a few parts of the myth that are significant for my mutual scaffolding style of analysis. At 248a–b, Plato delineates three different classes of charioteers depending on the heights reached by their journeys. The first kind he describes is that which proceeds in close proximity to the god it follows and keeps its head above the surface of the heavens. Therefore, it perceives reality, although perception is somewhat impaired. The second class bobs above and below the surface and sees only a part of reality. And the third kind of charioteer does not reach the surface

---

[35] White defines the four different kinds of madness in relation to Socrates's two speeches and explains Socrates's use of collection and division ([1993] pp. 42–44).
[36] Griswold (1986) p. 74.

and lacks a depository of knowledge to recollect; this third kind of charioteer only develops opinions once born into the world. The journey is repeated and Socrates explains that if a soul had not acquired a vision of reality it becomes incarnated. When a soul has sufficient view of Forms before birth, then the first incarnation is the most conducive to seeking 'wisdom or beauty'. Alternatively, and equally as good, the soul becomes 'a follower of the Muses and a lover' (248d). Depending on the choices one makes in life, one either descends to a lower social and intellectual status or begins regaining wings after three successive incarnations at the top class. Therefore, the search to remember what was lost depends on the nature of the quest one embarks on while disembodied. The first kind of soul, who had better visions of reality, recognizes knowledge easier and clearer when encountering the physical world. The second kind to a lesser degree, and the third kind only ever holds opinions. According to the myth, the soul's prenatal performance determines a particular kind of mental capacity corresponding to a particular process of knowledge acquisition—a process practiced during embodiment. This means that knowledge acquisition must be interpreted as a physical performance—with the same structure as the prenatal journey.

There are many sections of the myth committed to incorporating the senses or physical activity into the search for knowledge. At 249c–251b, the myth presents an interesting perspective on interpreting the connection between the Form of beauty and perception. Socrates discusses how the sight of beauty reminds one of true beauty. Attracted by the earthy vision of a beautiful individual, the spectator becomes mad with love because the sight helps recollect the beautiful itself,[37] although much more than just sight is needed to arrive at knowledge.[38] It is only beauty that can have this effect on humans because Socrates explains how it was the only Form that was seen in its full grandeur while the soul was on its cosmic journey. However, those who have not been initiated or have been corrupted while embodied misinterpret the vision and descend into base physical pleasure and ignore the pleasure of beholding an example

---

[37] Nicholson (1999) pp. 198–199.
[38] Price (1992) pp. 244–245. Price compares and contrasts the role of sight in the *Phaedrus* with other dialogues.

of the ideal manifested in the beloved (250e–251a). Expressing one's love through physical affection is not rejected; it is encouraged but only at the correct moment—after the Form has been fully appreciated—and with the right intentions. The myth is important for elaborating the role of the senses; it helps place things like physical attraction, and the physical complement to erotic love, in context.[39]

Plato explains in significant detail how the lover attends to the beloved in both physical and non-physical ways. The beloved's beauty assists the lover's imagination of divine qualities. In reaction to the physical beauty of the counterpart, the lover honors and worships the beloved by trying to enhance the natural attributes the beloved contains—traits which resemble the god that attracted the lover during the pre-embodied state. Only once the beloved is in a mature state of love is physical contact advisable and is, in fact, described by Plato as destiny (255b). The myth describes sexual interaction in poetic style and compares the beloved's attraction to Zeus's longing for Ganymede.[40] The link between the sight of the Beautiful, physical beauty, and the soul is confirmed by describing the beloved's experience:

> ... the 'stream of longing' sets in full flood towards the lover. Part of it enters into him [the lover], but when his heart is full the rest brims over, and as the wind or an echo rebounds from a smooth and solid surface and is carried back to its point of origin, so the stream of beauty returns once more to its source in the beauty of the beloved. It enters in at his eyes, the natural channel of communication with the soul, and reaching and arousing the soul it moistens the passages from which the feathers shoot and stimulates the growth of wings, and in its turn the soul of the beloved is filled with love (255c–d).

Through the myth of the charioteer, Plato introduces the idea that Forms can be recognized through the senses (i.e., encounters with the physical world). One is tempted to assert that, in relation to earlier dialogues, a new theory is presented. But this is not the case. The interplay between

---

[39] Santas (1992) pp. 306–307.
[40] For more details concerning the connection between the symbolic details of this example and Plato's metaphysics of love, see White (1993) pp. 162–163.

beauty, passionate love, and the soul defines the hypothesis employed in the *Phaedrus* in contrast to the intellect-senses/soul-matter dualism hypothesis. One need not conclude that a theoretical shift has taken place. Instead, Plato is performing a smooth transition from a straightforward and conceptual theory of the soul-world relationship, designed to promote virtue and its connection to knowledge over carnal desire, to a more exhaustive account that appreciates the more emotional and phenomenological aspects of the soul-world experience. 'Thus desire has an inherent degree of rationality and rationality includes an element of desire'.[41]

According to the theory in the *Phaedrus*, the objects of love that different souls are committed to depend on their guiding divinity. The view that Plato encourages us to accept now involves love—an indispensable human emotion worth serious consideration whether we discuss sensation or cognition.[42] According to this position, a rational being desires to know something because she sees it as absolutely beautiful and because, consequently, she is truly in love with it. In terms of the literary setting of the dialogue, this may also explain why Socrates and Phaedrus are attracted to the topic and each other—because they both love speeches and those who present them.[43]

Plato's arguments in the *Phaedrus* regarding authorship and reader response deserve more attention here. Particular scenes in the text reveal insight and offer thoughtful suggestions pertaining to Plato's attitude toward, and use of, myth. Firstly, in the context of speech-writing, Plato argues that no man of affairs could criticize Lysias for producing speeches and that writing as such is not a bad thing. Socrates makes his point to Phaedrus by stating 'there is nothing disgraceful in speech-writing.... The disgrace comes, I take it, when one speaks and writes disgracefully and badly instead of well' (258d). For Plato, a speech is worthy of praise

---

[41] White (1993) pp. 156–157.
[42] White (1993) p. 42. For White, Plato's definition of love represents a merger of different kinds of desire, all akin to each other. This amalgamation helps explain the intensity of desires, the quality of the pleasures they provide, and the hybrid reality (beautiful bodies) of the things desired.
[43] Socrates's love of receiving and producing speeches in the *Phaedrus* is not shared by the attitude held by the Socrates depicted in other dialogues (Nehamas and Woodruff, introduction to Plato [1995] p. xi).

if the writer produces it with the knowledge of good and evil and his speech encourages his audience to do good and seek the truth (260c–d). Secondly, he touches on the method used by rhetorical speakers to mislead their listeners. According to Plato, some rhetorical speakers use the technique of moving in small degrees leading from one thing to its opposite so that their attempt to stray from the truth is difficult to detect (261e–262a).

From 262a to 263c, Plato explains that if one does not wish to mislead others or himself one must know the true nature of the subject of study and be able to determine whether the subject is ambiguous or unambiguous. Knowledge of a subject is a prerequisite to identifying what it resembles or opposes. Like the concept of love, myth is ambiguous and a complex genre of representation. In his first speech, the concept of love is referred to by Socrates as a curse to lover and beloved and, in the second speech, described as the greatest of blessings.

> The first speech introduces the need for methodological considerations essential for successfully pursuing reasoned discussion. Failing to establish a definition at the outset results in disagreement not only between the views of the discussants but also within each participant. Such disagreement will tell against success in inquiry, since the contesting views do not meet on common ground. And, more fundamentally, this lack of agreement entails that each participant will have internally incompatible views (quite apart from any incompatibility arising between views of two people).[44]

Socrates explains that his speeches are the result of applying two different methods of reasoning: one is based on 'collection' of particulars and establishing a *genus*, which leads to certain conclusions; the other method concentrates on the 'division' of a subject, followed by a skillful articulation of the individual parts. In the first method of inquiry, the focus is primarily on clarity and consistency. Plato believes that by approaching the issue with a synoptic view of a diverse range of particulars, the inquirer can unify the data under a generic term. This allows the formation of a definition, thus clarifying the exact nature of the subject under

---

[44] White (1993) p. 38.

question.[45] Plato states that at this point the most important thing is the progression of the argument in accordance with clarity and consistency rather than whether the proposed definition is good or bad. In the second method of inquiry, one is advised to divide the proposed genus into species once again, but this time the species are evaluated by proposing and using a definition. Returning to phenomena under these conditions—the re-evaluation of the definition through collection and division—opens up a more philosophically sophisticated process of analysis that enables the inquirer to determine the validity of his or her hypothesis and reasoning (265d–266a). 'And in trying to tell what the emotion of love is like it may be that we hit upon some truth…a not entirely unconvincing speech, a mythical hymn which celebrates in suitably devotional language the praises of Love' (265b–c).

After considering the virtues of the collection and division method, Lysias's speech is exposed as a badly arranged rhetorical exercise, and Socrates's first speech is critiqued as one that employs a hypothesis leading to undesirable conclusions. However, the second speech is both well arranged and leads to desirable conclusions—an outcome that is conducive to arriving at an understanding of Beauty (i.e., a philosophical endeavor for truth). The methodological advances and advantages of Socrates's second speech pay homage to Plato's positioning of the myth and its interrelation with the course of argument.[46] White explains:

> When, during their subsequent reflections, Socrates tells Phaedrus that the second speech was "really sportive jest" (265d), he excludes from this assessment those parts of that speech which adumbrated the method of determining truth by collection, division, and determining a thing's nature. The jest may then refer to the splendid mythic panorama of this speech,

---

[45] Collection and division are represented and used in different ways throughout the dialogue: four types madness; types of souls (divine and human); parts of soul (desire, emotion, and reason); twelve ruling gods and corresponding groups of souls; three kinds of experience depending on class of soul; and three types of experience producing three classes of soul and their numerous sub-classes.

[46] Griswold (1986) p. 142. Griswold recognizes the place of the myth in relation to the analysis of rhetoric and a network of other features in the text. However, he concludes that the myth can be translated into a non-mythic discourse; that is, myth is an economical and elegant way to express complex points (pp. 146–147).

engendered only after incompletely applying the method for securing truth in rhetoric. But it remains vital to interpret the myth according to the problem for the sake of which this myth has been introduced.[47]

The theme of lover and beloved is a device implemented in the *Phaedrus* to help represent the integration of the physical world, physical pleasure, and passion. Myth plays an important role in ordering and applying the new ideas and substantiating an all-encompassing perspective or worldview. The perspective involves Platonic love and physical love and, most importantly, explains the role of passionate love in our search for truth; knowledge and love must ultimately be understood in relation to each other. One significant example is the account of recollection explained through the example of remembering Beauty. The dialogue promotes interaction with real physical and emotional situations to arrive at knowledge rather than remembering the Forms by reading books or through pure abstract thinking.

Plato explicates the nature of his reformed theory and method and illuminates their philosophical intricacies and implications in the *Phaedrus*. He provides new investigative philosophical tools to address more nuanced and complex issues. The prelude to the myth and the myth itself repeatedly use the method of collection and division. The introduction of this approach has important consequences for the latter part of the dialogue—the discussion of rhetoric—and the techniques used for analysis in later dialogues.[48] Plato begins by dividing madness into four types (244c–245c), followed by distinguishing the soul's 'divine and human' parts 'by observing it in both its passive and its active aspects' (245c–246a). At 246a–b, he separates the soul into a ruling element, a good element, and a bad element.[49] This is not yet division in the profound sense, but Plato then explains the different classes of charioteers and the various incarnations they might enter (248d–e); he gives some form of hypothetical starting point for understanding different capacities and personal and social idiosyncrasies in various individuals.

---

[47] White (1993) pp. 88–89.
[48] Gill (1992) p. 162; White (1993) pp. 277–291.
[49] White (1993) pp. 38–41.

From 252e, he describes the characteristics and peculiarities of the range of souls depending on the god they followed during their pre-embodied state. The method of collection and division runs throughout and Plato elaborates on the approach in the second section of the dialogue to show the steps and benefits of collection and division.[50]

## 6.6 Plot Structure

The myth of the charioteer has a plot structure that conditions the meaning of the dialogue and features a number of consistent themes. The theme of cosmic dualism (247a–c) is represented along with the 'gnostic' theme of physical entrapment (250a–c) as minor contextual threads in the plot. But the main story line involves a ritual initiation leading to transformation. A number of important concepts characterize the myth—ideas that pertain to the fusion of intellectual and sensual soteriology, the significance of salvation and atonement, and their connection to mental and physical pleasure. The plot is archetypal and shares affinities with similar mythic paradigms such as deliverance, eschatology, and reincarnation. The ritual initiation form of plot promotes actual physical performance as a vital concomitant to initiation, and the myth created to reflect the plot accentuates the role of the body. Plato introduces the myth to acknowledge the importance of the body in relation to salvation and its role in intellectual enlightenment. There is a significant interplay between knowledge acquisition, embodiment, and the forms and features of ritual.[51] Passionate love is combined with the Idea of Beauty within the literary and cultural context of ritual initiation; this nexus interprets the body as playing a significant role in metaphysics and epistemology.[52]

---

[50] Scolnicov (1992) p. 251.
[51] See Socrates's encounter with Diotima in the *Symposium* which shares affinities with the plot and themes of the *Phaedrus*. However, each dialogue has its own context, perspective, and concerns which play active and vital roles in the plots and themes. Some cross-dialogue comparisons and inter-textual communication is inevitable but must be analyzed with caution.
[52] De Vries mentions some of the most influential views concerning the unity (both artistic and thematic) of the *Phaedrus* and offers his own interpretation ([1969] pp. 22–24).

## 168   Myth and Philosophy in Platonic Dialogues

The plot is characterized by the notion of deliverance through ritual, and the *Phaedrus* incorporates a master/student or sage-guide/initiate dynamic into its structure.[53] Also, the topic of *eros* is introduced to facilitate the connection between passion and knowledge. The role of *eros* represents a critical development and reinterpretation of the customary 'homo-erotic' relationship in ancient Greece.[54] In Socrates's second speech, the relationship is explained to include education of divine knowledge. The character roles remain the same, but the function of the roles and their significance for the purposes of Plato's philosophy are transformed. The relationship between Socrates and Phaedrus follows a general pattern and power dynamic that fashion the interaction between an older lover and a younger beloved manifested in many cultures, including ancient Greek society. One version of this pattern is represented in the myth of the charioteer and its elaborate and fantastic representation of ritual initiation. This pedagogical social dynamic characterizes the interaction between the pair of interlocutors; the pattern orders the sequence of events involving Phaedrus's educational rite of passage or personal development through transition. Griswold analyzes this agreement between Socrates and Phaedrus by identifying connections between the different sections of the text, particularly the second part that deals with rhetoric.

The description at the end of the *Phaedrus* of the relationship between dialectician and student (a relationship explained in the context of a discussion about rhetoric) is grounded in the present description of Zeus-like lover and beloved. In this manner the teaching of the palinode continues to frame the subsequent discussion of rhetoric and dialectic.[55]

---

[53] Gill explains that one of the themes in the *Phaedrus* is a form of shared inquiry (dialectic) in which the questioner assists the respondent in his assent through each step of the argument. In addition, the mutual participation between questioner and respondent represents a more dialectically engaging style of philosophy in contrast to reading and listening to lectures. Gill also elaborates on the question-and-answer method in combination with other methods (1992). Also, refer to further comments on the dynamics of the relationship on pp. 166–167.

[54] For details concerning the role of homosexual relationships and the references to it in the different speeches, see Nehamas and Woodruff, introduction to Plato (1995) pp. xv–xvii. For background information on the topic and its use in the context of the *Phaedrus*, see Nicholson (1999) pp. 109–114. For the educational and initiatory function associated with homosexual relationships, particularly in Athens, see Tanner (1992) p. 218.

[55] Griswold (1986) p. 130.

## 6.7 Character Selection[56]

### 6.7.1 Master

The dialogue consists of only two characters, and Socrates occupies the role of master, instructor, or sage-guide. The dialogue depicts Socrates and Phaedrus as companions, but the roles they occupy in the friendship clearly resemble a master/student relationship. Socrates is enthusiastic about listening to Phaedrus read Lysias's speech because he is confident that he can dominate and persuade Phaedrus to critique and re-evaluate his admiration for Lysias and, consequently, undergo a more profound progressive change in his understanding of topics such as love, knowledge, and rhetoric. In connection to mystic master/student relationships, Socrates is similar to the spiritual guide who is also a lover and wishes to enhance the qualities he loves in the beloved. Consistent with most mystic ritual traditions, Socrates's intention is to make Phaedrus, the beloved, into a lover himself.[57]

### 6.7.2 Student

> Thus the beloved finds himself being treated like a god and receiving all manner of service from a lover whose love is true love and no pretence, and his own nature disposes him to feel kindly towards his admirer (255a).

Prior to the above statement, the myth shifts to explain a hypothetical example depicting the interaction between a lover and his beloved. Many elements from the myth are used to structure this section, particularly the initiation paradigm. At 255a–d, Socrates illustrates in poetic style the dynamics at play when a true lover aims to attract the beloved and the interaction resembles mystic rites involving a master/student relationship. The master loves the beloved because of his potential to become a lover of the Forms, which leads to the beloved recognizing his potential in the gaze and affection of the lover. Socrates describes the first steps taken by

---

[56] Colloud-Streit (2005) pp. 178–181.
[57] De Vries (1969) p. 5. De Vries lists a number of other important character traits that stand out in the figure of Socrates depicted in the *Phaedrus*.

an initiate toward true knowledge. The parallels with this framework and Phaedrus's education in the dialogue are identical. Phaedrus as initiate is dependent on Socrates as sage-guide. This dialectic demonstrated by the interlocutors and the hypothetical example is conditioned by the structure of the story line and its symbolic intricacies. Also, the role of Phaedrus in the dialogue is a literary device crafted for the purposes of transition or transformation within liminal space and through ritual performance. After illustrating the spiritual and intellectual interaction between master/lover and student/beloved, the dialogue moves away from explicit use of the mythic symbols and focuses primarily on the friendship between the two. The second half of the dialogue follows and addresses the topic of rhetoric. The myth provides structural cohesion and interpretative assistance throughout the text. Once transformation takes place, a discussion of rhetoric can be readdressed by using the enhanced methodology and reformed metaphysics and epistemology. However, the impact of the myth continues to resonate and the liminal elements and setting remain: the location, the plot, the prescribed character roles, and the themes and motifs.

> One notable feature of the description [description of oral discourse in Phaedrus 276a-277a] is the presence of language which indicates some kind of active participation on the part of the person taught as well as the teacher. The desiderated discourse, impossible to achieve in writing, is 'living', capable of defending or helping itself; it has to be 'implanted' in a suitable mind or character (*psuchen prosekousan*), that is, one which is capable of generating logoi to implant in other *ethe* and thus of rendering the process of such generation *athanaton*. What is characterized is not, for the most part, the contribution of teacher or pupil, but the logos in which they both participate.[58]

## 6.8 Conclusion

Selected cultural traditions and religious elements feature in the *Phaedrus* in order to project Plato's philosophical discourse and communicate with a specific set of contemporaries. The themes of ritual initiation and

---

[58] Gill (1992) p. 164.

transition are developed and applied to facilitate progress from Plato's earlier concerns regarding metaphysics, epistemology, and ethics to a new and more nuanced view that incorporates love, the body, and the method of collection and division. His own philosophical project is enhanced and guided by paradigms and symbols from religious culture and practice, and the dialogue embodies Plato's intellectual vision through recognition of cultural standpoint and acknowledgment of narrative power.

Transition from an earlier philosophical perspective and approach to an enhanced charter is coupled with the layers of Phaedrus's own transformation in the dialogue. The ritual plot manifests itself through philosophy, drama, and religious commentary and helps defines Phaedrus's character as student or initiate. Socrates's first speech represents a negative interpretation of the body characteristic of earlier dialogues. The palinode introduces the structure and themes informing the literary and philosophical direction of the *Phaedrus* including a more positive and philosophical understanding of the body, senses, and empirical analysis. These factors are reinforced in Plato's later period supporting intertextual interpretations that connect the dialogues by linking methodological, conceptual, and literary indicators.

The method of collection and division is initiated by Plato when analyzing good and bad speeches, demonstrating key parts of the palinode, and discussing rhetoric. The *Phaedrus* demonstrates the use of method in the context of dramatic and philosophical transition; Plato introduces his approach framed within the ritual initiation trope. An integral part of the *Phaedrus* is the prelude to the myth in which madness is divided into four types. The myth also devotes attention to identifying and categorizing individual gods; kinds of souls; stages and types of prenatal experience; different experiences of reality during the soul's journey; degrees of desire, emotion, and reason; and the classes of human beings embodying various kind of souls. Collection and division feature as valid philosophical methods and appear in the context of religious performance. The approach is essential to Plato's examination and applied consistently when addressing both philosophical issues and emotional experiences.

The dialogue also combines love, the soul, and knowledge. Plato illustrates the relationship by using the soul's journey and justifies the link through examples of lived experience. The association of love with the soul and knowledge is based on a number of factors, including the analysis of madness, a reformed interpretation of the senses, the immortality of the soul, the theory of Forms, and *anamnesis*. Justification for the intersection between love, the soul, and knowledge culminates in the presentation of the myth, and its sociocultural relevance is demonstrated by using the ritual initiation trope. These factors are supported by the emphasis on performance which facilitates the different levels of transition; ritual activity is contextualized further by incorporating themes such as liminal space, the master/student dynamic, and rite of passage processes. Analysis of the polyfunctionality of myth encouraged by Doty is necessary for elucidating the layers of symbolism and philosophical complexity of the dialogue. A polymythic hermeneutics encourages deeper philosophical exploration of scenes, narrative order, and the practices suggested by the religious and cultural tropes pervading the *Phaedrus*.

# 7

# The Atlantis Myth and Cultural Identity: *Timaeus* and *Critias*

## 7.1 Nationalism and Myth

The re-emergence of myth in the eighteenth and nineteenth centuries as a significant area of research produced wide-ranging scholarship that forged relationships between disciplines and helped define approaches and movements. In relation to politics, high culture, and popular culture, studies in mythology became part of a series of processes associated with the rise of nationalism. Writers and artists at the end of the eighteenth century became particularly fascinated and inspired by myths. A new discourse established around the idea of *Volk* theorized the literary and cultural passion for mythology. The Romantic movement was heavily influenced by the euphoria elevating the interest in myth to new levels, particularly in philosophy and the arts. The same developments contributed to artificial social constructions such as the Aryan-Semitic racial binary. Bruce Lincoln's work on modern theories of myth explores the intersections between comparative mythology, theories of race, the modern history of racism, and the rise of European fascism. In *Theorizing Myth* (1999), he examines the growing interest in mythology during the eighteenth and nineteenth centuries. As part of an emerging trend, myth studies scholars looked for a historical and linguistic basis or foundation for the identity and sociocultural characteristics of newly formed nation-states. Lincoln's theories and analyses are important for exposing the inherent potential of myth to project social and political fantasies—an imaginary for dividing and marginalizing in order to create and enforce meaning for privileged groups. He interprets myth as ideology presented through narrative. Lincoln examines the typologies of difference proliferated by mythology and the ways artists, political figures, and myth scholars interpret them to exploit and victimize the Other. The literary beauty and appeal of sacred narrative and the different forms of knowledge it conveys should not detract analysis from tendencies in myth writers/tellers to exclude and oppress.[1] Lincoln explains that idealizing heritage, heroes, national language, ancestors, or a traditional homeland through a canon of narratives has its own disreputable history; myth-makers and exegetes construct stories to communicate meaning that advances culture and ideas, but they also have the potential to stigmatize and marginalize.[2]

In the eighteenth and nineteenth centuries, Northern European nations led in terms of commitment and success in gathering evidence supporting a unique sense of Indigenous cultural identity.[3] Centuries-old historical texts (for instance, Tacitus's *Germania* and *Annals* for Germans) and sacred narratives (particularly the emergence of the *Eddas*, the Ossianic texts, *Nibelungenlied*, *Chanson de Roland*, and *Kalevala*) were discovered or revisited.[4] This meant scholars, such as Hamann and the Romantic philosopher Humboldt, could use facts and literary examples to create a basis for understanding identities specific to what was perceived as nations of culturally and ethnically distinct people or *Volk*.[5]

---

[1] Omidsalar (1993).
[2] Mythology also has the potential to act as a liberating factor. This is exemplified in the interpretation of African mythology and Greek classics among African-American writers and scholars. See Pugliese (2013) and Walters (2007). For the work of classicist and Plato scholar William Sanders Scarborough, see Scarborough (2005) and Ronnick (2006). For examples of other eminent African-American classicists, see Drake (1987), Rankine (2006), and Cook and Tatum (2010). For the relationship between African-American folklore, cultural practice, and literary production, see Gates (1988).
[3] Feldman and Richardson (1972) pp. 215–216.
[4] Feldman and Richardson (1972) pp. 166 and 199–202.
[5] Lincoln (1999) pp. 48–54. More details throughout Chap. 3.

## 7 The Atlantis Myth and Cultural Identity: *Timaeus*... 175

Discourse devised to interpret and analyze myth became a convenient and dangerous instrument for dividing groups of people by using imagined and often arbitrary distinctions. Theorists connected to nationalist movements argued that cultural and historical stories are the basis for distinguishing between groups of people and evaluating their identities, characteristics, and abilities. Many advocated social and racial hierarchy and separation based on essentialized linguistic, sociocultural, ethnic, and religious indicators. Romantic theories of myth, in particular, argued that myths are necessary for one's self-understanding and cultural situation and valuable to national continuity. Scholars began investigating mythology for evidence enabling them to trace nations back to their original common homeland.[6] The symbols, themes, and structures of myths were examined in connection to respective communities in order to decipher their unique values, social charters, and the relationships between physical characteristics and environmental factors. Visions of a homogenous *Volk* galvanized nations for war, and the myths and traditions of Northern Europe began to replace Biblical and Mediterranean stories and traditions as nations began looking for nationally distinct ways to unify their populations during periods of conflict.[7] Germans, Scandinavians, Anglo-Saxons, and others found evidence for their own heroes, sagas, sacred narratives, and rituals, and exploitation of literary and archaeological resources had enormous scholarly and political consequences.[8]

Herder's contributions to the now-discredited 'Aryan thesis' impacted discussions and research pertaining to race and its relationship to myth and language. He argued that myths created and propagated by a particular *Volk* are fundamental for understanding identity and inspiring a nation.[9] Herder posited Asia as the origin of all humans creating a narrative modelled on *Genesis*.[10] Sir William Jones was also inspired by the

---

[6] In particular, see Herder's *Reflections on the Philosophy of History of Mankind*. For Herder's Romantic views on myth and folklore, see Feldman and Richardson (1972) pp. 224–225. For comments and resources on the Romantic fascination with India and Aryan homelands and the influence of the Schlegel brothers, see Lincoln (1999) p. 56, fn. 27. Also, see Feldman and Richardson (1972) pp. 350–353 and 388.
[7] Lincoln (1989).
[8] Feldman and Richardson (1972) p. 302.
[9] See Mosse (1985) and Olender (1992).
[10] Lincoln (1999) pp. 52–53. For the contribution of Max Müller, see Feldman and Richardson (1972) p. 481.

Biblical account and introduced the idea that a set of distinct European languages originated from the same region, but he marked central Asia as the geographic point and selected languages later referred to as 'Aryan', 'Indogermanisch', and 'Indo-European'.[11] The combination of philology, mythography, and early forms of ethnography resulted in the emergence of pseudoscience that associated an original proto-language with a distinct ethnic group and a specific homeland. The Aryan thesis burgeoned out of this intellectual and cultural milieu dedicated to the systematic study of mythology and later functioned as the matrix for the rise of fascism in modern Europe.

Wagner and Nietzsche are notable examples of influential figures entranced by the endearing nature of myth studies.[12] Nietzsche's training in classical philology exposed him to the Aryan myth as explored by Indo-European comparative mythology scholar Adalbert Kuhn, whose work pronounced the importance of Prometheus in Aryan mythology.[13] Enamored with readings of myth by Kuhn, Welker, Wagner, and Goethe, Nietzsche distinguished the theft-of-fire theme from the Biblical account of the Fall in *Birth of Tragedy*.[14] Lincoln evaluates Nietzsche's dichotomy: 'Nietzsche used mythic narratives not just to stereotype peoples but also to erect a discriminatory structure of interlocking binary oppositions that conflated categories of race, gender, religion and morality'.[15] Lincoln outlines the sets and contrasting themes and categories suggested by Nietzsche: Prometheus/Eve; Greece/Israel; Aryan/Semite; male/female; bold sacrilege/mendacious deception; fire (cultural accomplishment)/fruit (sexual pleasure); tragedy/melodrama; ethic of evil/ethic of sin; proud defiance/neurotic guilt; suffering and strength/remorse and weakness. Nietzsche was part of a movement, including authoritative figures such as Herder, Müller, and Tylor, that studied mythology to justify and propagate pseudoscientific fantasies and specious linguistic, religious,

---

[11] Lincoln (1999) p. 54. Also, see Feldman and Richardson (1972) pp. 267–269.
[12] Lincoln (1999) pp. 57–62. Also, see Ruehl (2003).
[13] Lincoln (1999) pp. 64–66.
[14] For comments on Goethe's perspective on myth, creativity, and art, see Feldman and Richardson (1972) pp. 261–262.
[15] Lincoln (1999) p. 65.

# 7 The Atlantis Myth and Cultural Identity: *Timaeus*...

and political theories—often designed to elevate the fabricated Aryan racial category over others.[16]

For over a century, myth scholarship privileged Aryan or Indo-European myths and religions. It established a discourse based on the construction of hypothetical racial fictions—the notion of race-based *Volk* which had destructive and tragic social, cultural, and political consequences, especially in the twentieth century. Earlier allegorical readings of myth as coded taxonomy had transformed gradually into what Lincoln describes as 'ideology in narrative form'.[17] In the early twentieth century, comparative philologist Georges Dumézil emerged as one of the most prominent myth studies scholars. Together with a number of other academics, he was influential in improving the discipline in terms of scope, method, and depth. He raised new important questions and attracted interest in comparative mythology from other disciplines. Dumézil and a host of other colleagues were also connected with National Socialism to different degrees. Dumézil's work was particularly invested in advancing the 'Aryan thesis'. After the Second World War, the term 'Aryan' fell into disrepute but was elided into the more respectable term, Indo-European. However, the problematic and ideological notion of a proto-group remained, together with associated ideas such as a proto-language and a common social structure, religion, and mythology.

The cultural identity and political vision of communities are grounded in origin narratives, and Plato constructs the Atlantis myth to function as the founding myth of Athens. However, the narrative represents both application and critique of myth; Plato demonstrates the sociocultural role of storytelling, and he also manipulates the tale to act as a form of self-reflexive exercise. I examine the use of fantasy in the *Timaeus* and *Critias* and how Plato creates space in the dialogues to intersect cultural identity, history, and aesthetic detail in place of elaborate arguments.[18]

---

[16] Other notable examples of the interdisciplinary nature of pseudoscientific movements are Galton's eugenics and Gobineau's views on race, politics, myth, and religion. For analysis of the connections between racism, nationalism, and imperialist expansion, see Weinbaum (2004). For studies critically analyzing connections between European nationalism and scholarship, particularly in modern Germany, see Brennan (2014); Goldenhard and Ruehl (2003); Marchand (2003).
[17] Lincoln (1999) p. xi.
[18] Consider Brochard's work on fiction (1974). On the literary freedom provided by myth writing in Plato, see Frutiger (1930).

The Atlantis myth signals social and philosophical theories; the two major myths in the *Timaeus* and *Critias* are marked by the influence of Plato's epistemology, politics, and metaphysics.[19] The arguments occupy a place in the text through implication, and the narrative offers many indications regarding a relationship with *logoi*. The *Timaeus* and *Critias* do not include dialectic arguments but make reference to ideas; references to the ideal state are essential components of the narrative and function interdependently with the myth.

My analysis of myth and philosophy addresses the interdependent coexistence of *mythos* and *logos* in the same text. The two major parts of the *Timaeus* and all of the *Critias* are narrative monologues, and examples of dialectic argument are missing; the history of ancient Athens and Atlantis has no didactic or argumentative counterpart. However, the prelude to the Atlantis myth alludes to a previous conversation about the ideal city, possibly implying some of the arguments constituting the first five books of the *Republic*. I investigate how the Atlantis myth functions in connection to Plato's philosophy and critically analyze the relationship by using mutual scaffolding—the logic of interdependence between myth and argument in the two dialogues. I also make reference to the creation myth only insofar as it supports my structural and stylistic analysis of Critias's story. Timaeus's cosmogony/cosmology renders arguments for how the universe came to be, analyzes the structure of the universe, and describes its properties and purpose. The accounts presented in the *Timaeus* and *Critias* are both conditioned by beliefs about historical events and the basic elements constituting the physical world.[20]

The Atlantis myth is not a moral allegory, an example for educative purposes, or a strategy used to arrive at theoretical knowledge. The philosophical myth engages with Plato's previous arguments on two fundamental topics: epistemology and politics. However, Plato uses the myth as a form of self-reflection or critique indicating problems associated with

---

[19] For an interesting study of the Atlantis myth that draws on Benjamin's understanding of the interaction between mind and built environment, see Akkermann (2013).

[20] Timaeus's cosmology goes against Plato's advice in the *Phaedo* to reject pre-Socratic attempts to explain causation in terms of physical conditions. In the *Timaeus*, Plato acknowledges causation as significant and indispensable (see Johansen [2004] pp. 16–21). Also, consider Timaeus's account in relation to the notion of transition in the *Phaedrus*—a dialogue that introduces and incorporates a new view of the physical world (refer to the previous chapter).

constructing narratives that represent cultural identity. The myth is a historical account in response to formal and rational principles instrumental in the theory of recollection and the account of the ideal state. The Atlantis myth is both *mythos* and *logos*: a narrative that takes particular arguments as backdrop and presents them in the dialogue setting as history. Through the myth and the details of the setting, Plato creates a dramatic framework for questioning epistemology and political theory.[21]

## 7.2 Theme Introduction, Setting, and Narrative Mode

The dialogue begins with Socrates clarifying the number of companions present; friends whom he had been in conversation with the previous day. He indicates an individual missing due to illness, but he is left unnamed. The characters accompanying Socrates in the dialogue are Timaeus, Critias, and Hermocrates. All in attendance are described as statesmen trained in philosophy. They are not explicitly referred to as 'philosopher-kings' but there are indications that they resemble ideal guardians and Plato chooses these characters for the dialogue to help bring his ideal state to life.[22] The politicians and philosophers share affinities with Plato's views on leadership, are trained in philosophy, and model their activities on ideal principles and an ideal state.[23] Critias is the narrator of the mythic history of Athens and the fact that he is a philosophically trained statesman influences the status and meaning of the story.[24] Plato chooses a politician from the Athenian ruling class to tell the myth; Critias's

---

[21] For an earlier study using myth theory to interpret the Atlantis myth, see Fredericks (1978). For a brief account of the different readings of the Atlantis myth with reference to theories from folklore studies, see Forsyth (1980).

[22] Johansen (2004) pp. 32–33. For issues pertaining to reception, see Tarrant et al. (2011).

[23] Gill (1977) pp. 288–289. Gill recognizes that the philosopher-statesmen differ from poets in their predispositions and therefore can produce a good representation of the ideal state. He extrapolates certain comments made from the *Republic* and asserts that the interlocutors in the *Timaeus* have good knowledge of the real nature of the state and produce a good representation: 'a representation which attributes to its subject its proper character and shows that its moral goodness leads to its success in the world'.

[24] See Finkelberg (1996) p. 391.

monologue is unquestioned and Critias remains unchallenged throughout the dialogue.[25]

Socrates does not participate in most of the two dialogues but his role is crucial for understanding the stories, their status, and the characters who tell them. Why does Socrates express so much respect toward the three politicians? He is younger than all of them, but youth does not deter his critical approach to interlocutors in other dialogues. Timaeus, Critias, and Hermocrates are philosophers active in politics, and they are introduced in magisterial fashion in the opening scene of the *Timaeus*. The sociocultural and political power dynamics are clear, and Socrates is represented as respectful and compliant with convention. In the *Timaeus*, Socrates's interlocutors step into the dialogue with grand reputations—with privilege to speak free of scrutiny. Socrates is presented here by Plato as an admirer—a believer waiting to be told the truth. He trusts that the politicians will give him exactly what he anticipates; Socrates is certain that, being statesmen educated in philosophy, they will bring his ideal state to life. He does not test his interlocutors or pass judgment; there is no indication he could challenge or reject their views.

Critias and Timaeus function as narrators at different points but Plato is unclear about whether he employs them as reliable philosophers and statesmen (reliable narrators). The presentations by the 'philosopher-kings' in the *Timaeus* and *Critias* are accepted by Socrates and not necessarily analyzed by the rest of the group. In terms of their credentials and their respect for ideal principles, they live up to expectation; that is, they are the philosopher-rulers valorized by Plato in the *Republic*. However, their expositions reflect personal interests and affiliation, and Plato designs the dialogues to express critical commentary concerning the delicate nature of ideals and their precarious application in intellectual and creative accounts.

Plato does not elaborate or explain the environment in which the interaction between interlocutors takes place; details pertaining to space do not concern the *Timaeus* and *Critias*. In contrast, the Atlantis myth devotes a great deal of attention to describing the typology and society of a lost civilization and ancient Athens (the *Timaeus* also describes the genealogy

---

[25] I examine the character of Critias in more detail in 'Character selection'.

of the story and, after the Atlantis myth, offers a detailed account of the cosmos). This stylistic decision directs attention to the imagery and vivid events of the Atlantis myth. Early in the dialogue, the interlocutors engage in conversation, mentioning topics resembling certain arguments from the *Republic*. The conversation incorporates an intellectual context, replacing mise-en-scène, and the myth is a direct response to the conversation. The political discussion is a backdrop and an alternative to physical setting; that is, the intellectual framework setting up the dialogue is sufficient replacement. Lacking a description of space, the context for the conversation and presentation of myth includes a hypothetical constitution or, more accurately, principles for an ideal state.

Reference to the earlier conversation about the ideal state represents recollection, and the *Timaeus* and *Critias* explore the complexities of memory in preparing and delivering a 'true' account.[26] Prior to presenting his account, Critias tries to remember the philosophical discussion from the previous day about the principles of an ideal state. This leads to remembering a story told to him during childhood. He elaborates on the two experiences from different periods in his life and draws connections between them. Timaeus's account is also a response to Socrates's description of an ideal state; he too is influenced by, and must remember, the earlier conversation and responds by beginning his account with some basic details concerning the theory of Forms.[27]

The conversation the interlocutors continue in the *Timaeus* analyzes an example of an ideal state and the topics recapped by Socrates before Critias's monologue. The arguments discussed on the previous day somewhat resemble arguments from the *Republic*. Lee clarifies that the previous day's conversation referenced in the *Timaeus* is distinct from analysis in the *Republic*.[28] The dramatic details of each dialogue differ significantly,

---

[26] Burnyeat (2005).

[27] Timaeus's case differs slightly from Critias's. Timaeus must also remember a conversation with Critias from the day before when they left Socrates and regrouped at Critias's house. For a list of the essential features of the opening passage of Timaeus's cosmogony/cosmology, see Runia (1997) p. 103. Also, in relation to the link between Timaeus's myth and the theory of Forms, see Brochard (1974).

[28] See Lee's introduction to Plato (1977) p. 23. Also, see Clay (1997) pp. 50–51. For arguments supporting the view that the *Timaeus* is a sequel to the *Republic*, see Voegelin (1947) p. 308 and Johansen (2004) p. 7–23.

and the recapitulation of topics in the *Timaeus* refer only to issues raised in the first five books of the *Republic*; it leaves out some of the most important philosophical elements of the earlier dialogue. Understanding the *Timaeus* as a sequel to the *Republic* limits interpretative possibilities. The *Republic* contains significant discursive material specific to its context and literary structure and has its own myths, themes, and motifs. Plato carefully selects topics for the *Timaeus*—the same for the *Critias*—and describes them in the form he does with the Atlantis myth in mind.

Socrates invites the myth after expressing his dissatisfaction with the state he described previously. He is disappointed that it lacks life and resembles pictures or motionless objects rather than a real state. Socrates's description of his earlier account marks it as clearly different from the discourse regarding the ideal state from the *Republic*. The *Republic* contains vivid metaphors, examples, and its own monumental myth at the end. The pretext for defining the ideal state in the *Republic* is to arrive at a convincing account of a just man; Socrates's method is to describe the pattern of a just state in order to describe the model of a just man. In the *Timaeus*, however, Socrates requests an account that uses the abstract model of an ideal state and illustrates it as a functioning society. He hopes his comrades describe his perfect society, but not in the act of performing what actual societies normally do on a daily basis and not in reference to the profundity with which the state would react to serious and complex legal, cultural, or other philosophically pertinent problems. Socrates wants to see his state performing, strangely, only two very particular functions. In addition Socrates asked his interlocutors to 'transactions with other states', Socrates asks that his ideal state be described in the act of 'waging war successfully and showing in the process all the qualities one would expect from its system of education and training, both in action and negotiation with its rivals' (*Tim.* 19c).

Critias proceeds as narrator for the Atlantis tale in the *Timaeus*, followed by Timaeus for the cosmological account. Socrates excludes himself from the dialogue after he acknowledges that he is incapable of describing his ideal city in a real situation. He realizes that such a task is beyond his experience and best left to the others, who are referred to as both philosophers and statesmen. As a result, Critias's genealogy and presentation of the myth become a monologue. Critias is the one who, in response to Socrates's account of an ideal state, remembers a childhood story; he is the only one who has access to the history of ancient Athens and, therefore, the only one who can tell the myth. Critias is the only Athenian among Socrates's companions and the only one from a high-standing family; he was a relative of Plato. He is related to the line of transmission both ancestrally and socially; the first Greek to transmit the tale is Solon, and Critias is linked to him not just as a fellow citizen but also on the level of class and ideology.[29]

The introduction of the *Critias* begins with Timaeus transferring the narrator's role to Critias, who continues the conversation by asking for a degree of leniency from his audience and making some interesting comments regarding the mimetic nature of statements. He explains that all statements are essentially 'pictures or images' and the acceptance or rejection of a statement is strongly influenced by the severity with which we judge it (*Crit.* 107b). Critias raises this point and asks his interlocutors to avoid harsh criticism when evaluating his story. He contrasts the difficulty of Timaeus's account with his task, explaining that his is more complex because it attempts to describe human subjects rather than divine ones. Critias explains that divine themes are easier to account for because we are all ignorant about the gods and, therefore, a likely account is sufficient.[30] When engaging with human topics, description and analysis become subject to strict criticism because of our familiarity with many features of the account.

> So in what immediately follows, you should make allowances if my narrative is not always entirely appropriate; for you must understand that it is far from easy to give satisfactory accounts of human affairs (*Crit.* 107d–108a).

Socrates grants Critias this favor and there are no objections to giving Hermocrates the same allowances afterward (*Crit.* 108a). Critias's introductory comments about the difference between rendering an account

---

[29] I address these factors in further detail when analyzing Critias in the Sect. 7.7.
[30] See Burnyeat (2005).

of divine topics in contrast to human issues are unsupported, and he does not provide a meaningful basis for respecting his request for leniency; the interlocutors agree without questioning. Socrates has faith in the philosopher-statesmen.

## 7.3 Myth Aanalysis

After Socrates finishes praising the interlocutors for their philosophical and political talents in the *Timaeus*, Hermocrates mentions a follow-up conversation that took place after the previous day's discussion (*Tim.* 20c–d). The conversation did not include Socrates and was held at Critias's house, where the others were staying. The passage reveals that the dialogue took place in Athens and that the story is first recalled and told by a reputable Athenian in the surroundings of his own home in Athens. The place of historically significant Athenian figures in the transmission of the myth is acknowledged when Critias explains how the myth was passed onto his great-grandfather, Dropides, by Solon. Dropides was archon of Athens after Solon and, therefore, the first to carry on Solon's reforms. The myth was then passed down within the family until it reached the Critias featured in the dialogue. Plato infuses the Atlantis myth with a strong sense of Athenian identity. The genealogy is also part of the myth and adds to the philosophical significance and nature of the historical account; the characteristics of the transmitters, place of transmission, and other relevant details function as literary devices.

> It [the myth] relates many notable achievements of our city long ago, which have been lost sight of because of the lapse of time and destruction of human life. Of these the greatest is one that we could well recall now to repay our debt to you and to offer the Goddess on her festival day a just and truthful hymn of praise (*Tim.* 20e–21a).

Critias remembers attending a festival with his grandfather when he was about ten years old; his grandfather was also named Critias and was almost ninety at the time. The boys who recited poetry at the festival mainly chose Solon's poetry—a popular choice during that era. Critias then narrates how

## 7 The Atlantis Myth and Cultural Identity: *Timaeus...*

a fellow clansman and his grandfather spoke of Solon's poetic pre-eminence, and during this discussion grandfather Critias mentions the story Solon brought back from Egypt. The older Critias explains that Solon would have surpassed Homer and Hesiod in poetic creations had he not been preoccupied with statesmanship. The story brought back from Egypt tells of the 'greatest and most noteworthy' achievement of Athens (i.e., an account that fits the genre of epic). By detailing the process of transmission, Plato has Critias perform an important cultural practice in sociopolitical rhetoric. An Athenian political figure provides a 'folktale' or a patriotic historical account defining Athenian identity and distinguishing Athens as a distinct and privileged culture due to its noble origins and innate potential.[31]

Another crucial aspect of the genealogy is the symbolic and cultural place of Egypt in ancient Greek culture.

'Tell us from the beginning,' came the reply; 'how and from whom did Solon hear the tale which he told you as true?' (*Tim.* 21d).

According to Critias's genealogy, an Egyptian priest from the city of Sais in the district of Saitic told Solon the story while he was visiting Egypt. The Egyptian king Amasis hails from this city, where the patron god is Neith, the equivalent to Athena. Critias informs us that the Saisians were very friendly to Athenians because they believed the two people were related. Throughout the narrative, Critias portrays Athenians with respect and praise, particularly when describing Egyptian perceptions, in general, and Solon, in particular. Plato's details in these passages are significant for a number of reasons. First, King Amasis II, or Ahmose II, established close ties with the Greeks in many respects; the most significant were his contribution to rebuilding the temple of Delphi and his marriage to a Greek princess. Herodotus writes about this particular king at length and praises his achievements, thereby increasing his popularity—and possibly the popularity of the Egyptians in general—within Greek society and culture.[32] Second, the city Sais is the Egyptian sister city of Athens and Critias acknowledges its protection by the goddess

---

[31] Their potential is described as resulting from geographical and social factors.
[32] See Johansen (2004) p. 39 for contrasts between Herodotus's comments about the Egyptians and Critias's account.

Athena. And third, Solon hears about the existence of ancient Athens for the first time by a local priest in the Egyptian city; the priest is the equivalent to a priestess of Athena. Plato incorporates a sense of cultural and historical legitimacy to the myth by connecting the genealogy of transmission to Athenian glory and pride. The priest tells Solon that he has historical records to prove his narrative and says he will show Solon in due time. The genealogy contributes to interpreting the tale and adds a number of important dimensions to the myth.[33]

The priest tells Solon that pre-deluge Athens was exceptional in many respects, particularly in governance and war. There is a parallel, the priest notes, between the laws of Egypt at that time and ancient Athenian institutions and he begins to list some of the features of Socrates's ideal state mentioned at the beginning of the dialogue. In addition to these laws, one of the advantages of ancient Athens was its geographical location, which their Goddess originally chose for them and which influenced their characteristics. From among their many successful activities and exploits, one stood out as exceptional: their victory in defeating a belligerent Atlantis.

At the time of the battle between the two Greek powers, Atlantis, under the rule of a king, controlled not only the island of Atlantis but 'many other islands as well and parts of the continent; in addition, it controlled, within the strait, Libya up to the borders of Egypt and Europe as far as Tyrrhenia' (*Tim.* 25a–b). The priest claims they planned to conquer most of the known world, including Egypt and Athens, until the army of Athens, in the face of formidable odds, defeated them and quelled their imperialist aims. After briefly describing the battle, Critias finishes the story with an account of the deluge that submerged the island of Atlantis and killed the majority of Athenians.

According to Critias, the society and its inhabitants described by Socrates on the previous day bore an uncanny resemblance to the details concerning ancient Athens. The *Critias* describes how the gods divided up the earth and then allocated the rule of each region to a particular god according to intelligent agreement and justice. They ruled over their terrain using these same virtues, which they passed on to the

---

[33] There is no historical accuracy in relation to the contents of the myth, or for its transmission, 'it is introduced exclusively for the purpose of conveying the meaning which it has within the fabric of the *Timaeus*' (Voegelin [1947] p. 316).

native inhabitants. Athens was ruled by Hephaestos and Athena, who together had a reputation for their love of knowledge and skill, which they passed on to the Athenian people. After the deluge, the advanced members of the community perished, leaving only unlettered mountain dwellers. Therefore, pre-flood Athenian history was lost and owing to a primary concern for survival no effort was made to recover it. War is a central theme in Critias's narrative and he mentions Solon's account of the war that includes women partaking in military activity—a role natural to both genders. Critias indicates that the myth he heard resembles Socrates's ideal city in terms of its most important aspects—particularly issues concerning military power (*Crit.* 110e–111a). After briefly explaining the forgotten origin of some Greek names and the benefits of the original natural environment, Critias provides some of the dimensions of the Acropolis as it existed then and some basic demographic information concerning the different classes of people. Critias mentions how the Egyptians translated the Greek names in the story, which Solon then translated back into Greek after researching the meanings, and that Poseidon ruled Atlantis, which was occupied by an earth-born population. Poseidon's own offspring, which he begot with one of the mortals born of the soil, became the dynasty of kings who ruled the different regions of the island. Critias's narrative continues to describe features of the island's typology, the guardians of each region, its natural resources, architecture, military service, governance, the court of law, and political ceremony. The dialogue cuts off when Critias begins to tell of Atlantis's regression from a well-functioning state of citizens, akin to the gods, to a power-mongering empire made up of people who are more mortal than divine and who are punished and disciplined by Zeus.[34]

## 7.4 The Philosophical Arguments

The *Timaeus* lists the topics from the previous day's discussion on politics and society—subjects explored in other dialogues, particularly the *Republic* (*Tim.* 17b–19c). The *Timaeus* and *Critias* are conditioned by

---

[34] For an interpretation of the abrupt ending that considers the possibility that Plato intentionally ended it the way he did for specific literary and philosophical reasons, see Clay (1997) pp. 51–52.

narrative plot and individual themes and motifs particular to each text, in addition to core sociopolitical, epistemological, and metaphysical ideas. When Critias remembers a childhood story, he enacts *anamnesis*; by connecting his memory of listening to his grandfather's tale with Socrates's discussion of an ideal state, Critias recollects the Forms necessary for constructing the perfect society. The act of remembering his past experiences is not a mundane non-philosophical type of remembering but a more sophisticated, intellectual kind of memory function. The theory of recollection has a constitutive role in Critias's account of Atlantis and its genealogy.

Socrates stipulates the principles of the ideal city after Timaeus asks to be reminded (*Tim.* 17b). First, society is to be divided into classes each with its appropriate training and vocation. The segregation is justified by the impact it has on the development of guardians, particularly in relation to their performance in war.[35] As part of their training, they develop character in terms of both spirit (fortitude and determination) and philosophical thinking and this means that physical conditioning must accompany philosophical education. Also, guardians must live a modest and humble life and avoid distraction from responsibility to the state. In addition, women need to receive training similar to that of men and share the same occupations. Children should be the responsibility of the whole community; raising children is not solely the role of parents. Finally, marriages are to be arranged, clandestinely, by the state with the view of coupling the citizens who best match each other in terms of their excellence (*Tim.* 18c–19a).

## 7.5 Mutual Scaffolding

The *Timaeus* and *Critias* use fantasy tropes, including apocalypse, a device often used in narrative constructions about lost civilizations or to describe phases in the history of a civilization separated by catastrophic events. The narratives (Atlantis and cosmogony/cosmology) influence arguments by enacting them in a narrative scenario and indicating potential

---

[35] It is unclear whether the type of guardians referred to are the military as a whole or only the military leaders.

criticism. Through myths, Critias and Timaeus frame principles pertaining to the state and metaphysics; they portray individual or personal ways of using philosophical theories. In the process of justifying arguments, the Atlantis myth also exposes the kinds of mistakes fallible humans make when interpreting an 'ideal'.[36] The two dialogues demonstrate the problems with using theory in different situations and the complexity associated with narrative depictions of lived experience; I address these issues with a focus on epistemology (the theory of recollection), politics (the ideal state), and metaphysics (theory of Forms) consecutively. To address metaphysics, I move from the Atlantis myth to Timaeus's cosmogony/cosmology. Examining Timaeus's myth supports my analysis of Critias's narrative by demonstrating the consistency of plot structure and *mythos/logos* interdependence.

> What really happens is that the story-maker proves a successful "sub-creator." He makes a Secondary World which your mind can enter. Inside it, what he relates is "true:" it accords with the laws of that world. You therefore believe it, while you are, as it were, inside.[37]

The structural characteristics of the plot in the *Timaeus* and *Critias* are regulating factors in the Atlantis myth and signal arguments. In Greek mythology, the term 'golden age' is used to describe an original pure ideal period or utopia. This fictional historical era is represented in the literature and oral stories of many cultures. The different accounts depicting a culture's original perfect stage share a similar narrative framework and literary themes with Critias's myth, especially since many golden age tales often end with some form of catastrophe. This plot structure is used to tell the Atlantis myth. The *Timaeus* begins with a politician and philosopher considering ideal principles and subsequently applying them to illustrate a functioning society. The following cosmogonic/cosmological account also begins with an ideal—the theory of Forms—and aims toward a perfect creation.[38] However, the situation in both myths regresses; the

---

[36] Gill (1977) p. 289.
[37] Tolkien (1966) p. 37.
[38] Runia ([1997] pp. 105–107). Also, see Johansen (2004) pp. 21–22 for structural comparisons between the Atlantis myth and the cosmology.

Atlantis myth ends with the flood, and the cosmology describes certain corruptions such as disease and the emergence of immoral creatures, which are the outcome of previous unethical lives.

### 7.5.1 Rethinking Recollection

Critias's recollection in the *Timaeus* expresses a refined critical stance on *anamnesis* and represents an epistemological dimension to the dialogue. Critias remembers a childhood story perfectly but is unsure of the earlier philosophical conversation.[39] In response to Hermocrates, Critias mentions the goddess Memory, mother of the muses: 'Meanwhile I must follow your encouraging advice and call on the gods, adding the goddess Memory in particular to those you have mentioned. For almost all the most important parts of my speech depend upon this goddess' (*Crit.* 108d). Reference to the goddess Mnemosyne is also made in the myth of Er from the *Republic* and holds an important place in Orphic traditions. In the *Timaeus*, Critias remembers and seriously considers Socrates's description of an ideal state—one based on the Form of justice—and uses his memory to bring the blueprint to life.[40] He is a statesman and a philosopher and, therefore, Socrates and the others express complete faith and grant him liberty to demonstrate how the perfect society operates. Socrates's request is not philosophical but an invitation for Critias to tell a nationalist folktale; Critias responds with the Atlantis myth, which is extreme on many levels. Critias's story is more a glorification of Athens—or, more accurately, the aristocratic class of Athens—than a narrative focused on the idea of Justice. And he selects the narrative framework of a fallen utopia—the 'Paradise Lost' paradigm arranges his ideas, information, themes, and motifs—to achieve the same patriotic purpose. The plot is characterized by imagined cultural, social, and political oppositions designed to enforce a particular Athenian identity; the myth characterizes a form of moral and cultural superiority. The apocalyptic ending avoids blaming Athenians for regressing into the period

---

[39] Voegelin (1947) pp. 313–314.
[40] Osborne contrasts Critias's unoriginal, handed-down, story to Timaeus's novel, inaugural, account (Osborne [1996] pp. 185–186).

contemporary with Plato. And the catastrophe confirms the purity of the Athenians by depicting them as victims of unfortunate and unpredictable natural circumstances. The outcome of applying ideals or Forms by Critias is open to criticism; simply looking to the Forms or recollecting the Forms is insufficient when influences and prejudices weigh heavily on individual interpretations.

Plato's philosopher-kings recollect the Forms but interpret them according to their social and cultural standpoints. Socrates is represented as being in awe of his interlocutors, in contrast to Socrates the dialectician, and accepts their accounts without scrutiny.

> That was why I was so quick to agree to your conditions yesterday, thinking that I was pretty well placed to deal with what is always the most serious difficulty in such matters, how to find a suitable story on which to base what one wants to say (*Tim.* 26a).

Critias's statement regarding the best way to provide a narrative basis for one's thoughts indicates the interpretative work involved in applying principles of justice in one's current social situation. Plato draws attention to the place of a literary plot in theoretical deliberation; Critias's comments on the narrative he presents to the group at *Timaeus* 26a–e. Critias expresses amazement at how childhood stories remain in our memories in contrast to Socrates's account from the previous day which he remembers only in part. He describes his intention of connecting the structure of an ideal city with a story:

> We will now transfer the imaginary citizens and city which you described yesterday to the real world, and say that your city is the city of my story and your citizens those historical ancestors of ours whom the priest described (*Tim.* 26c–d).

Critias's attempt to transfer the imaginary state into a real state is an exercise in *anamnesis*; however, there are no competing theories and no hostile or doubting interlocutors and the conversation and relationship between interlocutors is amicable. Critias's account is based on his memory of the previous day, which in turn sparked memory of a childhood story. The scene is an example of recollection taking placed in lived experience; philosophical theory is animated by personal factors and the cultural and political context. The situation is a realistic act of storytelling conditioned by Critias's social conditions and aesthetic and philosophical influences. The storyteller, Critias, arranges recollected elements and events for impact and appeal. Plato depicts him remembering an ideal and combining it with an intimate memory or a chronicle of events. Critias finds the most appropriate narrative plot to structure it and present as the 'most likely' of accounts.[41]

## 7.5.2 Revisiting the Ideal State

After Critias's monologue in the *Timaeus*, Socrates commends him for telling a 'true history' and one that is suited for the day on which the dialogue takes place—the day marking the festival of Athena. The day on which the dialogue takes place is significant and informs certain details of the story. Critias is the storyteller and represents the Athenian ruling aristocracy. Consistent with his character as a proud and active citizen, he renders a historical account glamorizing the profound and unique nature of Athenian society and government. The myth describes the most virtuous time in Athenian history; and the great period of Athenian history contrasts with the problem-ridden era of Plato's Athens in its most important aspects.[42]

Critias avoids Athenian responsibility in regress and demise and inserts the event of a natural catastrophe to separate the golden age from the less-than-ideal situation of fifth- and fourth-century Athens. The representation of ancient Athens is a romantic and grandiose depiction with patriotic sentiments. It is an idealistic fantasy in many aspects, including the values of the state, the principles of society, its innocence, and the epic nature of its tragic end. For the Athenian patriot and politician, the Atlantis myth is

---

[41] Johansen (2004) p. 24, fn. 2.
[42] Morgan interprets the truth status of the account, following Rowe, as ironic (Morgan [1998] pp. 102–103). She states that the use of the myth as irony and the emphatic way it is presented instruct the reader to distinguish between the dramatic construction and appeal of the text and whatever the author's intended message may have been. Morgan bases her interpretation on criticism of myth in the *Republic* and the use of the 'Noble Lie' (pp. 102–104).

## 7 The Atlantis Myth and Cultural Identity: *Timaeus*...

self-affirming, and acknowledging it as true and ideal history has important consequences for imagined identity. Socrates's ideal city and the myth are arranged, interwoven, and presented as true by an aristocratic Athenian statesman; Plato demonstrates the construction of history and how veracity is contingent on those who tell it and those who believe it.

> But what should be the status of the evoked idea if it failed to be embodied in a historically real order? What is the meaning of the well ordered polis when its evocation is not the first step to its embodiment in reality? Is it, after all, an irrelevant velleity, the impractical program of a philosopher dabbling in politics? And, quite generally, what is an idea which neither remains set up in heaven, nor becomes the form, the "measure" of some piece of reality in the cosmos? Is it an ideal at all; or perhaps no more than a speculative opinion?[43]

The Atlantis myth revitalizes an old theory; Plato redefines the ideal state by framing it within a new plot. He places the structure of the best city in the hands of an Athenian politician and the result is the tale of ancient Athens. The myth is acknowledged and unquestioned by Socrates and his group of friends; the narrative is a series of true events, consisting of appropriate characters, places, actions, and reactions and imbued with the ideal principles of the best city.[44]

> The power of national myths on the popular mind dramatizes the need for philosophical control, and the Atlantis myth is an example of such manipulation, as the genres of philosophy, history, and oratory intersect. Both the myth and the cosmology are constructed to make a point about the way the world should be, the principles upon which we should construct it, and the means by which such models are rendered believable.[45]

The structure of the ideal state is comparable to the framework on which the Spartan state functioned. Drawing inspiration from the legacy of his

---

[43] Voegelin (1947) p. 311.
[44] Some scholars suggest that the myth reflects contrasts between Athens and imperial Persia (Johansen 2004, p. 11). In addition, the tale may function simultaneously as a critique of Athens's maritime imperialist exploits.
[45] Morgan (1998) p. 118.

ancestors and Solon, Critias advises and promotes a particular style of governance for his home state. Critias has this responsibility in the dialogue because of his status as a high-ranking political figure, and Socrates vehemently agrees and supports him. The content and delivery of the Atlantis myth are akin to those of the historical narratives created and exploited by romantic nationalists. The context and response to Critias's account represent extremely favorable or ideal circumstances for the presentation of a political speech.[46] Plato illustrates how a special kind of *mythos* is linked to abstract laws. And the Atlantis myth reflects Critias's interpretation of the laws and the influence of his level of knowledge, social standing, personal experiences, and idiosyncrasies.

### 7.5.3 Metaphysics

> ...the solution has to be found within the myth of nature and its cosmic rhythms. The idea of the well ordered polis is not embodied at present in a historical society; if we ascribe to it, nevertheless, objective status as a "measure" in reality, the ascription of objectivity must be based on an earlier or later embodiment of the idea; moreover, we need a theory which explains the temporary disembodiment. Into the creation of this myth of the polis, as the "measure" of society which in its crystallization and decay follows the cosmic rhythm of order and disorder, has gone the ripe art of Plato the poet.[47]

The second narrative in the *Timaeus*, the cosmogony/cosmology, shares structural and thematic similarities with the Atlantis myth and proves the consistency of Plato's method.[48] The introduction of Timaeus's monologue summarizes the theory of Forms followed by a discussion of the differences between the cosmos and its eternal model.[49] The early

---

[46] Johansen (2004) p. 38.
[47] Voegelin (1947) p. 312.
[48] However, Finkelberg describes the *Timaeus* as a cosmogonic account that does not necessarily reflect Plato's position on creation or generation (Finkelberg [1996] p. 393).
[49] For a detailed account and analysis of Timaeus's preamble, see Runia (1997) pp. 101–118. Also, see Burnyeat (2005) pp. 150–153 for comments on the distinction between Timaeus's account and the *Republic*.

section contrasts being and becoming and introduces a perfect paradigm into the text.[50] Timaeus's cosmogonical/cosmological account follows or builds on the paradigm.[51] Timaeus's story of the origins and nature of the cosmos is also influenced by the conversation from the previous day, but rather than produce a political treatise he presents a cosmogony/cosmology. His religious and philosophical sensibilities influence his interpretation and appropriation of the ideal principles; Timaeus's Pythagorean affiliation and training under Philolaus characterize his rendition in the same way Critias's sociopolitical standing influences his monologue. The narratives share the same plot structure but in Timaeus's account the apocalyptic end is replaced by a form of cosmic corruption. Timaeus employs the Demiurge in his myth to explain the creation of the cosmos—the most authentic and original act of creation imaginable.[52] The Demiurge is devoid of physical, historical, and sociocultural characteristics; it is transparent, like the receptacle, and exhibits no characteristics particular to humans. Timaeus is a philosopher-king and presents an account of the cosmos committed to conveying the theory of Forms. Both Critias and Timaeus attempt to replicate the Demiurge's activity—they look at the previous day's argument and attempt to create accordingly—and receive emphatic approval from Socrates.

## 7.6 Plot Structure

The cosmology reflects the story line from the Atlantis myth; both begin with a golden age or pure origins and deteriorate. Athens and Atlantis originally functioned perfectly by implementing the rules of an ideal state. Athens's success in the war with Atlantis was primarily due to its continuous commitment to justice.

---

[50] Runia (1997) pp. 112–113.
[51] Osbourne (1996) pp. 191–193.
[52] Cornford describes the Demiurge as being driven by unrestricted purpose (commentary in Plato [1997] p. 165). Analysis of the demiurge that addresses a diverse range of interpretations is found in Benitez (1995). I interpret the role of the demiurge in relation to a view of aesthetics that diverts from earlier dialogues at Tofighian (2009).

The Forms serve as paradigms both for the physical world created by the demiurge, and for the world in discourse created by Timaeus: his discourse gains its validity not from faithfulness to the way things appear, or the way particular things 'actually happened', but in virtue of its attempt to express in words a likeness of the perfect and eternal reality.[53]

The plot used to structure, characterize, and direct the different elements in the *Timaeus* and *Critias* belongs to a network of golden age or utopian myths.[54] The Atlantis myth shares the literary and cultural model exemplified in Hesiod's *Works and Days*:

> If you see fit, I will tell you another story right to the end, well and skillfully. Toss it about in your chest, how gods and mortal people are sprung from the same source.[55]
>
> At the very first the deathless ones who have Olympian homes made a golden race of mortal people,[56] who existed at the time of Cronus, when he was *basileus* in heaven. They lived like gods with woe-free spirit, apart from and without toils and grief; wretched old age did not hang over them, but unchanged in feet and hands, they delighted in festivities beyond all evils. They died as if overcome by sleep. They had all good things. The grain-giving plowland of her own will bore her produce, much of it, and without grudging. And they enjoyed the fruits of their works in ease and peace with many good things, [rich in sheep, dear to the blessed gods]. But ever since the earth covered over this race, they are divinities in accordance with the plans of great Zeus, and good ones on the ground, guardians of mortal people [—they watch over *dikai* and cruel works, wrapped in mist,

---

[53] Osborne (1996) p. 179.

[54] Other Greek myths that represent this plot structure include Orphic myths and the poetry of Empedocles. For examples from other cultures and eras, see Virgil's *The Georgics*, Ovid's *Metamorphoses*, Plutarch, the Hindu epic Mahabharata, Christian millennialism, the book of Isaiah, the Book of Enoch, and early modern and positivist notions about the historical and cultural role of the European Enlightenment. Also, see comments by Murray (2011) pp. 180–81 about other literary influences on Plato's myth. She refers to similarities with Hesiod on p. 183. For studies on the relationship between Plato and Hesiod, see Boys-Stones and Haubold (2009).

[55] 106–109 (Hesiod [1996]). See comments on p. 66, note 39: '*sprung from the same source*. Ordinarily this should refer to people and gods being descended from the same blood source. But here it must refer to the Golden Race, who "lived like gods" (112)'.

[56] See p. 66, note 40 for the influence of the Near East on Hesiod's tale of the degenerative races of heroes (Hesiod [1996]).

## 7 The Atlantis Myth and Cultural Identity: *Timaeus*...

wandering everywhere over the earth], givers of wealth: and this is the excellent prize that they got.[57]

Later those who have Olympian homes in turn made a second race, much worse, from silver, resembling the golden one in neither physique nor thought. By contrast a child was nurtured playing at his devoted mother's side for a hundred years in his *oikos*, an utter fool. But precisely when [each] reached puberty and reached the peak of his youth, they lived for a very short time, having pains on account of their follies: for they were not able to hold back outrageous violence[58] from each other, and they did not see fit to serve the deathless ones, not even to do actions at the holy alters of the blessed ones, which is proper behavior for people according to their customs. These then Zeus, the son of Cronus, hid away in his anger, because they did not give honors to the blessed gods who hold Olympus. But ever since the earth covered over this race, these are called blessed mortals under the ground; they belong to the second rank, but honor attends upon them all the same.[59]

The sequence of these passages represents the golden age plot structure and emphasizes a fall from glory. At 108, Hesiod establishes the homogeneous origins of gods and humans.[60] The original humans create a golden race of people during the time of Cronus and enjoy a utopian existence. They are guardians over mortals and successful in cultivating the land. At 127, a second, inferior race emerges and becomes part of society. This 'silver' race is proud, abusive, and impious and elicits punishment from Zeus. The Atlantis myth acknowledges and praises the golden era of Athens and Atlantis.[61] Inhabitants of Athens and Atlantis were originally akin to the gods and both civilizations enjoyed a utopian culture. The people of Atlantis degenerate because of their greater and more rapid degree of mixture with 'people of the soil'. Described as a second inferior race, they strayed from their commitment to the principles and cohesion indicative

---

[57] 109–127 (Hesiod [1996]).
[58] By violence the translators mean *hubris* as the antithesis of *dike*.
[59] 127–143 (Hesiod [1996]).
[60] See Burnyeat (2005) p. 145.
[61] The genealogical account, the narrative about the transmission from the Egyptian priest down to Critias, also reflects the regression theme constitutive of Hesiod's plot—an old wise civilization handing the tale down to children with no historical memory (Voegelin [1947] p. 312).

of their original state and began an imperialist mission. Critias's myth is modeled on the same paradigm as that of Hesiod's account. Regardless of the differences distinguishing Hesiod and Plato as thinkers and writers, the narrative paradigm influences both authors by determining the selection and arrangement of information, the movement and significance of the scenes, and the interaction of the elements within the story.

## 7.7 Character Selection

### 7.7.1 Socrates

Socrates's position and attitude in the *Timaeus* and *Critias* are unique in contrast to his role in other dialogues. Dialectical exchange in a philosophical sense is missing, and the younger Socrates represents a facilitator and fan of the speakers and their independent speeches. He does not respond to the narratives with questions but instead uncritically accepts and praises the stories without sufficient justification. Socrates steps back, observes, and refuses to play a prominent role or contribute in a significant way; there is no need for intervention by Socratic dialectic when more capable thinkers are in control. Plato's ideals are left in the hands of politicians and philosophers described as fully qualified for the task and encouraged by the young Socrates.

### 7.7.2 Critias

There is much debate regarding the identity of Critias in the two dialogues. Most agree he was an aristocratic Athenian, a statesman and a philosopher, and member of the family whose lineage connects him to Dropides and Critias, his grandfather. If the character is Critias from the Thirty Tyrants, Plato's choice enforces the patriotic and aristocratic sentiment and political pride expressed in the nature and delivery of the myth. However, Critias was a well-known name in Plato's aristocratic family and he may be just an invented character.[62] Critias demonstrates

---

[62] Voegelin (1947) p. 316.

how an ideal constitution is validated through historical writing, and the combination of charter and myth is used to justify a particular political vision and agenda.

### 7.7.3 Timaeus

The character of Timaeus is either completely fictional or possibly modeled on a figure such as Archytas of Tarentum.[63] Many scholars agree that he is a fictional Pythagorean philosopher known as Timaeus of Locri. In Plato's dialogue, he is a philosopher and politician who expresses Pythagorean views. Cicero refers to Timaeus of Locri as a Pythagorean philosopher and close acquaintance of Plato.[64] Also, Proclus, in his commentary on the *Timaeus*, refers to Timaeus as a Pythagorean.[65] Examples of Timaeus's Pythagorean background are detailed by Huffman in *Philolaus of Croton*, in which he draws similarities between Philolaus's theory of attunement and Timaeus's account in the *Timaeus*.[66]

### 7.7.4 Hermocrates

Hermocrates, according to Proclus (on 20A) and modern scholars, is the Syracusan who defeated the Athenian expedition to Sicily in Plato's childhood (415-413 B.C.). Thucydides (vi, 72) describes him as a man of outstanding intelligence, conspicuous bravery, and great military experience.[67]

Socrates informs the group at the beginning of the *Critias* that Hermocrates will present his own account after Critias completes the Atlantis myth. The *Critias* ends before the narrator finishes his story and there is no third dialogue presenting Hermocrates's narrative. Cornford is correct in stating that based on the evidence from the two dialogues we can only speculate regarding his character and what he may have

---

[63] Lee's introduction to Plato (1977) p. 29.
[64] Cicero (1999) I.X.
[65] Proclus (1820) pp. 187 and 199.
[66] Huffman (1993).
[67] Cornford commentary in Plato (1997) p. 2.

discussed in his speech. In the dialogue, Hermocrates panders to Critias, advising him to evoke Pan and the Muses to assist in glorifying ancient Athens; Pan assisted the Athenians at Marathon and this possibly initiated worship of the god in Athens for the first time.[68] Hermocrates was a Syracusan general and his activities, particularly military operations, are documented by Thucydides, Xenophon, Plutarch, and Polyaenus. And he was instrumental both in battle and as advisor in opposing Athenian imperialist ambitions. During the Peloponnesian War, he occupied the role of general against the Sicilian Expedition launched by the Athenians.

In the dialogues, there is little evidence to help decipher the balance between Hermocrates and Critias—individuals from warring states. Hermocrates is obliged to listen to a patriotic folktale that admonishes Atlantis as a belligerent and ruthless imperialist force, while Athens was engaged in a similar enterprise. However, the group seems to agree in relation to philosophical and political issues—or at least they are considerate of each other's positions and willing to cooperate—and from the amicable and intellectually nature of the meeting it seems Plato incorporates the character Hermocrates purely as a symbol of statesmanship—a symbol representing a city connected to Plato's own political activities.

> In the present gathering of philosophers and statesmen he is pre-eminently the man of action… He had also attempted to reform from within his native city, Syracuse, the scene of Plato's own abortive essays towards the reconstruction of existing society.[69]

## 7.7.5 Egypt and the Egyptian Priest

> Solon has been given a charter myth for Athens from the Egyptians, conveniently fetishized as preservers of accuracy about the past.[70]

Egypt occupies an important place in the ancient Greek imaginary and is supported by many examples of ancient literature. Egyptians are

---

[68] Fink (2014) p. 139.
[69] Cornford commentary in Plato (1997) p. 2.
[70] Morgan (1998) p. 104. Also, see fn. 11.

associated with perennial wisdom and the origin of knowledge[71]—particularly, mystical knowledge. The Atlantis story is preserved in Egypt by an Egyptian priest and transmitted back to the Greeks. The genealogy of the transmission reflects a recurring pattern of regress: the tale begins with the Egyptians as keepers of wisdom who preserve history and is transferred down to Critias as a child, but he forgets the story until the period described in the dialogue.

### 7.7.6 Solon

Solon is the first Greek figure in the transmission of the myth and represents the philosopher-statesman outlined and praised in the *Republic*.[72] Many of his qualities are exemplified in the three philosopher-politicians in the dialogue. The narrators of the myths are trusted and respected on the grounds that in character and action they resemble Solon—the Athenian statesman who returns to Greece with the historical account of ancient Athens and Atlantis. Solon's character is the archetype that contextualizes the other three characters; that is, Solon is the quintessential outstanding Greek guardian, an exceptional and complete statesman, and model of excellence.[73]

### 7.7.7 Atlantis

The conflict between the two civilizations, Athens and Atlantis, is a standard binary of good versus evil. The concept of an archenemy or 'Other' used for the depiction of Atlantis—the quintessential enemy—functions as a literary trope and characterizes Critias's glorification of Athens. The political and cultural dichotomy also supports the essentialism in

---

[71] Johansen (2004) pp. 39–40; p. 36.
[72] Compare with Morgan (1998) pp. 108–109. On page 112, Morgan expresses a different view by arguing that the role of Solon 'is closer to a parody of contemporary practice than an appropriation of it ... Whereas the interlocutors must accept the noble lie at face value, we must not do so, but must recognize that Atlantis is a speculative exercise in political rhetoric, albeit philosophically based. Our focus must be on the construction'.
[73] Voegelin argues that Solon represents the author, Plato, and the passages explaining Solon's poetic skills are autobiographical (Voegelin [1947] pp. 318–319).

describing the golden age period of ancient Athens in contrast to the decline and threat of Atlantis.[74]

## 7.8 Conclusion

The Atlantis myth described in the *Timaeus* and *Critias* is infused with a sense of Athenian cultural identity and functions as history, art, and a form of self-reflection. The tale signals Plato's theories and adds new dimensions to epistemology, politics, and metaphysics. The *Timaeus* and *Critias* describe an operating model of the ideal state, and the convergence of myth and philosophy in the historical tale demonstrates new possibilities for Plato's methods. By evoking an earlier conversation, arguments pertaining to principles of justice enter the discussion—stipulations suggestive of those pronounced in the first five books of the *Republic*. The Atlantis myth is informed by Plato's philosophical views and provides critical distance by illustrating how philosopher-statesmen remember and interpret ideas and arguments and attempt to apply them in different contexts. The creation myth also represents this self-reflexive strategy, is structured similarly, and shares stylistic features with Critias's story. The two myths presented in the *Timaeus* and *Critias* situate history and the origins and structure of the universe within a narrative framework that resonates with a particular sense of cultural identity familiar to the interlocutors and Plato's audience.

Rather than reading the Atlantis myth as allegory, I suggest interpreting the story as an example of philosophical rhetoric that communicates knowledge but also reflects biases associated with the narrator. A commentary on epistemology and politics, the myth demonstrates the complexities associated with applying theory, problems pertaining to partiality, and the influence of culture and social status; the monologues indicate how philosophers are also impacted by various forms of affiliation and community commitment. Lincoln's critique of mythology and myth theories raises awareness of the intersections between mythology, privilege, and politics. The rise of European fascism reminds scholars that

---

[74] See Morgan (1998) pp. 114 and 117 for a comparison between Atlantis and the Persian Empire.

erudite and critically aware intellectuals are also susceptible to the temptations of myth; sacred narrative has the potential to unite and galvanize, in addition to its insidious ability to divide and oppress. In the *Timaeus* and *Critias*, Plato introduces a historical basis for Athenian identity and presents sociocultural characteristics as ideal universal models. The dramatic context of the account indicates critical ways of reading Critias's story in order to expose elements of nationalism and the social and political privilege associated with the narrator.

Lincoln interprets myth as a narrative that codes and reinforces ideology. He examines mythology in relation to the discourse of difference ingrained in narrative structures and mythic paradigms. Division, exclusion, and stigmatization can be either subtle or explicit but often are elided by the poetic beauty of myth and its power to speak to and bolster cultural identity. Lincoln's perspective exposes how scholars become part of the legacy of myths when disclosing their philosophical and aesthetic significance. Theorists also enhance and perpetuate patterns in myth that strategically construct and marginalize the Other. The Atlantis myth and the genealogy of the tale idealize ancestors, Athenian statesmen, Athenian homeland, Athenian patron gods, and the notion of innate Athenian capabilities and talents. Critias's cultural imagination drives his selection and appropriation of elements of history and influences how he frames them within his epic narrative; Plato creates a dialogue that raises questions about the role of cultural standpoint in practicing philosophy and how lived experience impacts philosophers.

# 8

## Where Does Myth Belong?

Theories of myth and myth studies scholarship provide new methodological tools and conceptual frameworks for interpreting the relationship between myth and philosophy. Recognition of the development of modern theories and movements assists in describing, analyzing, and appreciating the significance and nuances of Plato's myths. A vibrant and sophisticated interdisciplinary tradition of myth research exists, and since the late eighteenth century, philosophers have been an integral part of it. Schilbrack and others criticize the disconnect between contemporary philosophers and the mythography tradition which encompasses a body of growing research on myth and ritual.[1] Until at least the end of the nineteenth century, prominent Western philosophers—and poets and writers contemporary with them—such as Schleiermacher, Humboldt, Schelling, Marx, Feuerbach, Nietzsche, and scholars from the Cambridge Ritualist school, exhibited profound interest in mythology and interacted with academic discourse on the topic to various degrees.[2] After a decrease in enthusiasm and productivity in the academic study of mythology following the

---

[1] Schilbrack (2002a, 2004a).
[2] Feldman and Richardson (1972) pp. 297–527.

Second World War and after recovering from the stigma attached to it due to associations with European fascism, the last few decades have experienced a revival in myth studies. Scholars specializing in a range of different fields have begun directing their attention toward myth or expanding and reinforcing their work in the area.[3] Historical, philological, and ethnographic work on mythology has been consistent over the last century; however, significant philosophical contributions to theorizing myth and philosophical studies of mythology have had limited output.

Many modern scholars use the term 'myth' for categorizing a divergent range of tales, whereas others acknowledge that fundamental problems persist with using general definitions for myth. Monomythic definitions detract from efforts to distinguish myths with philosophical import and obstruct investigation of the relationship between the myth and philosophy throughout the history of philosophy. After around three centuries of myth studies as an established discipline, philosophers are well placed to identify the subtle ways that myth and philosophy communicate. The potential for collaborative studies is immense and must include both cross-cultural and interdisciplinary projects. In particular, serious engagement with Indigenous research, Indigenous research protocols, and Indigenous methodologies is indispensable for the progress and significance of myth scholarship.[4] Indigenous voices can also inform philosophical investigations of myth and raise critical questions in philosophy about epistemic injustice and the existence of exclusory practices and methods.[5] Philosophical approaches to myth studies contribute to expanding knowledge in the field, and more research and institutional commitment are required to broaden the conceptual and methodological resources necessary for a genuinely inclusive understanding of mythology.[6] The damaging cultural, political, and intellectual influence of many

---

[3] Particularly contributions by Doty (1986); Segal (1999, 2004); Hawes (2014); Csapo (2005); Dundes (1984); Lincoln (1999); Bremmer (2010, 2011).

[4] Smith (1999) p. 4. Denzin et al. (2008) Chap. 1. Cruikshank (1998). Jackson (2012). Also, related work in Arctic studies is published by the journal series *Contributions to Circumpolar Anthropology*.

[5] Fricker (2009); Rigney (2006); Anderson (2014); Anderson (2002); Smith (1999); Park (2013); Buck-Morrs (Summer 2000); Jean-Marie (2013).

[6] Henrdy and Fitznor (2012); Grounds et al. (2003); Emeagwali and Sefa Dei (2014); Maaka and Andersen (2006); Semali and Kincheloe (1999) p. 15; Denzin et al. (2008) Chap. 1; Jackson (2012).

past Western thinkers and schools of thought manifest in contemporary mythography, and dedication to producing collaborative scholarship on myth that prioritizes the perspectives of researchers from marginalized knowledge systems is urgent.[7] An approach to studying myth dedicated to cognitive justice restores dignity and integrity to groups of people whose unique understanding of myth characterizes connections with identity, country, ritual, and lived experience.[8] A decolonial approach to transforming the way knowledge is produced benefits the development of myth studies; more importantly, it dismantles the asymmetrical way research is conducted concerning peoples whose links with sacred narratives have been disrupted and severed as a result of colonialism and its associated modes of scholarly endeavor.[9]

Philosophers are reluctant to invest in contemporary myth studies and have been slower than scholars from other disciplines to forge ties with religious studies, comparative mythology, myth theory, and the many approaches constituting these fields. The difficulties with using many modern theories of myth in a philosophical context result partly from the ambiguous, conflicting, and fluctuating evaluations of myth in the history of Western philosophy. The narrative constructed to define the place of myth in the Western philosophical tradition assigns a special place to Plato.[10] In particular, his scathing attack on poetry in the *Republic* is regularly referred to as the cornerstone of his views on myth and functions as the 'point of origin' in Western philosophy's foundation narrative; a particular interpretation of Plato becomes the myth that establishes the status of myth in post-Enlightenment thought. In this story, Plato is often valorized in heroic terms as the pioneer who broke with poetry, and this view is reinforced by associating him with people who emerged much later to challenge religious authority.

---

[7] Denzin et al. (2008) Chap. 1; Nakata (1998, 2004, 2007); Martin (2003); Rigney (2006); Coleman et al. (March 2012).
[8] De Sousa Santos (2007). Also, see Nakata (1998).
[9] Nakata et al. (1998, 2012); Bishop (2005) pp. 110–112; Smith (1999); Arashiro and Barahona (2015); Connell (2007); Yancy (2008); Alcoff and Caputo (2011); Alcoff and Mendieta (2000); Weinbaum (2004). Consider the early views of myth in the context of colonialism by Banier (Feldman and Richardson [1972] pp. 86–87).
[10] Detiene (1986, 2009); Snell (1953); Vernant (1962b, 1974); Buxton (1999).

Plato wrote philosophical myths that belong in a category distinct from myths employed without interdependent relationships with arguments. The philosophical myths I analyze and other relevant examples require a heterogeneous theory of myth or require that certain theories be appropriated in order to understand the dialectical theatre directed in Plato's dialogues. I emphasize the need to engage with the myth studies tradition and contemporary theorization of myth for contextualizing approaches and developments in Plato studies. However, including disciplinary critiques, ideas, and methods is only an initial step; application is another matter. Theories of myth have been designed and applied by theorists for other research projects, and in most cases the communication between myth theories and philosophy has been indirect or minor. In order for a theory, or a combination of theories, to benefit scholarly approaches to Plato, a well-defined systematic strategy is necessary—a strategy that links methodologies pertaining to myth with scholarship devoted to the dialogues. By examining specific elements and mythemes integral to selected dialogues and combining them by using my mutual scaffolding approach, I have demonstrated a procedure that acknowledges the advances in myth studies and is simultaneously sensitive to Plato scholarship. Mutual scaffolding also promotes an intimate reading of the text that pays special attention to understudied or marginal features and symbols, partnering them with the major philosophical positions and dominant mythic components.

A systematic project distinguishing between the various kinds of myth in the dialogues has not been undertaken and deserves attention by classicists and philosophers working on Plato. To differentiate between myths used in the dialogues, new comparative methods and transdisciplinary work are required to reposition Plato as philosopher/religious exegete/myth-maker/cultural innovator rather than solely a Greek philosopher. Integration of the important work from myth scholars adds significant tools, insights, and perspective; collaboration and interdisciplinary vision are necessary and need to be combined with a critical awareness of the cultural and political history of modern myth scholarship. As a result of important research from scholars such as Morgan, Brisson, Tarrant, Benitez, Partenie, Collobert et al., and Werner, we have some understanding of Plato's special kind of philosophical myth. Outside of a Plato studies context, philosophical myths have received little attention and few have entered debates or responded to philosophical questions posed by theorists from different disciplines. Identifying philosophical myths and highlighting their distinguishing features and functions demand an interdisciplinary strategy involving both philosophers and myth theorists. Illuminating the nuances of philosophical myths and constructing principles and categories for their study are critical tasks. But potential for misinterpretation is increased when one incorporates approaches originally developed for other purposes and examples. Influenced by Doty's approach to myth, I suggest a polymythic hermeneutics for reading myths rather than an approach based on all-encompassing definitions or prescription of clearly defined pathways. Focusing on the function of myth to decipher its meaning and role is an important first step. Beginning with the unique function and status of each individual myth enables researchers to find, advance, or construct theories and methods best suited for analysis.

Traditional and conventional interpretations of the relationship between myth and philosophy feature in modern studies of Plato's myths, but few inquiries indicate connections with the recent history and developments of myth scholarship. Plato studies has been affected by similar sociocultural and intellectual influences as myth studies, and overlapping patterns and shifts are obvious to Plato scholars who are familiar with theories of myth. Research in both fields is characterized and limited by many of the same theoretical and methodological problems and obstacles: interpreting and integrating analysis of language into cultural and philosophical investigation; balancing particular literary content with structural concerns; considering historical factors and recognizing social and political context; and theorizing the relationship between myth and argument. Addressing the disconnect between myth studies and Plato scholarship in practical terms is another concern. Moving beyond acknowledgment of the mutual influences and interests between areas of study, the formation of a transdisciplinary field that integrates various techniques, methods, and research topics enhances philosophical appreciation of myth, in general, and Plato's myths, in particular.

My own approach in this area of study draws on disciplines such as religious studies, myth studies, philosophy, cultural studies, symbolic anthropology, and literary criticism. I have examined Plato's dialogues, characterized by interdependence and diversity, with tailored approaches sensitive to the nuances of individual myths and the narrative dimensions of each dialogue. I used mutual scaffolding as a methodological device to foreground interdependence between elements in Plato's philosophy. The method reveals how Plato's vision both resists rigid binaries and uses narrative to represent the fluidity and uncertainty associated with using argument in complex and diverse situations. Plato's dialogues are transgressive in nature and his critique of political, religious, and intellectual matters is a combination of philosophical commitment and sociocultural experiment; his dialectical unity involves myth and philosophy represents hermeneutical spaces for introducing and testing knowledge and exposing opinions. Plato's literary techniques are a challenge to authority and reflect a savvy and audacious attitude to philosophical practice.

Plato's metaphysical, epistemological, and ethical concerns are intertwined with his construction and application of myth. Complex philosophical theory and critique are framed in narratives introducing legend, epic, homily, and devotion. The dialogue format incorporates competing discourses and situates them such that they become cross-genre accounts and invite interdisciplinary approaches in order to unpack it. An appropriate method for understanding Plato's dialogues requires decentering rational inquiry and examining his experimentation with hybrid forms of explanation and analysis; myth and philosophy are combined, but the collaboration is not uniform across dialogues. Plato's myths challenge conceptions of genre, both modern and ancient. Character, mythic themes, narrative plots, mise-en-scène, and literary tropes take center stage and dictate the direction, purpose, and terms of the discursive parts of the text. An inversion takes place in the dialogues: rather than theory determining narrative, the literary frameworks manage philosophy. However, Plato does not prioritize one over the other or construct standard hierarchies that span his oeuvre; he negotiates the terms and conditions depending on the questions, situation, intellectual aims, and the way myth and philosophy are introduced in a text.

Study of the function of Plato's myths within each dialogue clarifies their relationship with structural and thematic elements and projects an interpretative frame for analyzing the polymythic quality of his narratives. The modern tradition of myth studies has overemphasized definition. An approach based on function reveals deeper meanings and is not limited by the constraint of inquiries led by definitions—particularly, monomythic definitions. Using function as a starting point does not suggest a method restricted to the version espoused by functionalists such as Malinowski.[11] Investigating Plato's myths by determining the active role they play in the dialogues, one can develop an interpretation based on the individual operations of the philosophical myths. In particular dialogues, Plato expresses a perspective on narrative through his application of myth and confirms its potential to introduce philosophical features that facilitate debate and support argument.

The narrative features of Plato's myths and their interaction with philosophical arguments unfold in various ways as his dialogues develop, and the form and content of the myths activate structural principles in the texts. In each chapter, I explained the philosophical potential of literary features and how they illuminate the structural, contextual, and symbolic aspects of narrative. I gave special attention to plot structure, literary themes and tropes, construction of characters, narrative voice, mythic symbols, and religious factors such as liminality and ritual. My investigation demonstrates the value of interdisciplinary research and uncovers the cross-genre approach Plato uses to construct the dialogues. The design of the myth/argument relationship cannot be unpacked within the constraints of disciplinary boundaries, and I have used a method inspired by recent interdisciplinary scholarship of myth. Philosophical rigor is pivotal, but elements and insights from other fields help address assumptions and contextualize concepts, categories, and techniques.

The formation of myth studies and the directions it has taken since its inception are important for addressing Plato's dialogues. My aim has been to establish a framework and conceptual strategy for understanding philosophical myth and disclosing how Plato constructed and implemented sacred narrative. Modern discourse pertaining to myth presents a range of central questions and a number of core theories and evaluations

---

[11] For sociofunctionalist views of myth, see Doty (1986) pp. 44–45.

pertaining to the status and function of mythology. I considered these in my discussion of Plato:

1. I distinguished between myth and philosophy on the basis of how they manifest in discourse, themes, symbols, and structures.
2. I distinguished between the different kinds of Platonic myths and identified philosophical myths.
3. I discussed the interdependent relationship between philosophical myths and the arguments in the dialogues by analyzing different elements and reintegrating them through mutual scaffolding.

At the beginning of my study, I considered a series of pivotal questions as a guiding framework for interpreting myth. These questions assist in critically readdressing some fundamental theoretical presuppositions, methods, and trends characteristic of myth studies—presuppositions, methods, and trends that also surface in many examples of Plato studies. In the opening chapter, I argued that an interdependent approach combining *mythos* and *logos* and engaging with the literary and conceptual nuances of Plato's style of writing must acknowledge a set of significant factors and answer related questions. My study acknowledges the following issues as fundamental: (1) the literary and performative aspects, (2) structural authority, and (3) hermeneutical matters.

Exploring the complexities of these issues, I attempted to include interpretative themes and techniques from myth studies and Plato scholarship. I drew on theories and previous studies without reducing individual myths to a particular definition or interpretation originally employed for other myths. Instead, I prioritize the unique context and function of Plato's myths in order to investigate their multidimensional referents and the multilayered messages they suggest. Commitment to one category or genre misleads interdisciplinary inquiries, and single-genre or monomythic accounts do not reflect Plato's mythic project; instead, they emphasize logical order over imaginative curiosity when analyzing his systematic approach. Reducing the rational and the emotional to a dichotomy and abstracting philosophy from social, religious, and personal considerations marginalizes Plato's careful literary design and disconnects philosophy from a total human experience; Plato communicates a complete reflection of intellectual inquiry to elicit complex and multidimensional reception.

My interpretation of each of the six dialogues was ordered to illustrate the importance of dramatic scenes and literary elements, discursive arguments, and the social and religious factors that impact the text.

Theme introduction, setting, and narrative: I examined the opening scenes and the significance of narrative voice. The setting introduces the theme of the dialogue—the introduction of the philosophical question and how particular problems arise, the character who raises them, and the contexts that create the dilemmas. Narrative mode identifies explicit or implicit narrator(s) and narratee(s) and the messages behind Plato's choice of narrator(s) and narratee(s).

Myth analysis: I illustrated the details of the dialogue's myth and its interaction with the philosophical sections. I also addressed specialized literary techniques used to construct the myth, such as liminality or deliverance.

The philosophical arguments: I outlined the steps involved in Plato's discursive arguments, indicating the features that link them to the myth.

Mutual scaffolding: My method detailed the interdependent connection between myth and philosophy, interpreting the relationship as a dialectical unity in which the two discourses are represented as complementary.

Plot structure: The structural importance of the plot highlights the logical sequence of literary and philosophical sections.

Character selection: I described details of Plato's characters and how their personalities inform important aspects of the philosophical dramas.

Plato creates possibilities for interpreting myth in relation to argument. Many of the prominent features I identified and used to analyze the myth/philosophy dynamic apply to both discourses and must be dealt with in order to illuminate the aesthetic and philosophical theatre orchestrated in the dialogues. I explain these features as:

1. plot structure
2. character selection (determined by the plot)
3. the use of literary tropes to both combine and separate elements
4. the meaningful selection and use of mythic themes and motifs.

In my analysis of the six dialogues, I explored the myth/philosophy interdependence by using an interdisciplinary method guided by the sets of concerns stipulated above—the literary and performative features, structural factors, and hermeneutical issues.

Chapter 3: *Myth and Instruction*. In the *Meno*, myth instructs one on how to practice philosophy correctly. Socrates guides the inquirer by introducing a form of instruction manual that refers to myth and religious traditions in order to challenge Meno's paradox and indicate the personal and cultural influences operating in our cognitive processes. Socrates and the slave represent the use of the mythical trickster device: a character who introduces liminality, transformation, and renewal—aspects that are part of the theme and structure of the dialogue.

Chapter 4: *Myth and Partnership*. My study of the *Protagoras* reveals how a sophist combines myth with arguments in order to critique Socrates's views on virtue and whether it can be taught. Partnership is central to the myth, the arguments, and the dramatic setting, and the theme contextualizes the discussion on political skill and virtue. I consider how Laurence Coupe's discussion of radical typology elucidates the ability for myth to create conditions for interpretation and perpetuate meaning.

Chapter 5: *Myth and Regulation*. Myth in the *Phaedo* regulates the arguments and counter-arguments and administers three prominent themes: deliverance, dualism, and a Pythagorean/Platonic dynamic. Myth as an organizing principle positions and connects the arguments in the text with particular literary and religious features. My interpretation of dramatic and philosophical aspects in the dialogue is influenced by Lévi-Strauss's theory of myth involving binary opposition. The myth of the soul's journey is interpreted as a meaning-generating narrative that mediates a particular binary system, impacting the philosophical arguments and literary construction.

Chapter 6: *Myth and Transition*. Transition is a central theme in the *Phaedrus* and Plato designs the myth to evoke a sense of physical performance through ritual transformation. The phases within a rite-of-passage ritual correspond with the phases of Plato's arguments and the developmental message of the text—a message that signifies a move from one philosophical vision to a more advanced approach. William Doty introduces a complex and exhaustive working definition of myth which

I employ to illuminate the relationship between cultural standpoint and the presentation of epistemological and metaphysical nuances—details that explore the significance of love and the body for Plato's philosophy.

Chapter 7: *Myth and Cultural Identity*. For the Atlantis myth presented in the *Timaeus* and *Critias*, I focus on how myth operates as a mode of self-reflection and criticism. By examining Critias's account, I demonstrate how cultural and political affiliation and influence determine interpretation of philosophical principles. Bruce Lincoln's interpretation of myth as ideology in narrative form assists in understanding the exclusion and marginalization ingrained in mythic accounts and how sacred narratives like the Atlantis myth are susceptible to nationalism; the story is depicted as an expression of Athenian cultural identity that reflects hierarchy, power, and political ambition. My approach to Plato's myths argued that the dichotomy paradigm must be criticized and rethought. Whether explicit or implicit, dichotomous paradigms have dominated many of the theories and schools of thought in the myth studies tradition, and one of my aims has been to challenge this tendency. Serious consideration of the intellectual history of fields such as religious studies, anthropology, and folkloristics is fundamental. Their effects on the study of myth are important for moving toward a polymythic hermeneutics—a perspective that I argue leads to an appreciation of the philosophical potency of Plato's mythic project. My multidisciplinary outlook integrates contemporary methods and devices used to study myth and questions methodological restrictions placed on analyses of myth in the dialogues. Consequently, this study has created a horizon for a more dynamic and interdependent understanding of the *mythos/logos* relationship.

I also challenged the demand for verifiability in the study of myth— the view that myth is non-falsifiable and non-argumentative and, therefore, not subject to the scrutiny applied to logical discourse. My analysis involved criticism of perspectives that contrast the narrative discourse of myth, the referents of which are not accessible to sense or intellect, with the dialectical reasoning of Plato's philosophy. Plato criticizes myth, but would he critique his own philosophical myths as having the same referents and the same relation to logic as the myths contained in epics and tragedies? Do his philosophical myths occupy an inferior status? Are philosophical myths useful only in the realm of ethics and politics as an instrument of persuasion? The view that myth is unfalsifiable and therefore only a likely account is committed to the dichotomy paradigm and does not accommodate Plato's diverse, fluid, and vivid modes of philosophical expression.

Brisson explains how the Atlantis myth differs from other historical accounts based on actual historical events such as the Median and Peloponnesian wars. He distinguishes between historical accounts and Plato's tale about the war between Atlantis and ancient Athens in terms of accuracy and precision in dating the events. Brisson states: 'Myth is distinguished from true discourse about the past by its inability to precisely state when the events which it mentions took place'.[12] According to Brisson, the Atlantis myth, with its own contentious dating and unverifiable source, is akin to a story such as the *Odyssey* in that it is completely independent of anything but the reality which it creates for itself. He states that the discipline of history, which objectifies events, renders myth void because it documents an occurrence, subjecting it to validation—something that myth is unable to do.

However, my approach to Plato's myths investigates the structural and regulatory reasons behind inserting myth into the dialogues rather than attempting to verify the content. In most cases, Plato does not attempt to doubt or prove conclusively the existence of gods, daimons, heroes, the activities of the immortal soul, and the past exploits of gods and humans, because their verifiability is not central to the issues under investigation in the dialogues.[13] Instead, the working relationship of these elements in the framework of a plot, and their unique collaboration with elements in his arguments, justify their implementation in the text. Philosophical discussion invites the use of various forms of discourse and rhetorical expression but also requires an understanding of the appropriate context in which to make use of them. Therefore, if different discourses and expressions are indispensable parts of a unity—interdependently connected—then the target of criticism must be the coherence of the whole rather than the validity of the parts. Particularly in later dialogues, Plato's characters

---

[12] Brisson (1998) p. 22.
[13] See Veyne (1988) regarding the ambiguous distinctions between belief and disbelief in myth and legend in ancient Greece.

focus on the scope of paradigms, to what extent one should explicate them, and the proper form of discourse one should use.[14] Recognition of the mutual cooperation between Plato's two most dominant forms of explanation—both carefully crafted and thoughtfully arranged—reveals the counterproductive nature of comparing and contrasting *mythos* and *logos* and encourages one to move toward more meta-questions: the appropriate length of exposition, paradigm application, the limits of the question-and-answer form of dialectic, and the place of figurative language in philosophical discussion.[15] Questions targeting the truth status of myth are relevant but it is more important to transcend this form of analysis and concentrate on a critique of method.

Plato's philosophical myths belong to a completely different genre to other myths. The idiosyncrasies of this form of myth pertain to Plato's style and are relevant to his philosophical mission. His own myths are not subject to the same criticism targeted at other myths, even though they share content. Plato's myths constitute a distinct form of sacred narrative, unprecedented in his time. His mythic accounts share common features and patterns exhibited by the structure of the dialogues and the philosophical sections. The selected works I have addressed indicate a particular attitude toward the use of literary devices in philosophy. 'Philosophical tales are often newly invented because they have a point to make that does not fit into previous narrative formats, but most importantly because they must demonstrate how to employ myth correctly'.[16] A hermeneutics appropriate for Plato's use of myth accepts different stories, encourages multiple forms of interpretation, and allows various definitions to modify, change, merge, and transform. Myth is irreducible to a single theory; sacred narratives continuously reform and reposition as interpreters and myth-makers engage with them. The theoretical, methodological, and sociocultural limits conditioning interpretations of mythology indicate the potential for misguided readings and the inaccurate presuppositions associated with definitions and universal accounts. Analysis of Plato's myths must be interpreted as part of the same tradition;

---

[14] Morgan (2000) p. 157.
[15] Morgan (2000) p. 157.
[16] Morgan (2000) p. 16.

modern myth studies and recent Plato studies have run parallel and share theoretical, methodological, and sociocultural influences. Regardless of the subject matter or the identity of the myth-maker, one must exercise caution when studying myth and avoid demythologizing for the purposes of replacing sacred narratives with something more convenient. Myth has always resisted being reduced to scientific explanation, a translation of an ideal account of reality, a reflection of ritual, a psychological state, values from an original phase of history, or a sociopolitical charter. Where does myth belong? It belongs within an inclusive horizon that accommodates unconstrained narratives voicing many different things.

# Bibliography

## Primary Texts

Cicero, M.T. (1999). *'On the Commonwealth' and 'On the laws'*, Trans. by J.E.G. Zetzel. Cambridge: Cambridge University Press.
Diogenes Laertius. (1925). *Lives of Eminent Philosophers*, Trans. by R.D. Hicks. Cambridge, Mass.: Harvard University Press.
Euripides. (written 410 B.C.E) *Iphigenia in Aulis*. http://classics.mit.edu/Euripides/iphi_aul.html, retrieved on February 2016.
Hesiod. (1996). *Hesiod's Works and Days*, Trans. and commentary by D.T. Tandy and W.C. Neale. Berkley: University of California Press.
Kant, I. (2002). *Groundwork for the Metaphysics of Morals*. Trans. by A.W. Wood with essay by J.B Schneewind. New Haven: Yale University Press.
Pausanias. (1978). *Description of Greece, Volume I, Books 1–2 (Attica and Corinth)*. Loeb Classic Library 93. Trans. by W.H.S. Jones. Cambridge, Mass.: Harvard University Press.
Plato. (1955). *Plato's Phaedo*. Trans. with introduction and commentary by R. Hackforth. Cambridge: Routledge & Kegan Paul Ltd.
Plato. (1961a). 'Meno', in *The Collected Dialogues of Plato, Including the Letters*. E. Hamilton. and H. Cairns. Princeton: Pantheon Books.
Plato. (1961b). 'Protagoras', in *The Collected Dialogues of Plato, Including the Letters*. E. Hamilton and H. Cairns. Princeton: Pantheon Books.

Plato. (1973). *Phaedrus and Letters VII and VIII*. Trans. with introductions by W. Hamilton. Harmondsworth: Penguin Classics.
Plato. (1977). *Timaeus* and *Critias*. Trans. with an introduction and an appendix on Atlantis by D. Lee. London: Penguin Books.
Plato. (1985). *Meno*. Ed. with trans. and notes by R.W. Sharples. Warminster: Bolchazy Carducci Pub.
Plato. (1992). *Protagoras/Plato*. Trans. by S. Lombardo and K. Bell with introduction by M. Frede. Indianapolis: Hackett Publishing Company Inc.
Plato. (1993a). 'Phaedo', in *The Last Days of Socrates*. Trans. by H. Tredennick and H. Tarrant, introduction and notes by H. Tarrant. Harmondsworth: Penguin Classics.
Plato. (1993b). *Plato, Phaedo*. Trans. by C.J. Rowe. Cambridge, Mass.: Cambridge University Press.
Plato. (1995). *Phaedrus*. Introduction by A. Nehamas and P. Woodruff. Indianapolis: Hackett Publishing Company Inc.
Plato. (1996). *Protagoras*. Trans. with notes by C.C.W. Taylor. Oxford: Oxford University Press.
Plato. (1997). *Plato's Cosmology: The Timaeus of Plato*. Trans. with commentary by F.M. Cornford. Cambridge: Hackett Publishing Company, Inc.
Plato. (2004). *Protagoras and Meno*. Trans. with notes and interpretive essays by R.C. Bartlett. Ithaca: Cornell University Press.
Proclus. (1820). *The Commentaries of Proclus: On the Timaeus of Plato, in Five Books; Containing a Treasury of Pythagoric and Platonic Physiology*. Trans. by T. Taylor. London: The author.
Vico, G. (1999). *New Science*. Trans. by D. Marsh and into. by A. Grafton. London: Penguin Books.

# Secondary Texts

Akkermann, A. (2013). 'Gender Myth and the Mind-City Composite: From Plaot's Atlantis to Walter Benjamin's Philosophical Urbanism', *GeoJournal*. 78 (4): 727–741.
Alcoff, L.M. and Mendieta, E. (eds.). (2000). *Thinking from the Underside of History: Enrique Dussel's Philosophy of Liberation*. Lanham: Roman & Littlefield.
Alcoff, L.M. and Caputo, J.D. (eds.). (2011). *Feminism, Sexuality, and the Return of Religion*. Bloomington: Indiana University Press.

Anderson, P.S. (2002). 'Myth and Feminist Philosophy' in *Thinking Through Myths – Philosophical Perspectives*. K. Schilbrack (ed.) London: Routledge, 101–122.
Anderson, D.G. (2014). 'Cultures of Reciprocity and Cultures of Control in the Circumpolar North'. *Journal of Northern Studies*. 9 (2): 11–27.
Annas, J. (1982). 'Plato's Myths of Judgment', *Phronesis* 27 (2): 119–143.
Arashiro, Z. and Barahona, M. (eds.). (2015). *Women in Academia Crossing North–South Borders*. Lanham: Lexington Books.
Araújo, M. and Maeso, S. (eds.). (2015). *Eurocentrism, Racism and Knowledge: Debates on History and Power in Europe and the Americas*. New York: Palgrave Macmillan.
Auerbach, E. (2003). *Mimesis: The Representation of Reality in Western Literature*. Trans. by W.R. Trask with introduction by E.W. Said. Princeton: Princeton University Press.
Babcock-Abrahams, B. (1975). 'A Tolerated Margin of Mess: The Trickster and his Tales Reconsidered', *Journal of the Folklore Institute* 11 (3): 147–186.
Bal, M. (1997). *Narratology: Introduction to the Theory of Narrative*. Toronto: University of Toronto Press.
Barash, J. A. (2011). 'Myth in History, Philosophy of History as Myth: On the Ambivalence of Hans Blumenberg's Interpretation of Ernst Cassirer's Theory of Myth', *History and Theory* 50: 328–340.
Barthes, R. (1975). *S/Z An Essay*. London: Hill and Wang.
Barthes, R. (1996). 'Introduction to the Structural Analysis of Narratives', in *Narratology. An Introduction*. S. Onega and J.A.G. Landa (eds.). London: Routledge, 45–60.
Benitez, E. E. (1995). 'The Good or the Demiurge: Causation and the Unity of the Good in Plato', *Apeiron* 28 (2): 113–140.
Benitez, E. (2007). 'Philosophy, Myth and Plato's Two-Worlds View', *The European Legacy* 12 (2): 225–242.
Benitez, E. (2016). 'Boy! What Boy? (A Plea for Meno's Slave)', *Ancient Philosophy* 36 (1): 107–114.
Bernal, M. (1987). 'The Fabrication of Ancient Greece, 1785–1985', in *Black Athena: The Afro-Asiatic Roots of Classical Civilization, Volume I*. New Brunswick: Rutgers University Press.
Bernal, M. (1991). 'The Archaeological and Documentary Evidence', in *Black Athena: The Afro-Asiatic Roots of Classical Civilization, Volume II*. New Brunswick: Rutgers University Press.
Bernal, M. (2001). *Black Athena Writes Back: Martine Bernal Responds to his Critics*. D.C. Moore (ed.). Durham: Duke University Press.

Bernal, M. (2006). 'The Linguistic Evidence', in *Black Athena: The Afro-Asiatic Roots of Classical Civilization, Volume III.* New Brunswick: Rutgers University Press.

Bernasconi, R. (1997). 'Philosophy's Paradoxical Parochialism: The Reinvention of Philosophy as Greek', in *Cultural Readings of Imperialism.* K. Ansell-Pearson, B. Parry and J. Squires (eds.). London: Lawrence & Wishart.

Bernasconi, R. (Spring 1995a). 'On Heidegger's other sins of omission: his exclusion of Asian thought from the origins of Occidental metaphysics and his denial of the possibility of Christian philosophy', *American Catholic Philosophical Quarterly* 69 (2): 333–350.

Bernasconi, R. (October 1995b). 'Heidegger and the invention of the Western philosophical tradition', *Journal of the British Society for Phenomenology* 26 (3): 240–254.

Bernasconi, R. (2000). 'Krimskrams: Hegel and the current controversy about the beginnings of philosophy', in *Interrogating the Tradition: Hermeneutics and the History of Philosophy.* C.E. Scott and J. Salis (eds.). Albany: SUNY Press, 191–208.

Bernasconi, R. (2002). 'Religious Philosophy: Hegel's occasional perplexity in the face of the distinction between philosophy and religion', *The Bulletin of the Hegel Society of Great Britain* 45/46: 1–15.

Bernasconi, R. (2003). 'With what must the history of philosophy begin? Hegel's role in the debate on the place of India within the history of philosophy', in *Hegel's History of Philosophy: New Interpretations.* D.A. Duquette (ed.). Albany: SUNY Press.

Bertens, H. (1995). *The Idea of the Postmodern: A History.* London: Routledge.

Bishop, R. (2005). 'Freeing ourselves from neo-colonial domination in research: A Kaupapa Māori approach to creating knowledge', in *The SAGE handbook of qualitative research* (3rd ed., pp. 109–138). N. K. Denzin and Y. S. Lincoln (eds.) Thousand Oaks, CA: Sage.

Blok, J. H. (1994). 'Quest for a Scientific Mythology: F. Creuzer and K.O. Müller on History and Myth', *History and Theory*, Vol. 33. No. 4, Theme Issue 33: Proof and Persuasion in History, 26–52.

Blondell, R. (2002). *The Play of Characters in Plato's Dialogues.* Cambridge: Cambridge University Press.

Bluck, R.S. (1964). *Plato's Meno.* Cambridge: Cambridge University Press.

Boedeker, D. (2002). 'Epic Heritage and Mythical Patterns in Herodotus', in *Brill's Companion to Herodotus.* E.J. Bakker, I.J.F. de Jong and H. van Wees (eds.) Leiden: Brill, 97–116.

Booth, W.C. (1987). *The Rhetoric of Fiction.* Harmondsworth: University of Chicago Press.

Bottici, C. (2007). *A Philosophy of Political Myth*. Cambridge: Cambridge University Press.
Bottici, C. and Challand, B. (2010). *The Myth of the Clash of Civilizations*. New York: Routledge.
Boys-Stones, G.R. and Haubold, J.H. (2009). *Plato and Hesiod*. Oxford: Oxford University Press.
Bremmer, J.N. (2010). The Greek Gods in the Twentieth Century, in J.N. Bremmer and A. Erskine (eds.). *The Gods of Ancient Greece: Identities and Transformations*. Edinburg: Edinburg University Press.
Bremmer, J.N. (2011). 'A Brief History of the Study of Greek Mythology', in *A Companion to Greek Mythology*. K. Dowden and N. Livingstone (eds.) Oxford: Wiley-Blackwell, 527–547.
Bremmer J.N. (2012) 'Introduction: The Greek Gods in the Twentieth Century'
Brennan, T. (2014). *Borrowed Light: Vico, Hegel, and the Colonies*. Stanford: Stanford University Press.
Brisson, L. (1998). *Plato the Myth Maker*. Chicago: University of Chicago Press.
Brisson, L. (2006). 'Platon et la cosmologie', *Cahiers critiques de philosophie* 3: 31–43.
Brochard, V. (1974). 'Les mythes dans la philsophie de Platon', *Etudes de philosophie ancienne et la philosophie modern*: 46–59.
Buck-Morrs, S. (Summer 2000). 'Hegel and Haiti', *Critical Inquiry* 26 (4): 821–865.
Burger, R. (1984). *The Phaedo: A Platonic Labyrinth*. New Haven: Yale University Press.
Burke, K. (1966). *Language as Symbolic Action: Essays on Life, Literature, and Method*. Berkeley: University of California Press.
Burke, K. (1970). *The Rhetoric of Religion: Studies in Logology*. Berkeley: University of California Press.
Burkert, W. (2007). *Babylon, Memphis, Persepolis: Eastern Contexts of Greek Culture*. Massachusetts: Harvard University Press.
Burnet, J. (2003). 'Pythagoras and Pythagoreanism', in *Encyclopedia of Religion and Ethics, Part 20*. J.R. Hastings and J.A. Selbie (eds.). Edinburgh: Kessinger Publishing.
Burnyeat, M.F. (2005). 'Eikos Muthos', *Rizai. A Journal for Ancient Philosophy and Science*. Issue 2: 143–165.
Buxton, R. (ed.). (1999). *From Myth to Reason? Studies in the Development of Greek Thought*. Oxford: Oxford University Press.
Campbell, J. (1949). *The Hero with a Thousand Faces*. New York: Pantheon Books.

Campbell, J. (1988). *An Open Life: Joseph Campbell in Conversation with Michael Toms*. J.M. Maher and D. Briggs (eds.). Burdett: Larson Publications.
Capps, W.H. (1995). *Religious Studies, The Making of a Discipline*. Minneapolis: Fortress Press.
Capra, A. (2010). 'Plato's Hesiod and the Will of Zeus: Philosophical Rhapsody in *the Timaeus and the Critias*', in *Plato and Hesiod*, G.R. Boys-Stone and J.H. Haubold. (eds.) Oxford: Oxford University Press, 200–218.
Carroll, N. (2001). 'Interpretation, History, and Narrative', in *Beyond Aesthetics – Philosophical Essays*, N. Carroll (ed.) Cambridge: Cambridge University Press, 133–156.
Carroll, N. (2006). *Philosophy of Film and Motion Pictures – An Anthology*. N. Carroll and J. Choi (eds.) Oxford: Wiley-Blackwell, 7–18.
Cassirer, E. (1946). *Language and Myth*. S.K. Langer (trans.). New York: Harper & Bros.
Cassirer, E. (1955). *The Philosophy of Symbolic Forms, Vol. 2: Mythical Thought*. New Haven: Yale University Press.
Cassirer, E. (1961). *Myth of the State*. New Haven: Yale University Press.
Chance, J. (1994). *Medieval Mythography: From Roman North Africa to the School of Chartes, AD 433–1177*. Gainesville: University Press of Florida.
Clay, D. (1997). 'The Plan of Plato's Critias', in *Interpreting the Timaeus-Critias: Proceeding of the IV Symposium Platonicum – Selected Papers*. T. Calvo Martinez and L. Brisson (eds.). Sankt Augustin: Academia Verlag, 49–54.
Coleman, D., Glanville, E.G., Hasan, W. and Kramer-Hamstra, A. (eds.). (2012a). *Countering Displacements: The Creativity and Resilience of Indigenous and Refugee-ed Peoples*. Alberta: The University of Alberta Press.
Coleman, D., Battiste, M., Henderson, S., Findlay, I.M. and Findlay, L. (March 2012b). 'Different Knowings and the Indigenous Humanities', *English Studies in Canada*, 38 (1): 141–159.
Collobert, C. (2012). 'Epistemic Status and Functions of Platonic Myth', in *Plato and Myth: Studies on the Use and Status of Platonic Myth*. C. Collobert, P. Destrée, F.J. Gonzalez (eds.). Leiden: Brill, 87–108.
Collobert, C., Destrée, P. and Gonzalez, F.J. (2012). 'Introduction', in *Plato and Myth: Studies on the Use and Status of Platonic Myth*. C. Collobert, P. Destrée, and F.J. Gonzalez. (eds.). Leiden: Brill, 1–12.
Colloud-Streit, M. (2005). *Funf platonische Mythen im Verhaltnis zu ihrem Textumfeldern*. Fribourg: Academic Press.
Compton, T.M. (2006). *Victim of the Muses – Poet as Scapegoat, Warrior and Hero in Greco-Roman and Indo-European Myth and History*. Washington D.C.: Center for Hellenic Studies.

Connell, R. (2007). *Southern Theory: The Global Dynamics of Knowledge in Social Sciences*. Crows Nest: Allen & Unwin.
Cook, W.W. and Tatum, J. (2010). *African American Writers and Classical Tradition*. Chicago: University of Chicago Press.
Coupe, L. (2006). *Myth*. London: Routledge.
Crombie, I.M. (1971). *An Examination of Plato's Doctrines*. London: Routledge & Kegan Paul.
Cruikshank, J. (1998). *The Social Life of Stories. Narrative and Knowledge in Northern Canada*. Lincoln: University of Nebraska Press and Vancouver, UBC Pres.
Csapo, E. (2005). *Theories of Mythology*. Oxford: Wiley-Blackwell.
Cupitt, D. (2002). *Is Nothing Sacred? The Non-Realist Philosophy of Religion: Selected Essays*. New York: Fordham University Press.
Currie, G. (2006). 'Unleliability Refigured: Narrative in Literature and Film', in *Philosophy of Film and Motion Pictures – An Anthology*. N. Carroll and J. Choi (eds.). Oxford: Wiley-Blackwell, 200–210.
Day, J. (1988). *Plato's Meno in Focus*. London: Routledge.
de Jong, I.J.F. (2004a, org. published 1987). *Narrators and Focalizers: The Presentation of the Story in the Illiad*. London: Bristol Classical Press.
de Jong, I.J.F. (2004b). *Narrators, Narratees, and Narratives in Ancient Greek Literature – Studies in Ancient Greek Narrative, Volume One*. I.J.F. de Jong, R. Nunlist and A. Bowie (eds.). Leiden: Brill, 1–10.
De Luise, F. (2007). 'Il mito di Er: significati morali', in *La Republica, libro X*. M. Vegetti (ed.). Napoli: Bibliopolis, 311–366.
Denzin, N.K., Lincoln, Y.S. and Smith, L.T. (2008). *Handbook of Critical and Indigenous Methodologies*. London: Sage Publications.
de Sousa Santos, B. (ed.). (2007). *Cognitive Justice in a Global World: Prudent Knowledges for a Decent Life*. Lanham: Lexington Books.
de Sousa Santos, B. (2014). *Epistemologies of the South: Justice Against Epistemicide*. London: Routledge.
De Vries, J. (1969). *A Commentary on the Phaedrus of Plato*. Amsterdam: Adolf M. Hakkert.
Detienne, M. (1981). *L'Invention de la mythologie*. Paris: Gallimard.
Detienne, M. (1986). *The Creation of Mythology*. M. Cook (trans.). Chicago: Chicago University Press.
Detienne, M. (2009). *Les grecs et nous*. Paris: Perrin.
Detienne, M. (1972). *The Gardens of Adonis: Spices in Greek Mythology*. Trans. by J. Lloyd and into. by J. Vernant. Princeton: Princeton University Press.
Dillon, J. (2003). *The Heirs of Plato: A Study of the Old Academy (347–274 BC)*. Oxford: Clarendon Press.

Dorter, K. (1982). *Plato's Phaedo: An Interpretation*. Toronto: University of Toronto Press.

Doty, W. (1986). *Mythography*. Alabama: University Alabama Press.

Doty, W. (2003) 'What's a Myth? Nomological, Topological, and Taxonomic Explorations', *Soundings: An Interdisciplinary Journal*. Vol. 86, No. ¾ (Fall/Winter): 391–419.

Drake, S. (1987). *Black Folk Here and There: An Essay in History and Anthropology, Vol. 1*. Los Angeles: University of California.

Droz, G. (1992). *Les Mythes platoniciens*. Paris: Éditions du Seuil.

Dundes. A. (ed.). (1984). *Sacred Narrative. Readings in the Theory of Myth*. Berkeley: University of California Press.

Ebert, T. (2002). 'Wenn ich einen schonen Mythos vortragen arf… Zu Status, Herkunft und Funktion des Schlussmythos' in *Platons Phaedon. Platon als Mythologe. Neue Interpretationen zu den Mythen in Platons Dialogen*. M. Janka and C. Schafer (eds). Darmstadt: Wissenschaftliche Buchgesellschaft: 251–269.

Ebert, T. (2003). 'The Role of the Frame Dialogue in Plato's Protagoras', in *Plato's Protagoras – Proceedings of the Third Symposium Platonicum Pragense*. Havlicek, A. and Karfik F. (eds.). Prague.

Eckstein, J. (1968). *The Platonic Method: An Interpretation of the Dramatic-Philosophic Aspects of the Meno*. New York: Greenwood Publishing Corporation.

Edelstein, L. (1949). 'The Function of the Myth in Plato's Philosophy', *Journal of the History of Ideas* 10 (4): 463–481.

Edmonds, III, R.G. (2004). *Myths of the Underworld Journey: Plato, Aristophanes, and the 'Orphic' Gold Tablets*. Cambridge: Cambridge University Press.

Edmonds, III, R.G. (2012). 'Whip Scars on the Naked Soul: Myth and Elenchus in Plato's Gorgias', in *Plato and Myth: Studies on the Use and Status of Platonic Myth*. C. Collobert, P. Destrée, F.J. Gonzalez (eds.). Leiden: Brill, 165–186.

Emeagwali, G. and Sefa Dei, G.J. (eds.). (2014). *African Indigenous Knowledge and the Disciplines*. Rotterdam: Sense Publishers.

Feldman, B. and Richardson, R.D. (1972). *The Rise of Modern Mythology: 1680–1860*. Bloomington: Indiana University Press.

Ferguson, K. (2008). *The Music of Pythagoras: How an Ancient Brotherhood Cracked the Code of the Universe and Lit the Path from Antiquity to Outer Space*. New York: Walker Books.

Ferrari, G.R.F. (1987). *Listening to the Cicadas – A Study of Plato's Phaedrus*. Cambridge: Cambridge University Press.

Ferrari, G.R.F. (2009). 'Glaucon's Reward, Philosophy's Debt: The Myth of Er', in *Plato's Myths,* C. Partenie (ed). Cambridge: Cambridge University Press, 116–133.
Ferrari, G.R.F. (2012). 'The Freedom of Platonic Myth', in *Plato and Myth: Studies on the Use and Status of Platonic Myth.* C. Collobert, P. Destrée, F.J. Gonzalez (eds.). Leiden: Brill, 67–86.
Fink, D. (2014) *The Battle of Marathon in Scholarship: Research, Theories and Controversies Since 1850.* Jefferson: McFarland.
Finkelberg, A. (1996). 'Plato's Method in Timaeus', *The American Journal of Philology* 17 (3): 391–409.
Flaig, E. (2003). 'Towards 'Rassenhygiene': Wilamowitz and the German New Right', in *Out of Arcadia: Classics and Politics in Germany in the Age of Burckhardt, Nietzsche and Wilamowitz.* I. Goldenhard, I. and M. Ruehl. (eds). London: Institute of Classical Studies, 105–129.
Flood, C. (2002). 'Myth and Ideology', in *Thinking Through Myths – Philosophical Perspectives.* K. Schilbrack (ed.). London: Routledge, 174–190.
Forsyth, P. Y. (1980). *Atlantis: The Making of the Myth.* London: Croom Helm.
Fowler, R.L. (2011) 'Mythos and Logos', *Journal of Hellenic Studies* 131: 45–66.
Fredericks, S.C. (1978). 'Plato's Atlantis: A Mythologist Looks at Myth', in *Atlantis: Fact or Fiction?* E. Ramage (ed.). Bloomington: Indiana University Press.
Fredericks, S.C. (1980) 'Greek Mythology in Modern Science Fiction', in *Classical Mythology in Twentieth Century Thought and Fiction.* W. Aycock and T. Klein (eds.). Lubbock: Texas Tech Press.
Fricker, M. (2007) *Epistemic Injustice: Power, and the Ethics of Knowing.* Oxford: Oxford University Press.
Frutiger, P. (1930). *Mythes de Platon: Etude philosophique et litteraire.* Paris: Librairie Felix Alcan.
Frye, N. (1957). *Anatomy of Criticism: Four Essays.* Princeton: Princeton University Press.
Furley, D. (1987). *The Greek Cosmologists – Volume 1, the Formation of the Atomic Theory and its Earliest Critics.* Cambridge: Cambridge University Press.
Gantz, T. (1993). *Early Greek Myth: A Guide to Literary and Artistic Sources.* Baltimore: Johns Hopkins University Press.
Gates Jr., H.L. (1988). *The Signifying Monkey: A Theory of African-American Literary Criticism.* Oxford: Oxford University Press.
Gaster, T.H. (1954). 'Myth and Story', *Numen,* 1: 184–212.
Genette, G. (1980). *Narrative Discourse: An Essay in Method.* Ithaca: Cornell University Press.

Genette, G. (1982). *Figures of Literary Discourse*. Trans. by A. Sheridan and intro. by M. Logan. New York: Blackwell Publishers.

Genette, G. (1988). *Narrative Discourse Revisited*. Ithaca: Cornell University Press.

Genette, G. (1992). *The Architext: An Introduction*. Trans. by J.E. Lewin. Berkley: University of California Press.

Gerhart, M. and Russell, A.M. (2002). 'Myth and Public Science', in *Thinking Through Myths – Philosophical Perspectives*. K. Schilbrack (ed.). London: Routledge, 191–206.

Gill, A. (1977). 'The Genre of the Atlantis Story', *Classical Philology*, 72 (4.): 287–304.

Gill, C. (1992). 'Dogmatic Dialogue in Phaedrus *276–7*', in *Understanding the Phaedrus: Proceedings of the II Symposium Platonicum*. L. Rossetti (ed.). Cambridge: Academia Verlag.

Gilroy, P. (1993). *The Black Atlantic: Modernity and Double Consciousness*. London: Verso.

Goldenhard, I. and Ruehl, M. (eds). (2003). *Out of Arcadia: Classics and Politics in Germany in the Age of Burckhardt, Nietzsche and Wilamowitz*. London: Institute of Classical Studies.

Gonzales, F. (2012). 'Combating Oblivion: The Myth of Er as Both Philosophy's Challenge and Inspiration', in *Plato and Myth: Studies on the Use and Status of Platonic Myths*. C. Collobert, P. Destrée, F.J. Gonzalez (eds.). Leiden: Brill, 259–278.

Goody, J. (2007). *The Theft of History*. Cambridge: Cambridge University Press.

Gould, E. (1981). *Mythical Intentions in Modern Literature*. Princeton: Princeton University Press.

Gould, T. (1990). *The Ancient Quarrel between Poetry and Philosophy*. Princeton: Princeton University Press.

Griswold, C. (1986). *Self-Knowledge in Plato's Phaedrus*. New Haven: Yale University Press.

Grosfoguel, R. (2013). 'The Structure of Knowledge in Westernized Universities: Epistemic Racism/Sexism and the Four Genocides/Epistemicides of the Long 16th Century', *Human Architecture: Journal of the Sociology of Self-Knowledge* 11 (1): 73–90.

Grounds, R.A., Tinker, G.E. and Wilkins, D.E. (eds). (2003). *Native Voices: American Indian Identity and Resistance*. Lawrence: University Press of Kansas.

Hack, R.K. (1935). 'Les Mythes de Platon: Etude philosophique et litteraire' by Percival Frutiger, *Classical Philology.* 30 (3): 270–272.

Halbfass, W. (1998). *India and Europe: An Essay in Understanding*. Albany: SUNY Press.
Hawes, G. (2014). *Rationalizing Myth in Antiquity*. Oxford: Oxford University Press.
Hendry, J. and Fitznor, L. (eds.). (2012). *Anthropologists, Indigenous Scholars and the Research Endevour: Seeking Bridges Toward Mutual Respect*. New York: Routledge.
Hartle, A. (1986). *Death and the Disinterested Spectator – An Inquiry into the Nature of Philosophy*. Albany: SUNY Press.
Hatab, L. (1990). *Myth and Philosophy: A Contest of Truths*. Illinois: Open Court Publishing Company.
Hatab, L. (2005). *Nietzsche's Life Sentence: Coming to Terms with Eternal Recurrence*. New York: Routledge.
Herder, J. G. (1968). *Reflections on the Philosophy of History of Mankind*. F.E. Manuel (trans.). Chicago: University of Chicago Press.
Huffman, C.L. (1993). *Philolaus of Croton, Pythagorean and Presoctratic*. Cambridge: Cambridge University Press.
Hynes, W.J. and Doty W. (eds.). (1993). 'Introducing the Fascinating and Perplexing Trickster Figure', in *Mythical Trickster Figures: Contours, Contexts, and Criticisms*. London: University Alabama Press.
Ionescu, C. (2007). *Plato's Meno: An Interpretation*. Maryland: Lexington Books.
Jackson, S.N. (2012). *Creole Indigeneity: Between Myth and Nation in the Caribbean*. Minneapolis: University of Minnesota Press.
Jakobson, R. (1985). *Selected Writings. Volume IV: Contributions to Comparative Mythology*. S. Rudy (ed.). New York: Mouton.
Janka, M. (2002). 'Sematik und Kontext: Mythos and Verwandtes im Corpus Platonicum' in *Platon als Mythologe. Neue Interpretationen zu den Mythen in Platons Dialogen*. M. Janka and C. Schafer (eds). Darmstadt: Wissenschaftliche Buchgesellschaft, 29–43.
Janka, M. and Schafer C. (eds.). (2002). *Platon als Mythologe. Neue Interpretationen zu den Mythen in Platons Dialogen*. Darmstadt: Wissenschaftliche Buchgesellschaft.
Jean-Marie, V. (2013). 'Kant and Trouillot on the Unthinkability of the Haitian Revolution', *Souls* 15 (3): 241–257.
Johansen, T.K. (2004). *Plato's Natural Philosophy – A Study of the Timaeus-Critias*. Cambridge: Cambridge University Press.
King, R. (1999). *Indian Philosophy: An Introduction to Hindu and Buddhist Thought*. Washington, DC: Georgetown University Press.
Kirk, G.S. (1970). *Myth: Its Meaning and Functions in Ancient and Other Cultures*. Cambridge: Cambridge University Press.

Kirk, G.S. (1984). 'On Defining Myths', in *Sacred Narratives: Readings in the Theory of Myth*. A. Dundes (ed.). Berkeley: University of California Press, 53–61.

Klein, J. (1989). *A Commentary on Plato's Meno*. Chicago: University of Chicago Press.

Kluckhohn. C. (1942). 'Myths and Rituals: A General Theory', *Harvard Theological Review*. 35: 45–79.

Kobusch, T. (2002). 'Die Wiederkehr des Mythos. Zur Funktion des Mythos in Platons Denken und in der Philosophie der Gegenwart', in *Platon als Mythologe. Neue Interpretationen zu den Mythen in Platons Dialogen*. M. Janka and C. Schafer (eds). Darmstadt: Wissenschaftliche Buchgesellschaft, 44–57.

Kovach, M. (2009). *Indigenous Methodologies: Characteristics, Conversations, and Contexts*. Toronto: University of Toronto Press.

Kovacs, G. and Marshall, C.W. (eds.). (2011). *Classics and Comics. Classical Presences*. Oxford: Oxford University Press.

Landry, E. (2012). 'Recollection and the Mathematician's Method in Plato's Meno', *Philosophia Mathematica* (III) 20: 143–169.

Larivée, A. (2012). 'Choice of Life and Self-Transformation in the Myth of Er', in *Plato and Myth: Studies on the Use and Status of Platonic Myth (Mnemosyne Supplements, 337)*. C. Collobert, P. Destrée, F.J. Gonzalez (eds.). Leiden: Brill, 235–258.

Le Doeuff, M. (1989). *The Philosophical Imaginary*. Stanford: The Athlone Press.

Lefkowitz, M.R. and Rogers, G.M. (eds.). (1996). *Black Athena Revisited*. Chapel Hill: University of North Carolina Press.

Lentricchia, F. (1980). *After the New Criticism*. London: University of Chicago Press.

Lévi-Strauss, C. (1955). 'The Structural Study of Myth', *The Journal of American Folklore* 68 (270): 428–444.

Lévi-Strauss, C. (1963). *Structural Anthropology*. C. Jacobson and B.G. Schoepf (trans.). New York: Basic Books.

Lévi-Strauss, C. (1966). *The Savage Mind*. Chicago: The University of Chicago Press.

Lévi-Strauss C. (1969). *The Elementary Structures of Kinship*. Revised Edition. J.H.B. Bell (trans.), J.R. von Strummer and R. Needham (eds.). London: Beacon Press.

Lévi-Strauss, C. (1973). *Totemism*. Harmondsworth: Penguin Books.

Levin, S.B. (2001). *The Ancient Quarrel Between Philosophy and Poetry Revisited: Plato and the Greek Literary Tradition*. Oxford: Oxford University Press.

Lincoln, B. (1989). *Discourse and the Construction of Society: Comparative Studies of Myth, Ritual, and Classification*. New York: Oxford University Press.

Lincoln, B. (1999). *Theorizing Myth: Narrative, Ideology, and Scholarship*. Chicago: University of Chicago Press.
Lock, H. (2003). *Transformations of the Trickster*, www.southerncrossreview.org/18/trickster.htm, retrieved on September 2007.
Louis, M.K. (2005). 'Gods and Mysteries: The Revival of Paganism and the Remaking of Mythography through the Nineteenth Century', *Victorian Studies* 47 (3): 329–361.
Lundquist, S.E. (1991). *The Trickster: A Transformation Archetype*. San Francisco: Edwin Mellen Press.
Maaka, R.C.A. and Anderson, C. (eds.). (2006). *The Indigenous Experience: Global Perspectives*. Ontario: Canadian Scholars' Press.
Manuwald, B. (2002). 'Platons Mythenerzahler', in *Platon als Mythologe. Neue Interpretationen zu den Mythen in Platons Dialogen*. M. Janka and C. Schafer (eds). Darmstadt: Wissenschaftliche Buchgesellschaft, 58–80.
Marchand, S.L. and Grafton, A. (1997). 'Martin Bernal and His Critics', *Arion* 5 (2): 1–35.
Marchand, S. (2003). *Down From Olympus" Archaeology and Philhellenism in Germany, 1750–1970*. Princeton: Princeton University Press.
Martin, K.L. (2003). 'Ways of Knowing, Ways of Being and Ways of Doing: a theoretical framework and methods for Indigenous re-search and Indigenist research', in 'Voicing Dissent' *New Talents 21C: Next Generation Australian Studies*. K. McWilliam, P. Stephenson and G. Thomspon (eds.). *Journal of Australian Studies*, No. 76: 203–214.
Martin, K.L. (2008). *Please Knock Before You Enter: Aboriginal Regulation of Outsiders and the Implications for Researchers*. Teneriffe, Qld: Post Pressed.
Mason, H. (1980). 'Myth as an 'Ambush of Reality'', *Olson*: 15–19.
Mattei, J. (1988). 'The Theatre of Myth in Plato', in *Platonic Writings, Platonic Readings*. C.L Griswold Jr., (ed.). New York: Routledge.
McGrath, E. (2009). 'Platonic Myths in Renaissance Iconography', in *Plato's Myths*. C. Partenie, (ed.). Cambridge: Cambridge University Press.
Mehta, J.L. (1985). 'The Concept of Progress', in *India and the West – Selected Essays of J.L. Mehta*. California: Scholars Pr.
Mignolo, W. (2011). *The Darker Side of Western Modernity: Global Futures, Decolonial Options*. Durham: Duke University Press Books.
Mills, C.W. (1997). *The Racial Contract*. Ithaca: Cornell University Press.
Moellendorf, D. (Summer 1992). 'Racism and rationality in Hegel's philosophy of subjective spirit', *History of Political Thought* 13 (2): 243–255.
Moors, K. (1982). *Platonic Myth: An Introductory Study*. Washinton, DC: University Press of America.

Morgan, K.A. (1998). 'Designer History: Plato's Atlantis Story and Fourth-Century Ideology', *Journal of Hellenic Studies* 118: 101–118.
Morgan, K.A. (2000). *Myth and Philosophy from the pre-Socratics to Plato*. Cambridge: Cambridge University Press.
Morgan, K.A. (2004). 'Plato', in *Narrators, Narratees, and Narratives in Ancient Greek Literature – Studies in Ancient Greek Narrative*, Volume One. I.J.F. de Jong, R. Nunlist and A. Bowie (eds.). Leiden: Brill, 357–374.
Morgan, K.A. (2010). 'The Voice of Authority: Divination and Plato's Phaedo.', *The Classical Quarterly* 60 (1): 63–81.
Morgan, M. L. (1992). 'Plato and Greek Religion', in *The Cambridge Companion to Plato*. R. Kraut (ed.). Cambridge: Cambridge University Press.
Mosse, G. (1985). *Toward the Final Solution: A History of European Racism*. Madison: University of Wisconsin Press.
Most, G. (2002). 'Platons Exoterische Mythen', in *Platon als Mythologe. Neue Interpretationen zu den Mythen in Platons Dialogen*. M. Janka and C. Schafer (eds). Darmstadt: Wissenschaftliche Buchgesellschaft, 7–19.
Most, G. (2012). 'Plato's Exoteric Myths', in *Plato and Myth: Studies on the Use and Status of Platonic Myth*. C. Collobert, P. Destrée, F.J. Gonzalez (eds.). Leiden: Brill, 13–24.
Müller, M. (1882). *Introduction to the Science of Religion;* four lectures delivered at the Royal Institution, February 19. London.
Murray, P. (2011). 'Platonic 'Myths', in *A Companion to Greek Mythology*. K. Dowden and N. Livingstone (eds.) Oxford: Wiley-Blackwell, 179–194.
Nakata, M. (2007). *Disciplining the Savages – Savaging the Disciplines*. Canberra: Aboriginal Studies Press.
Nakata, M. (1998). 'Anthropological Texts and Indigenous Standpoints', in *Australian Aboriginal Studies* 2: 3–12.
Nakata, M. (2004). 'Ongoing Conversations about Aboriginal and Torres Strait Islander Research Agendas and Directions', in *Australian Journal of Indigenous Education, The* 33: 1–6.
Nakata, N.M., Nakata, V., Keech, S. and Bolt, R. (2012). 'Decolonial Goals and Pedagogies for Indigenous Studies', in *Decolonization: Indigeneity, Education & Society* 1 (1): 120–140.
Nicholson, G. (1999). *Plato's Phaedrus*. Indiana: Purdue University Press.
Olender, M. (1992). *The Languages of Paradise: Race, Religion, and Philology in the Nineteenth Century*. A. Goldhammer (trans.). Cambridge: Harvard University Press.
Omidsalar, M. (1993). 'Of the Usurper's Ears, the Demon's Toes, and the Ayatollah's Fingers', in *The Psychoanalytic Study of Society: Essays in Honour of*

*Alan Dundes.* L. B. Boyer, R. M. Boyer and S.M. Sonnenberg (eds.). Hillsdale: Analytic Press.
Osborne, C. (1996). 'Space, Time, Shape, and Direction: Creative Discourse in the Timaeus', in *Form and Argument in Late Plato*. C. Gill and M. M. McCabe (eds.). Oxford: Oxford University Press.
Park, P.K.J. (2013). *Africa, Asia, and the Philosophy of History: Racism in the Formation of the Philosophical Canon, 1780–1830*. Albany: SUNY Press.
Partenie, C. (2011). *Plato's Myths*. Cambridge: Cambridge University Press.
Patterson, R. L. (1965). *Plato on Immortality*. University Park: The Pennsylvania State University Press.
Paul, H. (2009). 'Hayden White and the Crisis of Historicism', in: *Re-Figuring Hayden White*. F. Ankersmit, E. Domańska, and H. Kellner (eds.). Stanford: Stanford University Press, 54–73.
Pender, E.E. (2000). *Images of Persons Unseen: Plato's Metaphors for the Gods and the Soul*. Sankt Augustin: Academia Verlag
Piaget, J. (1970). *Structuralism*. C. Maschler (trans. and ed.) New York: Basic Books.
Power, W.L. (2002). 'Myth and Pragmatic Semiotics', in *Thinking Through Myths – Philosophical Perspectives*. K. Schilbrack (ed.). London: Routledge, 65–84.
Price, W. (1992). 'Reason's New Role in the Phaedrus', in *Understanding the Phaedrus*. Rossetti, L. (ed.). Cambridge: Academia Verlag.
Propp, V. (1968). *Morphology of the Folktale*, second edition. Austin: University of Texas Press.
Pugliese, M. (2013). *Rewriting Medea. Toni Morrison and Liz Lochhead's Postmodern Perspectives*. Florida: Universal Publishers.
Quijano, A. (2007). 'Coloniality and Modernity/Rationality', *Cultural Studies* 21 (2–3): 168–178.
Radin, P. (1956). *The Trickster: A Study in American Indian Mythology*. London: Bell.
Rankine, P.D. (2006). *Ulysses in Black: Ralph Ellison, Classicism, and African American Literature*. London: University of Wisconsin Press.
Ricoeur, P. (1965). *History and Truth*. Evanston: Northwestern University Press.
Ricoeur, P. (1988). *Time and Narrative*. Chicago: University of Chicago Press.
Rigney, L. (2006). 'Indigenist Research and Aboriginal Australia', in *Indigenist Peoples' Wisdom and Power: Affirming Our Knowledge Through Narratives.'* J.E. Kunnie and N.I. Goduka (eds.). Hampshire: Ashgate, 32–50.
Ronnick, M.V. (ed.). (2006) *The Works of William Sanders Scarborough. Black Classicist and Race Leader*. Oxford: Oxford University Press.

Rosen, S. (1988). *The Quarrel Between Philosophy and Poetry: Studies in Ancient Thought*. New York: Routledge.
Rowe, C.J. (2007). *Plato and the Art of Philosophical Writing*. Cambridge: Cambridge University Press.
Rowe, C.J. (2012). 'The Status of Myth in the *Gorgias* or: Taking Plato Seriously', in *Plato and Myth: Studies on the Use and Status of Platonic Myth*. C. Collobert, P. Destrée, F.J. Gonzalez (eds.). Leiden: Brill, 187–198.
Ruehl, (2003). '*Politeia* 1871: Nietzsche *contra* Wagner on the Greek State', in *Out of Arcadia: Classics and Politics in Germany in the Age of Burckhardt, Nietzsche and Wilamowitz*. I. Goldenhard and M. Ruehl. (eds). London: Institute of Classical Studies, 61–86.
Runia, D.T. (1997). 'The Literary and Philosophical Status of Timaeus' Prooemium', in *Interpreting the Timaeus-Critias, Proceeding of the IV Symposium Platonicum:* selected papers. T. Calvo and L.Brisson. (eds.). Sankt Augustin: Academia Verlag, 101–118.
Russell, W.M.S. (1991). '"A Funny Thing Happened...." Humour in Greek and Roman Life, Literature and Theatre', in *Spoken in Jest*. G. Bennett (ed.). Sheffield: Sheffield Academic Press for the Folklore Society.
Saal, B. (2013). 'How to Leave Modernity Behind: The Relationship Between Colonialism and Enlightenment, and the Possibility of Altermodern Decoloniality', *Budhi: A Journal of Ideas and Culture* 17 (1): 49–80.
Santas, G. (1992). 'The Theory of Eros in Socrates' Second Speech', in *Understanding the Phaedrus*. L. Rossetti (ed.). Cambridge: Academia Verlag.
Saussure, F. de. (1983). *Course in General Linguistics*. Chicago: Open Court.
Scarborough, M. (2002). 'Myth and Phenomenology', in *Thinking Through Myths – Philosophical Perspectives*. K. Schilbrack (ed.). London: Routledge, 46–64.
Scarborough, W.S. (2005). *The Autobiography of William Sanders Scarborough: An American Journey from Slavery to Scholarship*. M.V. Ronnick (ed). Detroit: Wayne State University Press.
Scheub, H. (2012). *Trickster and Hero: Two Characters in the Oral and Written Traditions of the World*. London: University of Wisconsin Press.
Schilbrack, K. (ed.) (2002a). *Thinking Through Myths – Philosophical Perspectives*. London: Routledge.
Schilbrack, K. (2002b). 'Introduction: on the use of philosophy in the study of myths', in *Thinking Through Myths – Philosophical Perspectives*, K. Schilbrack (ed.). London: Routledge, 1–17.
Schilbrack, K. (2002c). 'Myth and metaphysics', in *Thinking Through Myths – Philosophical Perspectives*, K. Schilbrack (ed.). London: Routledge, 85–100.

Schilbrack, K. (ed.). (2004a). *Thinking Through Rituals – Philosophical Perspectives*. London: Routledge.
Schilbrack, K. (2004b). 'Introduction: on the use of philosophy in the study of rituals', in *Thinking Through Rituals – Philosophical Perspectives*, K. Schilbrack (ed.). London: Routledge, 1–30.
Schilbrack, K. (2004c). 'Ritual metaphysics', in *Thinking Through Myths – Philosophical Perspectives*, K. Schilbrack (ed.). London: Routledge, 128–147.
Schmitt, A. (2002). 'Mythos und Vernunft bei Platon' in *Platon als Mythologe. Neue Interpretationen zu den Mythen in Platons Dialogen*. M. Janka and C. Schafer (eds). Darmstadt: Wissenschaftliche Buchgesellschaft, 290–309.
Schmitz, T.A. (2007). *Modern Literary Theory and Ancient Texts*. Oxford: Wiley-Blackwell.
Scolnicov, S. (1992). 'Love and the Method of Hypothesis', in *Understanding the Phaedrus*. L. Rossetti (ed.). Cambridge: Academic Verlag.
Scott, D. (2006). *Plato's Meno*. Cambridge: Cambridge University Press.
Sedley, D. (1990). 'Teleology and Myth in the Phaedo', in *Proceedings of the Boston Area Colloquium in Ancient Philosophy 5*. C. Partenie (ed.): 359–83.
Segal, R.A. (ed.). (1990). *In Quest of the Hero*. Princeton: Princeton University Press.
Segal, R.A. (1999). *Theorizing About Myth*. Amherst: University of Massachusetts Press.
Segal, R.A. (2004). *Myth: A Very Short Introduction*. Oxford: Oxford University Press.
Segal, R.A. (2002). 'Myth as Primitive Philosophy: The Case of E.B. Tylor' in *Thinking Through Myths – Philosophical Perspectives*. K. Schilbrack (ed.). London: Routledge, 18–45.
Semali, L. M., & Kincheloe, J. L. (1999). 'Introduction: What is indigenous knowledge and why should we study it?' in *What is indigenous knowledge? Voices from the academy* (pp. 3–57). L. M. Semali, ed. & J. L. Kincheloe (Eds.) New York: Falmer.
Sharpe, E.J. (1975). *Comparative Religion: A History*. London: Macmillan Pub Co.
Sillitoe, P. (2005). *Indigenous Studies and Engaged Anthropology: The Collaborative Moment*. Farnham: Ashgate.
Simmons, E. (2013). *Indigenous Earth: Praxis and Transformation*. Penticton, BC: Theytus Books.
Smith, L. T. (1999). *Decolonizing methodologies: Research and indigenous peoples*. Dunedin, New Zealand: University of Otago Press.
Smith, C. and Wobst, H.M. (2005). *Indigenous Archaeologies: Decolonizing Theory and Practice*. New York: Routledge.

Snell, B. (1953). *The Discovery of the Mind*. Oxford: Blackwell.
Sternfeld, R. and Zyskind H. (1978). *Plato's Meno: A Philosophy of Man as Acquisitive*. Carbondale: Southern Illinois University Press.
Stewart, J.A. (trans.) (1905). *The Myths of Plato*. London: Centaur Press.
Strenski, I. (1987). *Four Theories of Myth in the Twentieth-Century History, Cassirer, Eliade, Lévi-Strauss and Malinowski*. Iowa City: University of Iowa Press.
Tanner, R.G. (1992). 'Plato's Phaedrus: An Educational Manifesto?', in *Understanding the Phaedrus*. L. Rossetti (ed.). Cambridge: Academic Verlag.
Tarrant, H. (2005). *Recollecting Plato's Meno*. London: Bristol Classical Press.
Tarrant, H., Benitez, E. and Roberts, T. (2011). 'The Mythical Voice in the Timaeus-Critias: Stylometric Indicators', *Ancient Philosophy* 31: 95–120.
Tarrant, H. (2012). 'Logos, Mythos, and Explanatory Values. From the Protagoras to the Timaeus-Critias', in *Literal and Deeper Meaning in Platonic Myths*. C. Collobert, P. Destrée, F.J. Gonzalez (eds.). Leiden: Brill, 47–66.
Thein, K. (2003). 'Teleology and Myth in the Protagoras', in *Plato's Protagoras – Proceedings of the Third Symposium Platonicum Pragense*. A. Havlicek and F. Karfik (eds.). Prague.
Thomas, J.E. (1980). *Musings on the Meno*. The Hague: Springer.
Thompson, E.S. (1901). *The Meno of Plato*. London: Kessinger Publishing.
Tofighian, O. (2009). 'Rethinking Plato's Theory of Art: Aesthetics and the Timaeus', *Literature and Aesthetics* 19 (2): 25–40.
Tofighian, O. (2010). 'Beyond the Myth/Philosophy Dichotomy. Foundations for an Interdependent Perspective', *Forum Philosophicum* 15 (1): 175–190.
Tofighian, O. (2013). 'Contemporary Liminal Encounters: Moving Beyond Traditional Plots in Majidi's *Baran*', in *Conflict and Development in Iranian Film*. A.A. Seyed-Gohrab and K. Talattof (eds.). Leiden: Leiden University Press.
Tolkien, J.R.R. (1966). *The Tolkien Reader*. New York: Penguin Random House.
Turner, V. (1969). *The Ritual Process – Structure and Anti-Structure*. Chicago: Aldine.
Turner, V. (1974). *Dramas, Fields and Metaphors*. Ithaca: Cornell University Press.
van Ophuijsen, J. M., van Raalte, M. and Stork, P. (eds.) (2013). *Protagoras of Abdera: The Man, His Measure*. Philosophia Antiqua, 134. Leiden: Brill.
Van Riel, G. (2012). 'Religion and Morality. Elements of Plato's Anthropology in the Myth of Prometheus', in *Plato and Myth: Studies on the Use and Status of Platonic Myth*. C. Collobert, P. Destrée, F.J. Gonzalez (eds.). Leiden: Brill, 145–164.

Vernant, J. (1962a). *Les origines de la pensée grecque*. Paris: Presses Universitaires de France.
Vernant, J. (1962b). *Mythe et pensée chez les Grecs*. Études de psychologie historique, Maspero, « Les textes à l'appui ».
Vernant, J. (1974). *Mythe et Société en Grèce ancienne*. Paris: François Maspero.
Vernant, J. and Vidal-Naquet, P. (1990). *La Grèce ancienne - Du mythe à la raison*, coll. Points. Paris: Le Seuil.
Vernant, J. and Vidal-Naquet, P. (1991). *La Grèce ancienne - L'espace et le temps*, coll. Points. Paris: Le Seuil.
Vernant, J. and Vidal-Naquet, P. (1992). *La Grèce ancienne - Rites de passage et transgressions*, coll. Points. Paris: Le Seuil.
Vernant, J. and Vidal-Naquet, P. (2000). *Mythe et tragédie en Grèce ancienne*. Paris: La Découverte.
Veyne, P. (1988). *Did the Greeks Believe in their Myths? An Essay on the Constitutive Imagination*. Trans. by P. Wissing. Chicago: University of Chicago Press.
Vlastos, G. (1952). 'Theology and philosophy in early Greek thought', in D.W. Graham (ed.). (1993). *Studies in Greek Philosophy: The Presocratics*. Princeton: Princeton University Press.
Voegelin, E. (1947). 'Plato's Egyptian Myth', *The Journal of Politics* 9 (3): 307–24.
Walters, T.L. (2007). *African American Literature and the Classicist Tradition. Black Women Writers from Wheatley to Morrison*. New York: Palgrave Macmillan.
Weinbaum, A.E. (2004). *Wayward Reproductions: Genealogies of Race and Nation in Transatlantic Modern Thought*. Durham: Duke University Press.
Weiss, R. (2001). *Virtue in the Cave: Moral Inquiry in Plato's Meno*. New York: Oxford University Press.
Werner, D.S. (2014). *Myth and Philosophy in Plato's Phaedrus*. New York: Cambridge University Press.
Wetzel, J. (2002). 'Myth and Moral Philosophy', in *Thinking through Myths – Philosophical Perspectives*. K. Schilbrack (ed.). London: Routledge, 123–141.
White, D.A. (1993). *Rhetoric and Reality in Plato's Phaedrus*. Albany: SUNY Press.
White, H. (1973). *Metahistory: The Historical Imagination in Nineteenth-century Europe*. Baltimore: Johns Hopkins University Press.
White, H. (2000). *Figural Realism – Studies in the Mimesis Effect*. Baltimore: Johns Hopkins University Press.
White, J.J. (1972). *Mythology in the Modern Novel: A Study of Prefigurative Techniques*. Princeton: Princeton University Press.
Wians, W. (2009). *Logos and Muthos: Philosophical Essays in Greek Literature*. Albany: SUNY Press.

Wiles. M.F. (1976). '"Myth" in Theology', *Bulletin of the John Rylands University Library of Manchester* 59 (1): 226–246.

Wilson, G.M. (2006). 'Le Grand Imagier Steps Out: The Primitive Basis of Film Narration', in *Philosophy of Film and Motion Pictures – An Anthology*. N. Carroll and J. Choi (eds.). Oxford: Wiley-Blackwell, 185–199.

Witzel, E.J.M. (2012). *The Origins of the World's Mythologies*. New York: Oxford University Press.

Woloshyn, C. (2008). 'Myth, Image, and Dianoia, Situating the Myth of Er on the Divided Line', presented at the conference *The Uses, Functions and Status of Platonic Myth*, May 28–31, University of Ottawa.

Woolf, V. (1925). 'On Not Knowing Greek', in *The Common Reader: First Series*. New York: Hogarth Press.

Wroe, E. (2005). 'Towards a "non-ghettocentric Black Brit vibe": A Trickster Inspired Approach to Storytelling in Diran Adebayo's My Once Upon a Time', in *Write Black, Write British – From Post Colonial to Black British Literature*, K, Sesay (ed.). London: Hansib Publications.

Wynter, S. (2003). "Unsettling the Coloniality of Being/Power/Truth/Freedom: Towards the Human, After Man, Its Overrepresentation -- An Argument", in *The New Centennial Review*, 3 (3): 257–337.

Yancy, G. (2008). *Black Bodies, White Gazes: The Continuing Significance of Race*. Forward by L. Alcoff. Lanham: Rowman & Littlefield.

Zilioli, U. (2007). *Protagoras and the Challenge of Relativism – Plato's Subtlest Enemy*. Hampshire: Ashgate.

Zima, P.V. (1999). *The Philosophy of Modern Literary Theory*. London: Athlone Press.

# Index

**A**

Acrocorinthus, 117n24
Acumenus, 151
Akkermann, A., 178n19
Alcibiades, 105, 105n46
Alcoff, L.M., 11n42, 12n45, 207n9
allegorical method, 34
*anamnesis*, 64, 65n33, 69, 72, 76, 79–81, 126, 172, 188, 190, 191
Anaxagoras, 128
Anderson, C., 11n40, 206n5
Anderson, D.G., 12n47, 206n5
Anderson, P.S., 18n64, 206n5
Anglo-American New Criticism and Russian Formalism, 8n29
Annas, J., 23n77

Aphrodite, 117n24, 154
*aporia*, 63, 74, 75, 78, 89
Arashiro, Z., 12n47, 207n9
Araujo, M., 11n40
archenemy concept, 201
Archytas of Tarentum, 199
Aryan myth, 176, 177
Aryan-Semitic racial binary, 173
'Aryan thesis', 175, 177
Asopus, 117n24
Athena, 185–7, 192
Athenian cultural identity, 202, 215
Atlantis myth, 42, 177–8, 178n19, 179, 179n21, 180–2, 184, 186–90, 192–197, 199, 201–3, 215, 216
attunement theory, 127, 128

Note: Page number followed by 'n' refers to notes.

© The Editor(s) (if applicable) and The Author(s) 2016
O. Tofighian, *Myth and Philosophy in Platonic Dialogues*,
DOI 10.1057/978-1-137-58044-3

## B

Babcock-Abrahams, B., 56n3, 57n5
Bal, M., 45n34
Barahona, M., 12n47, 207n9
Barash, J.A., 18n65
Barthes, R., 29n94, 44n30
Bartlett, R.C., 88n18
Benitez, E., 61n20, 133n63
Benitez, E.E., 47n46
Bernal, M., 11n40, 12n47
Bernasconi, R., 12n45
Bertens, H., 50n52
binary oppositions, 103, 111n1, 113–15, 176, 214
binary systems, 111–15, 140, 214
Bishop, R., 207n9
Blok, J.H., 32n103
Bondell, R., 44n32, 45n36
Bluck, R.S., 58n11, 59, 64n29, 65n34, 66n36
Blumenberg, H., 17
Booth, W.C., 150n22
Bottici, C., 9n34, 17n60, 44n29
Boys-Stones, G.R., 196n54
Bremmer, J.N., 19n66, 32n103, 206n3
Brennan, T., 12n45, 117n16
Briggs, D., 57n7
Brisson, L., 16n57, 22n74, 34, 34n3, 216, 216n12
Brochard, V., 27n87, 181n27
Buck-Morrs, S., 11n40, 13n50, 206n5
Burger, R., 119n29, 127n50
Burke, K., 83, 83n1–83n2
Burkert, W., 1n1
Burnet, J., 116n23
Burnyeat, M.F., 38n16, 181n26, 183n30, 194n49, 197n60
Buxton, R., 46n41, 207n10

## C

Campbell, J., 2n3
Capps, W.H., 13n51, 29n97, 30n99, 32n103
Caputo, J.D., 11n42, 207n9
Carroll, N., 7n27, 46n40
Cassirer, E., 6n18, 9n34, 24n80
Cebes, 37, 38, 38n16, 115n16, 123, 125, 127, 128, 129n54, 131, 138, 139
Challand, B., 9n34, 17n60, 44n29
Chance, J., 4n13
Christian myth, 39n18
Cicero, M.T., 199, 199n64
Clay, D., 181n28, 187n34
Coleman, D., 12n46, 12n48, 207n7
Collobert, C., 23n77, 24n79, 37n14
Colloud-Streit, M., 10n37, 31n100, 33n1, 137n70, 169n56
complex philosophical theory, 210
Compton, T.M., 2n3, 139n74
Connell, R., 12n47, 207n9
contemporary myth studies, 11, 18, 143–4, 207
contemporary scholarly approach, 1
conventional definitions of myth, 3–4
Cook, W.W., 174n2
Cornford, F.M., 195n52, 199, 199n67, 200n69
cosmic dualism, 75, 80, 167
cosmic dualist framework, 77
Coupe, L., 6n6, 6n7, 9n20, 23n71, 33n100, 83, 84, 84n3–84n6, 84n8, 85, 85n9, 85n10, 86n12, 86n13, 87n16
*Critias*, 42, 198–200, 215. *See also Timaeus*

# Index

Croce, 8n29
Crombie, I.M., 58n9, 59n14
cross-cultural device, 56
cross-cultural mythic elements, 58
Cruikshank, J., 12n47, 206n4
Csapo, E., 11n41, 16n59, 112n4, 113n7, 144n3, 206n3
cultural identity, 147, 177, 179, 202, 203, 215–18
cultural productions, 2n4, 115
Cupitt, D., 83, 84n7
Currie, G., 46n40

## D

Day, J., 63n26, 75n56
definitive theory, 58
de Jong, I.J.F, 45n36, 45n37, 46n39
deliverance, 2n4, 3, 73, 117–20, 122–3, 130–4, 136, 136n68, 138–40, 167, 168, 213, 214
De Luise, F., 51n58
Demiurge, 195, 195n52
Denzin, N.K., 13n49, 206n4, 206n6, 207n7
de Sousa Santos, B., 13n50, 2078
Detienne, M., 21n70, 27, 207n10
De Vries, J., 167n52, 179n57
dialectical unity, 35–52, 96, 134, 137, 140, 210, 213
dichotomy paradigm, 15n55, 18, 18n64, 19, 34, 65n31, 215, 216
Dionysus, 154
Dorter, K., 116n21, 126n47, 127n48, 129n53, 134n64, 136n66

Doty, W., 3n9–11, 6n18, 8n28, 10n36, 10n38, 14n54, 17n55, 24n80, 29n97, 39n18, 44n30, 49n48, 50n51, 50n53, 56n1, 56n3, 112, 112n3, 112n5, 113n6, 143n1, 143n2, 144, 144n4, 144n5, 145, 145n6–8, 146n9, 146n10, 147, 147n12–15, 148, 148n18, 206n3, 211n11, 214
Drake, S., 174n2
Dropides, 184, 198
dualism, 73–5, 80, 81, 106, 118, 120, 122–5, 130, 132, 133, 136, 139, 140, 163, 167, 214
dualist mythologies, 76
dubious systems of knowledge production, 7
Dumézil, G., 177
Dundes, A., 2n1, 146n11, 148n17, 206n3
Durkheim, E., 112n4

## E

Ebert, T., 88n19, 88n20, 105n45, 106n51, 116n20, 130n56
Echecrates, 115–16, 118, 126, 127n49, 129n54, 131, 138, 138n72, 139
Eckstein, J., 43n28, 60n15
Edelstein, L., 28n91, 28n92, 35n7
Edmonds, III, R.G., 23n77, 24n79, 117n25, 118n26, 122n35, 124n43, 132n61, 135n65, 138n73
Egypt, 185, 186, 200–1

Egyptian priest, 185, 197n61, 200–1
Eliade, 4n12, 5n15, 5n16, 32n103, 48n47, 69n45, 85n9
Emeagwali, G., 13n49, 206n6
Enlightenment historiography, 47
Epicrates, 152
Epimetheus, 988n17, 92, 99, 102
*eros*, 117n24, 143, 154, 159, 168
Erskine, A., 19n66
Euhemerism, 5, 144
Euhemeros, 143
European colonial expansion, 11
European fascism, 173, 202, 206
exclusive structuralist approach, 6

F

Feldman, B., 2n1, 4n12, 5n15, 5n15, 8n30, 25n84, 32n103, 69n45, 174n3, 174n4, 175n6, 175n8, 175n10, 176n11, 176n14, 205n2
Ferrari, G.R.F., 36, 36n11, 40n21, 51n58, 150n21
Fink, D., 200n68
Finkelberg, A., 179n24, 194n48
Fitznor, L., 13n49, 206n6
Flaig, E., 19n66
Flood, C., 27n88
Forms, 20, 23n79, 125–9, 151n23, 154, 157, 161–2, 166, 169, 172, 188, 191, 196
Fowler, R.L., 21n71
Frazer, Sir James, 29n97, 144
Fredericks, S.C., 20n71, 179n21
Fréret, N., 8n31
Fricker, M., 206n5

*From Religion to Philosophy* (Cornford), 19n66
Frutiger, P., 177n18
Frye, N., 3n7, 6n18

G

Galton, 177n16
Gantz, T., 14n53
Gaster, T.H., 146, 146n11
Gates Jr., H.L., 50n53, 174n2
*Genesis*, 175
Genette, G., 45, 45n34, 45n38
*The Georgics* (Virgil), 196n54
Gerhart, M., 3n8, 44n29
Gill, A., 166n48, 168n53, 170n58, 179n23, 189n36
Gilroy, P., 11n42
Gobineau, 177n16
Goldenhard, I., 177n16
Gonzales, F., 51n58
Goody, J., 13n50
Gould, E., 5n17, 44n30
Gould, T., 15n55
Grafton, A., 11n40
Greek myth, 4, 8, 27, 29n93, 34n4, 86n14, 196n54
Griswold, C., 151n24, 159n33, 160n36, 165n46, 168n55
Grosfoguel, R., 11n43
Grounds, R.A., 13n49, 206n6

H

Hackforth, R., 120n32, 123n37, 124n41, 125n45, 128n51, 128n52
Hades, 37, 117n24

Halbfass, W., 12n45
Hartle, A., 124n42, 127n49, 131n59, 139n74
Hatab, L., 2n5, 28n93, 34n4
Haubold, J.H., 196n54
Hawes, G., 206n3
Heidegger, 17n60
Hendry, J., 13n49, 206n6
Hephaestos, 187
Herder, J.G., 47, 175n6
hermeneutical sensibility, 58
Hermocrates, 179, 180, 183, 184, 190, 199–200
Herodotus, 185, 185n32
Hesiod, 185, 196, 196n54, 196n56, 197, 197n61, 198
Hestia, 155
Heyne, 2n1, 22n75, 25n84, 32n103, 113n7
hierarchy of incarnations, 156
Hippocrates, 89, 89n21, 90, 102, 106n48
Holton, G., 3n8, 6n22
Homer, 15n56, 29, 29n95, 105, 105n46, 185
Huffman, C.L., 116n17, 124n40, 199n66
Humboldt, 174, 205
humor functions, 55
Hynes, W.J., 50n53, 56n1, 56n3
hypothetical method functions, 59

Indo-European myth, 176, 177
integrated meaning-generating system, 114

interdisciplinary approach, 19, 43n28, 84, 210
Ionescu, C., 58n12, 60n17, 65n31, 71n47

Jackson, S.N., 13n49, 206n4, 206n4
Jakobson, R., 113n7
Janka, M., 26n86
Jean-Marie, V., 11n40, 13n49, 206n5
Johansen, T.K., 179n22, 181n28, 185n32, 189n38, 192n41, 193n44, 194n46, 201n71
Jones, Sir William, 175–6
Jung, C., 56

Kant, I., 47, 47n44
Kerényi, K., 56
Kincheloe, J.L., 13n49, 206n6
King, R., 12n45
Kirk, G.S., 8, 8n30, 11, 12n44, 29n94
Klein, J., 60n15, 62, 62n23, 62n24, 65n32, 66n35, 76n60
Kluckhohn, C., 146n11
knowledge acquisition, 57, 61, 66, 75, 87, 136, 153, 157, 161, 167
knowledge and identity, 70
Kobusch, T., 29n93
Kovach, M., 13n49
Kovacs, G., 20n68
Kuhn, A., 176

# Index

## L

Laertius, D., 23n77, 29n96
Landry, E., 68n43
Larivée, A., 45n35, 46n39, 51n58
Le Doeuff, M., 18n64
Lee, D., 181, 181n28, 199n63
Lefkowitz, M.R., 11n40
*Les Mythes de Platon* (Frutiger), 22n76
Levin, S.B., 14n58
Lévi-Strauss, C., 9, 9n35, 14n52, 16n59, 111–14, 111n1, 112n4, 112n5, 113, 113n8–11, 114n12–14
   structuralist approach, 9n33
   theory of binary systems in myth, 3
   theory of myth, 214
'life-death-rebirth' structure, 73
liminality, 41n23, 49–50, 50n50, 51, 51n58, 52, 57, 58, 58n8, 77, 80, 138, 151, 151n23, 211, 213, 214
liminal phases, 49–51, 119, 151, 170
liminal themes, 49, 50, 57, 80
Lincoln, B., 7, 7n26, 7n27, 11n42, 32n103, 144n3, 173, 174, 174n5, 175n6, 175n7, 175n10, 176, 176n11–176n13, 176n15, 177, 177n17, 206n3
Lock, H., 50n53
*logoi*, 127, 159, 170, 178
*logos*, 13, 14, 17, 25, 26, 29n93, 31, 34, 42, 43, 47n46, 127, 132, 159, 170, 178, 179, 189, 212, 215, 217
Louis, M.K., 5n14, 19n66, 22n75
Lundquist, S.E., 77n63

## M

Maaka, R.C.A., 11n40, 206n6
Maeso, S., 11n40
Maher, J.M., 57n7
Manuwald, B., 34n2, 91n26
Marchand, S., 177n16
Marchand, S.L., 11n40
Marshall, C.W., 20n68
Martin, K.L., 13n49, 13n50, 207n7
Mason, H., 148, 148n16
Mattei, J., 23n78
McGrath, E., 86n15
Mehta, J.L., 2n6
Mendieta, E., 1n45, 207n9
*Meno*, 41n23, 42, 51, 88, 100, 119, 214
   character selection, 75–79
   mutual scaffolding, 70–3
   myth analysis, 63–68
   philosophical arguments, 68–70
   plot structure, 73–5
   theme introduction, setting, and narrative mode, 87–90
   trickster characters, 55–60
*Metahistory* (White), 46
*Metamorphoses* (Ovid), 196n54
metaphysical theory, 128, 129
Mignolo, W., 12n46
Mills, C.W., 11n42
Mnemosyne, 190
modern conceptions of myth, 19
modern mythography, 8n30, 11, 11, 20
Moellendorf, D., 12n45
monomythic definitions for myth, 148, 206, 211
Moors, K., 20, 20, 21n70

Morgan, K.A., 15n56, 21, 21n72, 21, 21n72, 21n73, 27n87, 31n101, 31n102, 35n6, 39, 39n20, 42n24, 45n34, 192n42, 193n45, 200n70, 201n72, 202n74, 217n14–16
Morgan, M.L., 65n34
*Morphology of the Folktale* (Propp), 2n1
Morychus, 152
Mosse, G., 175n9
Most, G., 19n67, 24n81, 26n86, 36n10, 63n26
Müller, M., 11n42, 32n103, 144, 175n10
mutual scaffolding approach, 35–52, 97, 178, 208, 213
*Meno*, 70–3
*Phaedo*, 130–5
*Phaedrus*, 159–67
*Protagoras*, 96–101
*My Once Upon a Time* (Adebayo), 50n53
*Myth and Philosophy* (Hatab), 29n95
'myth and ritual' schools, 29n97, 144, 146
*Myth: A Very Short Introduction* (Segal), 41
mythemes, 14n52, 112, 113, 115, 144, 145, 147, 208
*Mythical Intentions in Modern Literature* (Gould's), 39n17
mythic language, 146–7
mythic pluralism, 29
mythography, 4, 5, 11, 13, 18, 20, 30, 39n18, 49n48, 113n9, 176, 205, 207
*Mythography* (Doty), 3

mythological corpus, 144
mytho-religious dualism, 74
*mythos*, 2, 13, 14, 17, 26, 29n93, 31, 34, 42, 43, 47n46, 132, 214, 215, 217
*The Myths of Plato* (Stewart), 22

N

Nakata, M., 13n51, 207n7
Nakata, N.M., 12n46, 207n9
National Socialism, 177
Nehamas, A., 151n25, 159n34, 168n54
Nicholson, G., 151n24, 161n37, 168n54
Nietzsche, 17n60, 47, 176
non-Athenian, 107
non-Platonic myth, 34
non-realism, 84
non-realist allegory, 85, 85n11, 86
non-realist interpretations, 86
non-Western epistemologies, 12

O

*Odyssey*, 216
Oedipus myth, 114n14
Olender, M., 175n9
Omidsalar, M., 174n1
Orphic myths, 196n54
Orphic traditions, 65, 190
Osborne, C., 190n40, 195n51, 196n53

P

paradigmatic model, 16n59
'Paradise Lost' paradigm, 102, 190

Park, P.K.J., 12n45, 206n5
Partenie, C., 24n79
Patterson, R.L., 125n45
Paul, H., 46n41, 47n43, 47n45
Pausanias, 116, 116n22, 117n24
Peloponnesian War, 200, 216
Pender, E.E., 40n22
*Phaedo*, 38, 41n23, 42, 51, 68n44, 140–41, 178n20, 214
  binary systems and myth, 111–15
  character selection, 137–9
  mutual scaffolding, 130–5
  myth analysis, 120–3
  philosophical arguments, 123–29
  plot structure, 135–7
  theme introduction, setting, and narrative mode, 115–19
*Phaedrus*, 42, 51, 68n44, 146, 148–51, 170–2, 178n20, 214
  character selection, 169–70
  cultural standpoint and myth, 143–9
  literary language of, 147
  mutual scaffolding, 159–67
  myth analysis, 153–58
  philosophical arguments, 158–9
  plot structure, 167–8
  theme introduction, setting, and narrative mode, 149–3
Philolaus, 116, 116n17, 123–27, 131, 131n57, 138, 138n72, 195, 199
*Philolaus of Croton* (Huffman), 199
philosophical device, 69, 78
philosophical myths, 21, 21, 34, 35, 35n7, 39, 41, 48, 49, 74, 178, 208, 209, 211, 212, 215, 217

Phliasian Asopus, 117, 117n24
Phliasian territory, 117, 117n24
Phlius, 115, 116, 122, 125, 129n54, 131, 138
Piaget, J., 36n8
Pindar, 64, 65, 71–2, 77
pivotal literary, 69
Platonic metaphysics, 129
Platonic myths, 20, 28n91, 33, 35, 212
Platonic solid, 121, 121n33, 131, 131n57
Plato scholars, 19, 174n2, 209
Plato scholarship, 1, 20, 22, 34, 208, 209, 212
polyphasic definition, 28n92
pre-Socratic causation, 129
pre-Socratic philosophy, 123, 125, 126, 131
  interpretation and critique of, 114
  tenets and theories of, 118
pre-Socratic-Pythagorean factor, 139
Presocratics, 31
pre-Socratic theories, 120
pre-Socratic tradition, 116
Price, W., 161n38
Proclus, 199, 199n65
Prometheus, 86, 88n17, 92, 99, 102, 103, 176
Propp, V., 2n1, 3n8, 44n31, 111n1
*Protagoras*, 42, 149, 214
  character selection, 105–7
  mutual scaffolding, 96–101
  myth analysis, 90–3
  philosophical arguments, 94–96
  plot structure, 101–5
  radical typology, 83–7
  theme introduction, setting, and narrative mode, 87–90

Pugliese, M., 174n2
Pythagoras, 116, 121, 121n33
Pythagorean affiliation, 135, 195
Pythagorean attunement theory, 127
Pythagoreanism, 116, 118, 122, 124
Pythagorean philosophy, 115, 125, 129, 136n67
Pythagorean/Platonic contrast, 121, 131
Pythagorean/Platonic dialectic, 140
Pythagorean/Platonic dynamics, 116, 118, 124, 129n54, 133
Pythagorean/Platonic trope, 116
Pythagoreans, 115, 116, 121, 124, 126, 130–2, 132n60, 133, 135, 137–9
Pythagorean traditions, 65

Q

Quijano, A., 11n43

R

racism, 11, 12, 12n45, 173, 177n16
Radin, P., 56
Ramsey, A., 39n18
Rankine, P.D., 174n2
realism, 84
realist allegory, 85, 86, 109
reductionism, 5, 28
rhythmic ritual movement, 146
Richardson, R.D., 2n1, 4n12, 5n15, 5n16, 8n30, 25n84, 32n103, 69n45, 174n3, 174n4, 175n6, 175n8, 175n10, 176n11, 176n14, 205n2
Ricoeur, P., 17, 84n5

Rigney, L., 13n49, 206n5, 207n7
*The Rise of Modern Mythology: 1680–1860* (Feldman and Richardson), 32n103
ritual/ceremony, liminal phase of, 119
ritual movement, 153
Rogers, G.M., 11n40
Roman myth, 4, 11
Romantic movement, 4, 173
romantic theories of myth, 175
Ronnick, M.V., 174n2
Rosen, S., 15n55
Rowe, C.J., 23n77, 130n55
Ruehl, M., 177n16
Runia, D.T., 181n27, 189n38, 194n49, 195n50
Russell, A.M., 3n8, 44n29

S

Saal, B., 11n46
Santas, G., 162n39
Saussure, F. de., 113n7
Scarborough, W.S., 174n2
Scheub, H., 56n2, 57n6, 57
Schilbrack, K., 16, 17n60, 205, 205n1
Schmitz, T.A., 6n20, 44n30
Scolnicov, S., 167n50
Scott, D., 35n5, 66n37, 71, 71n49, 74n54, 75n56, 75n58, 76n61
Sedley, D., 22n80
Sefa Dei, G.J., 13n49, 206n6
Segal, R.A., 2n3, 6n19, 16, 17n61, 22n82, 23n79, 30n98, 144n3, 206n3
Semali, L.M., 13n49, 206n6

## Index

sexual interaction in poetic style, 162
Sharpe, E.J., 17n60, 23n78
Sicyonians, 117, 117n24
*The Signifying Monkey* (Gates), 50n53
Sillitoe, P., 12n46, 12n47, 13n49
Simmias, 115n16, 120, 125, 127, 128, 129n54, 131, 134, 138, 139
Simmons, E., 12n48
slave, 61, 61n20, 63, 67–70, 72–4, 74n55, 78–9, 79n65, 81, 89n21, 125, 137, 214
Smith, C., 12n48
Smith L., 13n49, 206n5
Smith, L.T., 11n40, 12n48, 207n9
Smith, W.R., 29n97
Snell, B., 207n10
social activity, 114
Socrates, 36–8, 46n39, 49, 58, 58n8, 59, 60, 63–70, 74, 76–8, 76n59, 77–9, 79n65, 88, 89, 89n21, 90, 91, 93–6, 99, 103, 104–6, 106n48, 107, 114–27, 115n16, 119n30, 119n31, 123n38, 124n39, 128n52, 131, 132n61, 133–40, 138n71, 139n74, 149–6, 151n25, 157, 158, 160, 161, 163–5, 163n43, 167n51, 168–72, 179, 182, 183, 186, 188, 190–4, 198, 199, 214
Solmsen, F., 19n66
Solon, 183–87, 194, 200, 201, 201n72, 201n73
Spencer, H., 23n82
state education system, 95

Sternfeld, R., 58n10, 60n16, 62n22, 67n40, 76n60
Stesichorus, 160
Stewart, J.A., 21, 22, 22n81, 23, 24, 24n84–6, 36,36n12
Strenski, I., 48n47
*Structural Anthropology* (Lévi-Strauss), 111
structural approaches, 111, 112n3
structuralist approach, 112, 114
syllogism, 23n83
symbolism, 21, 76, 77, 103, 131, 133, 137, 139, 140, 172

T

Tanner, R.G., 168n54
Tarrant, H., 23n82, 61n19, 61n21, 63n25, 63n27, 64n30, 65n33, 68n42, 71n48, 73n52, 91n26, 92n29, 96n35, 179n22
Tartarus, 121, 122, 132
Tatum, J., 174n2
Thein, K., 91n25
*Theorizing Myth* (Lincoln), 173
theory of Forms, 118, 119, 127, 131, 136, 157, 158n30, 172, 181, 181n27, 189, 194, 195
theory of recollection, 64, 64n29, 65, 65n32, 68, 69, 71–2, 125, 126, 128, 157, 179, 188, 189
Thomas, J.E., 59n13, 67n40, 69n46, 72n51, 79n62
Thompson, E.S., 61n18, 75n57, 78n64
Thucydides, 199

*Timaeus*
 character selection, 198–12
 mutual scaffolding, 188–5
 myth analysis, 184–87
 nationalism and myth, 173–79
 philosophical arguments, 189–90
 plot structure, 195–198
 theme introduction, setting, and narrative mode, 179–4
Timaeus of Locri, 199
Tofighian, O., 89n11, 195n52
Tolkien, J.R.R., 189n37
*Totemism*, 9
'traditional mythic pattern', 118n26
trickster characters, 50, 50n53, 55–60, 70, 74, 74n55, 79–81
*Trickster, The* (Radin), 56
Turner, V., 49n50, 50, 50n50, 50n54, 50n55, 51, 51n56, 51n57, 119n27, 119n28
'two-worlds' theory, 133
Tylor, E.B., 17, 23–n79
Tyrrhenia, 186

V
van Gennep, A., 50
van Ophuijsen, J.M., 102n40
Van Riel, G., 90n23, 90n24, 98n37, 104n41
Vernant, J., 21n70, 207n10
Veyne, P., 216n13
Vidal-Naquet, P., 21n70
virtue, 61, 62, 64, 67, 69, 71, 75, 76, 78, 79, 90–100, 102–4, 107, 108, 114

Vlastos, G., 18n69
Voegelin, E., 181n28, 186n33, 190n39, 193n43, 194n47, 198n62, 201n73
*Volk*, 173–5, 177
von Wilamowitz-Mollendorff, U., 19n66

W
Wagner, 176
Walters, T.L., 174n2
Weinbaum, A.E., 11n40, 11n42, 179n16, 207n9
Weiss, R., 64n28, 68n35, 67n38, 67n39
Werner, D.S., 149n19, 154n27
Western colonial expansion, 12
Western colonial powers, 11
Wetzel, J., 23n76
White, D.A., 159n31, 159n32, 160n35, 162n40, 163n41, 163n42, 164n44, 166n47, 166n49
White, H., 3n7, 6n22, 7n23, 7n25, 13n51, 42n25, 46, 46n42
Wians, W., 46n41
Wiles, M.F., 144n5
Wilson, G.M., 46n40
Witzel, E.J.M., 9n32
Wobst, H.M., 12n48
Woloshyn, 23n79
Woodruf, P., 151n25, 159n34, 168n54
Woolf, V., 45n33
*Works and Days* (Hesiod), 196
Wroe, E., 50n53
Wynter, S., 11n42

## 250　Index

Y
Yancy, G., 207n9

Z
Zeus, 36, 92, 102, 117n24, 155, 162, 168, 187, 196, 197

Zilioli, U., 91n27, 93n31, 98n36, 102n39
Zima, P.V., 16n58, 28n90, 29n93, 43n27, 45n33
Zyskind, H., 58n10, 60n16, 62n22, 67n40, 76n60

Printed in the United States
By Bookmasters